THE RELUCTANT
SHAMAN

A Woman's First Encounters
with the Unseen Spirits
of the Earth

Kay Cordell Whitaker

HarperSanFrancisco

A Division of HarperCollins*Publishers*

FIRST EDITION

Library of Congress Cataloging-in-Publication Data

Whitaker, Kay Cordell.
    The reluctant shaman : a woman's first encounters with the unseen spirits of the earth / Kay Cordell Whitaker. — 1st ed.
        p.   cm.
      ISBN 0-06-250953-5 (alk. paper)
      1. Shamanism. 2. Whitaker, Kay Cordell. I. Title.
BL2370.S5W55 1991
299'.8—dc20   90-55404
                                               CIP

91 92 93 94 95 RRD(H) 10 9 8 7 6 5 4 3 2 1

This edition is printed on acid-free paper that meets the American National Standards Institute Z39.48 Standard.

HarperSanFrancisco and the author, in association with the Rainforest Action Network, will facilitate the planting of two trees for every one tree used in the manufacturing of this book.

Dedication

This book is dedicated in respect and gratitude to our Mother, our planet Earth, for all that she has continually given to us, with a prayer for her rapid and gentle healing, that we may earn the opportunity to move into the future with her in a good way.

CONTENTS

INTRODUCTION

In the winter of 1974, it was my great fortune to fumble into the friendship and tutelage of an elderly Indian couple, Domano and Chea Hetaka, from the western Amazon basin of Brazil. We met in Santa Cruz, California, shortly after I moved there. I became their adopted granddaughter, and through the years that followed, they taught me about their religious belief system, which they referred to as shamanism.

There are many types and degrees of shamans throughout the world, ranging from herbalists and curers to ceremonial leaders and even clowns. Each culture has its own traditions, standards, and names for those who fill such roles.

My elders refer to themselves as belonging to the *kala keh nah seh,* or the medicine storyteller tradition. They help the group through the development of individuals in relation to themselves and their world; they do this by leading people to direct experience with the help of their stories and jesting.

The development of the shaman never ends. One spends one's whole life perfecting techniques and learning about oneself and one's world.

For the sake of clarity, I do not claim to be, by the definition of the North American Indians, a "medicine woman." I have been trained specifically as a *kala keh nah seh* and as a servant of the Earth.

The Hetakas required of me only that I not speak of their teachings to others and most important, that I not write down any of what I learned or record it in any other way. That kind of activity, they insisted, would only keep the lessons and my attention locked in my thoughts, and I would never be able to fully grasp and use the knowledge with the rest of my being.

Someday, they said, if things went well enough, they would ask me to teach what I had learned to others, perhaps many others. But until that time, I was to honor my promise.

In 1987, at our last meeting, they said that the time was well suited and I had learned what I needed, and they asked me to write about and publish the experiences that I had had with them. I was to do this for them, certainly, because they asked. But the true reason I should help them give these teachings to the public was and is for the sake of the healing and growth of humanity and our Mother Earth today and tomorrow. The Hetakas reminded me of the many prophecies around the world that say it will take the efforts of all people working together to pull the world back into balance.

I have received a great deal of help and support from my family and many others through the three years of preparation for this book and I would like to express my deepest appreciation to all of them.

The Hetakas requested that I change only proper names and some dates and locations for the sake of their privacy and safety and that of their people. Even though they had been in the United States for several years before we met, they spoke with a thick, gutteral accent, and their use of English syntax was very poor. In spite of this, their vocabulary seemed more than adequate, and as we spent more time together, I was able to understand them with increasing clarity. And so, to accommodate the need for accurate communication in this book, I have presented their dialogues in a more standardized English than they actually spoke.

As we were about to part, in that last meeting together, the Hetakas' final word of advice to me was to suggest to the readers that they read with more than their thoughts, that they enjoy the pages slowly, that they experience with their whole selves as they proceed.

1

THE INVITATION

Struggling against the force of the wind, I bent forward and walked toward the edge of the cliff. Drenched and cold, I stood looking out into the sea. This is what I was seeking. I wanted to feel the storm in my bones.

A movement caught my eye. I turned, and facing me was a man who seemed to appear from nowhere. The wind was blowing his white hair straight back. Thunder burst in my ears as the man stepped toward me, watching the waves as they broke over the path. He nodded his head and said with a quick glance, "I've been waiting for you. You wasted no time in getting here. That is good."

The wind drove the rain hard into my face. I heard a second thunderclap, and I could feel electricity tingling on the bottoms of my feet. I figured he must be one of the crazy derelicts who lived under the bridges. I stepped a few feet backward, afraid he was going to attack. But he didn't move. He just stood motionless, facing the sea. This was my chance to escape fast and abandon the storm.

Then, just over the howl of the wind, I heard him say, "We waited pretty long years to be able to meet with you."

Now I knew he was nuts. My stomach tightened up and my head ached at the temples. I started to walk away through the mud. Lightning filled the sky a third time. I couldn't move fast enough.

"Are you going to throw away so many years of preparation?" he asked calmly.

I was stopped in my tracks, and as if the old man and the thunder were in league together, the thunder and lightning jolted again. It must have been striking very close. I noticed for the first time that the man had an accent, though I couldn't place it. I turned to look at him. He still hadn't moved. He looked like he was in his late seventies or early eighties, maybe slightly over five feet tall, with darkish skin. He was wearing sandals, peasant pants, and an old, disheveled poncho. Despite his age, I felt physically threatened.

"Leave me alone," I yelled, stepping backward, the wind almost blowing me over. Lightning and thunder hit twice, once on either side of me. The sound immobilized me.

His words seemed to flow out of the sky around me: "It is time for you to learn the balance. *Ka ta see.* You have much work to do."

I was so cold and wet, I ached and buzzed. I could hear a seagull screaming in the distance off the cliff to my left as the thunder came the seventh and final time. I wanted to scream at him. Anything. Obscenities. It didn't matter. I even wished the wind would push him off the cliff. Then he lifted his head and opened his eyes fully for the first time.

These were not the eyes of a drunken derelict. They were calm, knowing, and caring. They were strong eyes reflecting something mysterious. His stare was softly compelling, which scared me even more. For a moment, I didn't know whether to stay or to run. The wind pushed around us furiously. I made up my mind and started for the car again. I wasn't going to let anything stop me this time.

I raced to the car, turning to see if he was following me. He still hadn't moved, but he held out his hand and yelled, "We will meet again. *Ka ta see.* Soon."

I opened the door as fast as I could, hopped in, and started the motor, never looking back.

Two weeks later I was sitting and writing, as I often did, in the coffee shop at Stevenson College on the University of California campus at Santa Cruz. My kids were in school, and I wasn't working, so I often rode into town with my husband on days when he was attending classes. A sudden huge gust of wind blew over one of the tables outside. I looked up, and to my astonishment I saw the same old man sitting at a table next to the window. I suddenly felt sick to my stomach. I could feel the same fear welling up inside me again. He nodded and kept his soft eyes fixed on me. He looked less like a derelict today and more like a very old simple man.

I was going to leave, but then I decided I'd be safer in the coffee shop. I'd just sit there and ignore him until he left. I was sure he'd get bored and leave within fifteen or twenty minutes.

Two hours later he was still there and still nodding his head politely. He looked a lot less threatening in there, and older, too old to be living under a bridge. I thought of going over to him and just telling him to go away and leave me alone, but I was much too intimidated. A true product of the 1950s, I had never learned how to stand up for myself to men, especially those much older than me. So I sat there sipping my French roast, getting angrier at myself by the minute. I was too afraid to leave and too afraid to confront him.

As I sat there heartily engrossed in my stewing, he quietly doddered over to my table and asked if he might join me. His demeanor was soft and small. I suddenly felt silly and ashamed for thinking such loathsome thoughts about this little old man. He seemed now so small and almost feeble. In his broken English he was consistently polite.

I said nothing to him, unintentionally allowing him to sit at my table. I wanted to leave, but I just didn't get up.

"Is it okay I can sit here? Yes? It's good we should talk now. You and I. It's a good time. We have much to talk about."

I said nothing. I thought nothing. I felt, however, as if

I were drowning in a whirlpool of pity, fear, and anger. I wondered if I had a sign on my head saying, "Gullible Woman—Easily Harassed."

"How 'bout if you eat some soup. You will feel better. You eat something. Please. I'll buy some soup so you will eat." His voice was concerned. He waved the nonserving clerk over and actually talked him into bringing a bowl of soup over to the table.

I still said nothing. The clerk brought my soup. The old man said softly, "Eat. Please. You will feel better. When your stomach is full maybe you will not see me as fear anymore."

All this time I was staring at his eyes, I had thought they were light colored, but as he spoke I noticed that they were really dark, almost black. If I had begun to settle down a little, that set me off again. I pressed up against the back of my chair, stiff and tense.

"It's nice," he said reassuringly. "I have eaten their soup before. It's good food. It is okay. Please eat. For an old man. Yes?"

I picked up the spoon. "What do you want from me?" I asked, still not eating, but holding the spoon.

"The time has come to talk to you," he said. "We have much to talk about. It would please this old man much to give to you what is time."

"What?" I asked. "You don't even know me. What are you talking about?"

"I am old," he answered quietly. "I have things to give to you, before I go."

"Well, that's quite nice of you, but I really don't think so." This was getting way out of hand, even for me. I picked up my purse and started to rise.

"You have no time to turn me down. These things belong to you. We have a job to give this. Soon. So soon! I'm very sorry I scared you the other day on the beach. My work is not to scare, but to give to you what belongs to you from the old ones."

4

I nodded my head up and down. "Sure," I said sarcastically. "I think you're very well meaning. But I don't think so. Goodbye." I got up to go. He seemed sincere but probably a bit senile. I hoped I hadn't been too harsh and hurt his feelings.

"If you go again I will meet you again soon. You don't have too much time, so maybe you will listen next time." His tone was quiet and so matter-of-fact, so congenial.

I stopped and looked at him again. He smiled gently. I no longer felt the whirlpool inside me, just confusion. I couldn't believe he was still laying that line on me. He was spooky. I wondered why he had picked me, and in an unusual wave of assertiveness I told him I'd give him five minutes and no more. "What do you want, *really*? Why me?"

"*Ka ta see,* as my people say. It means balance. I have a gift of many stories and the tradition of balance. For you. It is yours. This talk, this work, of *ka ta see,* is for you. You have so much work to do and so little time. It is good that you eat."

Without realizing it, I had picked up the spoon again and unconsciously begun eating the soup. I interrupted him. "Who *are* you? What are you talking about? Who are your people? Where are you from? How do I know you are not just some 'drug-rat' crazy?"

"You know already that I am not dangerous to you or a 'drug-rat.' You see that much from me. My name is Domano Hetaka. I have come from my people who are jungle people, from far away south."

"Come on," I interrupted. "What do you mean, 'far away south'? What country are you from? Are you an Indian? What do you do?"

He stopped me with his finger up to his mouth. "I came from South America, Brazil, and my people are Amazon people. I am their *kala keh nah seh.* You would say a storyteller. I give medicine to my people in their stories. It is now my time to give my medicine to the youth, the next generation. I am told to give to you. My desire is to give my talk—*ka ta see,* the balance of the spirit—to you."

Gasping, I said, "You want to pass your tradition on to me!" And with increasing agitation and volume, I said, "Why me? Where are your people? Why don't you pass it on to your people? Your knowledge and traditions belong to them, not me!" I was shocked. He was so sincere, so sure. "How did you get here?" I continued my barrage, a little quieter this time. People had started to turn around. "How long have you been here? Why did you leave your people to come all this way?"

"To find you," he said in such a convincing tone.

I nodded my head again as I stood up. "Sure. I think you've been reading some weird science fiction or something. You really are a very nice man. I appreciate the thought, really. I'm not ungrateful. But you have me mixed up with someone else, I'm sure. Thank you for the soup, it really did make me feel better. Now I'd better let you go so you can find who you're looking for. I need to get going home. I've got lots to take care of." I grabbed up my purse. "Husband." I took a step. "Kids." I turned back around. "House." I set my purse down. "Laundry."

He nodded his head up and down with a gentle smile. "Sure," he said, copying my intonation.

I had to laugh.

"Please, sit awhile," he asked gently, "to hear the song in an old man's heart?"

I realized that my mouth was hanging open and, I thought, as my mother used to say, ready to catch flies.

"Ready to catch some flies?" he asked with a soft chuckle.

My knees betrayed me, they buckled involuntarily and I was sitting again.

"More soup?" he asked. "You need some bread? Or sugar?"

I couldn't say anything. The bottoms of my feet felt the same electrical tingles that I had felt at the cliff in the storm, and my temples began to throb.

"You are certainly different, Domano," I finally said.

"Yes," he nodded. "That is *ka ta see*."

I asked him what that meant, and what it had to do with his storytelling.

"You want some sugar. That one there. I will get it for you." He pointed to a chocolate mousse. He was right. I had had my eye on it all day but didn't have enough cash to buy one.

"Oh no. Please. That's okay. You don't have to do that." But he was up and at the counter before I could stop him. Now I was embarrassed, too. Even though I had tried before and this would have been a perfect time to get up and run, I didn't. I was somehow getting caught up in his scenario and I never even thought to make a dash for it until much later.

The mousse was very good, and while I savored my rare treat he kept on talking.

"*Ka ta see* is balance. The balance of being perfectly whole. It is from the spirit. Here," he said as he tapped his heart. "It begins in the spirit. We can balance anything. Our voice. Our work. Our body. You can even balance your sadness."

"So you help your people by giving them balance?" I was having trouble understanding him, but he was beginning to sound interesting.

"No. No one can give such a thing to another person. I show them balance. I bring *ka ta see* to their doorstep with my storytelling. They need to do whatever they do. Now it is time for you to learn *ka ta see* and learn how to bring it to others, many others."

I thought, boy has he got the wrong number! Lots of people, eh? Well, that's not for me. I'm a recluse. I prefer solitude, my family, my few but very close friends. No crowds for me.

"This is the right time," he said. "My teachers came to teach me so when this time now is here, I can find you and teach you."

"That's very flattering, Domano. If I weren't such a hermit my ego could take that and run!"

7

"Yes," he nodded, grinning. "But it is still because you are you, and you are the one for *ka ta see*. You see?"

I shook my head from side to side, making a faint groaning sound. He leaned over and said in a teasing way, "Does the sugar hurt your stomach?"

I shook my head again and said, trying to sound authoritative and parental, "So tell me, Domano, what are you *really* doing?"

He paused, lowered his head, took a deep breath, and said in a submissive manner, "I'll tell you. My companion and I worked to make this trip. We worked for money and saved it. A long time. We have worked on *ka ta see* to make it perfect. We help our people when we are asked. We learned the Spanish language some, and the English language some better. Our teachers gave us information to find you. And when we were ready we set on a trip for this place. It was very exciting and very different from our home. We've had a real good time. Now we have found you, we must go to work, and work hard. There's not much time to finish."

"What work do you mean, exactly?" I asked. "Just what do you have in mind?"

Domano was so plastic in his mannerisms, and he had a child's sense of play. He had mocked my seriousness, and now he straightened his face, looked me squarely in the eyes, and spoke clearly: "We intend to teach you what our teachers taught us."

His English was very inconsistent, and sometimes difficult to understand. He seemed to have a fair vocabulary, but cared little about sentence structure and said things in improper order, leaving out whole parts and phrases at random. I assumed that his native language structure must be quite different from ours.

"But don't you think that that belongs to your people? It shouldn't be taken away from them. They'll lose it." I was very serious about that. I became worried about his people and envisioned them as poverty-stricken Amazon Indians, suffering disease and losing their lands.

He stopped me, saying, "They are fine, my people. My companion and I have taught many of the young folks of our tribe. My teachers, they were not one of us. They came from a long ways away just to teach us. Some of these things are not long with my people either."

"Oh," I said, wondering what all that meant. I wanted to ask where, exactly, he came from. And then I wanted to know where his teachers came from. It seemed odd to me that his teachers were not from his own people. Perhaps that was just a tradition of the natives of that area. The questions and what seemed incongruities poured into my head. How on Earth did I get into this odd situation? I wished I weren't so wishy-washy and timid. As my mind was grinding on, I began to feel huge pangs of inadequacy and powerlessness. Old bits and pieces of uncomfortable memories bubbled up from the deep. I wanted to be someplace else doing something pleasurable, but the inertia of the moment had me cemented to the spot.

Domano suggested some terms of a continuing relationship where we could both fulfill our destinies. "To work, we can meet one, sometimes two times a week. For half days, or maybe sometimes for whole days. Some days will be outside but very private, and some days in my apartment will be okay. You need to learn to be in the city. This is a new time. There is much that is city wise. People need to have balance with cities. Will you come see me in my apartment Tuesday, twelve-thirty?"

"Can I bring someone?" My throat was dry.

"No." Domano answered with finality, his eyes seeming to catch more light.

I don't know why, but I wanted to go. Overactive curiosity, maybe. I was frightened. My whole body was tight.

Women just didn't go to a bizarre stranger's home alone, if at all. I wondered what could possibly happen to me. I felt manipulated and confused. But I saw a spark in him that was thrilling and far departed from diapers and dishes. The words floated out of me as if someone else were answering, "Yes. Tuesday, twelve-thirty."

2

VIEW OF THE EDGE

I kept my appointment on Tuesday. It seemed like a foolish thing to do. I had barely mentioned the crazy old man on the beach to my husband, but I was reluctant to tell him about the coffee shop, and especially that I had agreed to go meet that weird old man whom I didn't even know, alone at his apartment. I was just a housewife and mother, for god's sake. I was sure he wouldn't understand. I didn't. Why should he? So I went without telling him my plans. I felt like a little kid on Halloween sneaking into the yard of the outcast neighbor that all the children had been forbidden to go to, just to see what was really there.

Although I didn't think Domano planned to cause me any harm, I was afraid of him, and even more afraid of being in his apartment. Once I arrived I began to wonder if I had made a mistake, and I wanted to leave. But as I had too often in the past, I let the momentum of the situation pull me on. I didn't notice it then, but sometimes I wasn't a very decisive person and was easily influenced by the circumstances around me. I had never learned how to stand up very consistently for what I thought or wanted. I suppose, like so many women of my era, I was raised to be an obedient daughter and wife, seen and useful but not heard.

At Domano's invitation, I stepped into the doorway with hesitation and wonder. His little apartment was sunny and bright. The furnishings were simple and sparse, with only a few artifacts, not as decoration but as necessary utensils. The hardwood floors were bare, and there were no curtains or drapes, only white pull shades on the two front windows. Instead of a sofa there were two very low-sitting rustic wicker benches with no pillows or cushions. A wooden orange crate sat against the wall with a plywood board on the top. A hand-made leather sack hung on one wall, four hand drums on another. There was an overhead light, and large candles on the floor with an abalone shell full of ashes.

He invited me in again and motioned for me to sit on one of the benches. As he went into the kitchen I turned around to look out the front windows at the ocean, and the sunlight was reaching through the windows in long beams. This place was peaceful. Unusual, but altogether comforting. Perhaps for the first time, I thought Domano might be telling the truth.

"I am happy you are here," he said as he returned from the kitchen. He seemed unstable on his feet. "Would you like hot water for tea? I have also coffee."

"That's very thoughtful, thank you. I don't want you to go to any trouble." I was worried that he might overdo it, that he might be in pain.

"It is not trouble that I seek, but to share the peace of my home." He seemed so generous and polite, a real foreign gentleman.

"Coffee," I quickly said, hoping I hadn't inadvertently offended him. "Can I help you?"

"No," he said smiling, "this is easy coffee. You be restful. You enjoy the sunlight." He returned in a moment with a tray and suggested that because I loved the light so much I should sit on the bench by the window while he talked.

He certainly was astute for an old "derelict."

"I am *kala keh nah seh*. That is a storyteller, or speaker of magic words. The one who learns to speak the fibers of Earth Spider's web, the old singer of the sounds that pull things apart. A *kala keh nah seh* is a dancer, a builder of webs of balance. By these webs I lead balance.

"The world is such a delicate place. Like a very thin spider web. We are so much like the spiders. Yes, the spiders of Earth. I am Spiderman, yes?" he laughed, flexing his arms.

I pictured him shinnying up a skyscraper in leotards. I laughed.

"As the little spider lives, so she works, she builds, even as she walks. So as we live we build our worlds. We can walk our world, or knot our world. Or think it. Some are makers from their heart. Or some birthers. Some build like the wind. I will tell you all these things. I will tell you how my teachers taught me to pull on the web. It takes a long time. First we find Patience. Perhaps you will meet Patience in this sunlight and become good friends. You have similar natures. I think you will like each other good."

I must have had a quizzical look on my face. He stopped and tilted his head and looked at me the way a dog does when it's confused.

"Don't you make any need to worry," he said, straightening his head and smiling. "I will tell you again. I will tell you again and again until your insides knows. It takes a long time to learn. You will make a new world. We will teach you how to be a Spider Woman," again flexing his arms and giggling. I laughed, too.

I didn't understand him, but he seemed to know exactly what he was saying. He was confident, clear, and perceptive. I didn't suspect or fear him any longer. I did still wonder if perhaps he had picked me by mistake. He seemed to have such a clear purpose. My mind strayed off, wondering what was involved in learning someone's whole tradition. It seemed overwhelming. How could I find the time for such a major undertaking? I had a family to take care of and a college career that I wanted to prepare for. I love studying and learning with a passion, and what Domano proposed was so very appealing, but I was convinced I couldn't do it. He must have the wrong person; he must have mistaken me for someone else.

I thought how exciting and beautiful, even exotic, it would be to study with him, but it couldn't be. I had my life, my all-consuming obligations and responsibilities. And he would be sure to find his mystery student any day. My mind zipped around at all the possibilities of what he might teach, his culture, his oral traditions, arts, histories, religion. I felt very envious of that lucky student.

"Patience tells me now that you have much work to do. You have given up already. You give your job away. You say, 'Ah, this can't be *my* job.' Yes? It is you I will teach. I'll tell you why.

"My teachers gave me a dream. They showed me where you live now and what you look like. I saw many things that would show me where you would be. Animals came and agreed to point you out when the time came.

"I saw you in the town here, and I thought she's the one. So I watched. I watched the animals. First a little white cat followed you and stopped and talked to you. I am sure he told you that we were near. You petted that cat just as you did in my dream. So I watched more, as my teachers instructed me. I saw many signs that the world gave me, just as they said it would. I went to the beach cliff in the storm and called you. You were very good. You waste no time. You were the only other person to come on the cliff all day. Yes. It is you.

"When you saw me on the cliff, you saw your destiny. It is a very shaky feeling the first time you see your destiny. Yes? There can be much fear. Destiny has a sister who is stuck to her body. Forever. She is Death. They grow together, these sisters. You knew they were there. That is good. You heard their cry. You thought it was a sea gull. The lightning pointed you out, too. It struck on both sides of you at once!" he giggled. "You are the one all right! Lightning never lies!" He sat back on his bench and giggled and giggled. He had such a sweet innocence and lightness. I didn't know whether to think he was pulling my leg or that he was just nuts. But one thing was certain, he was quite the charmer.

"I did the same thing as you," he continued. "Some day I will tell you the story of how I met my teachers." His eyes twinkled and he giggled again. "But right now I will tell you the story about my first lesson with them."

He gave me no chance to think or speak. He just started right along with his story, pulling me into his jungle environment. I felt dislocated. I wanted to analyze his justifications for selecting me, but I couldn't hold my mind on anything except the picture he was now painting of his tropical home.

"We were in my village. It's a small village. Only sixty-five people. Well, maybe I count a dog or two, too. We were preparing for a happy day. A special joy for all my people. One of our women chose a big happy man from the Zictato people downriver. They will be companions. And they chose our village to live. And have many children. They make a great joy in our village to bring the laughter of children for all. Everyone is happy. Everyone is very excited. There are not that many people, so there are not that many —'weddings'— as you say. We don't have a word like that. Taking a companion for life is a different way with my people.

"Among my people it is believed that all animals and plants are smart. They can be a friend if you are good. Some people believe rocks and dirt and mountains and rivers are smart, too. And will make very good friends. When I was young I had animal friends. And some plant friends, too. I was a pretty good guy. I didn't think so sure about rocks being smart, though. I thought maybe those people got hit in the head with a rock.

"My teachers said nothing. They just watch me and wait for a perfect time to show me. To lead me to the edge of my web.

"People are busy with this and busy with that. They make fancy grass-bark skirts and capes. And make paintings on their houses, carve special magic, fix lots of food, and prepare for the ceremonies. Everyone runs around. They practice songs and dances. Some men go into the jungle and cut large poles, branches, reeds. They bring them to the women, who build a new house for our young couple. The young woman's grandfather catches a pig for a gift to the young man. All is working very well for the village. Everyone is having lots of fun.

"My teachers had asked me what I thought about rocks and things being alive. Smart," he said, tapping his chest. "I said they didn't seem to be. They never talked to me like the animals did. They were brothers on this world to me, but they didn't seem to be like that. My teachers say, 'Hmmmmmmm. Hmmmmmmm.'"

"So how did your teachers lead you to the edge of your web, Domano?" I asked.

"Oh. That was not hard. My web was very small when I was young. I sure didn't have to go far. Your web is much bigger than mine was."

"What does that mean?" I asked.

"That the world you have built your web to be reaches farther, includes more. Weaves together with far more other webs. It is very complex. Mine was simple. It was very easy for me to fall off the edge," and he made a sudden and precise movement with his body, appearing to fall and tumble completely off the bench, flailing his arms and legs, giving the illusion that he had a far greater length to fall than one foot. Then he giggled. I felt as if the bottom had fallen out from under me. I was dizzy and disoriented. My stomach felt as if it had been dropped from an airplane, and I was becoming nauseated.

His "falling" was so sudden and so perfectly mimed, it took me completely by surprise. I believed in his oldness and doddering, and in one second he tore that image and belief

16

apart. In that moment his movements were the studied movements of a twenty-year-old acrobat. And then, just as quickly, he was up on the bench and back to his feeble self. I laughed. I had difficulty formulating thoughts and justifying to myself how such a doddering old man could also be so ominous, fearsome, youthfully agile, and comical.

"The other men in the tribe hunted wild pig for the feast," he just continued on with his story, his eyes flickering. "They were going to roast several in a big hole that was lined with fire, and many sweet leaves and fruit. Pigs like that taste very good." I had a hard time listening or concentrating. I felt as if my brain and stomach had been left back on the floor with Domano's fall.

"What did you say the pigs were roasted with?" I interrupted.

"The pigs were fired up with many sweet leaves." He grinned. "And fruit. It is very special. Very sacred. Only for the best ceremonies," he said, giggling. "Just watch my lips. You will be okay.

"Our celebration was getting a big momentum. It was the day before the ceremony and my teachers come to me with the young woman's father. They want me to be the singer of the sacred joining song. This was a great honor. I was very surprised they wanted me."

By now I was completely captivated by the story, imagining the jungle village around me with all the sights and sounds and excitement.

"Usually this is asked of a much older person. This song has to be brand new for each ceremony. There was not much time. I wasn't so sure, but my teachers said to the father, 'Oh, yes. Oh, sure. He can do it. He's good. There is plenty of time for him. Have no worries. Domano will provide your family with a most special song.'

"This worried me a whole lot. I have never made a song like that before. I never was even a very good singer. My teachers send him on his way to gather herbs to burn while I go make the song.

"I say to my teachers, 'Wait. I'm scared. I'm scared I can't do this special job. You better get an older person.' They pat my back, and look understanding and concerned. One hands me some meats and fruits. They say to go out and find the song. I did not know what that was. How does somebody 'find' a song? They tell me quietly, so no one else hears, to go to the giant rock not far from the little waterfall at the opening of snake's cave. Put my head close to the rock and ask for the sacred song that belongs to the woman's family. Then listen. The rock will tell me the song. I must remember perfectly and bring it back. This is the secret of sacred songs. They make me say not to tell the secret.

"So I go to the rock. I do not think this is a good idea. I spend lots of time wondering if a snake is coming out of the hole. I watch and watch and watch. I do not have my head close to rock. That is too close to snake's hole. I am pretty scared. After a while I see it is getting much later, and I have no song. I haven't even listened! So I worry about that, too. I think that if I don't bring back the song, maybe I better not go back at all. It would be a big disgrace. I feel very ashamed. But not enough shame for me to do such a silly foolish thing as listening to a rock and putting my head close to a snake's house. The later it gets, the more disgrace and silly I feel. It is a bad place to have one's self in.

"So the sun is getting kind of low. Now I think to myself, I better put my head to the stone and try. I bend my body in a very unstable place to keep as much of me as possible away from the snake's home. And set my head on the rock near the top so I can still see the hole and keep watch.

"I am all bent funny like this when out of the hole comes a very huge snake. Then I try to pull back as fast as possible. I am very full of fear. I cannot think. I jerk back, forgetting how unbalanced I put my body. Oh! I slip very good. And get myself wedged between the giant rock and some little rocks next to it. I cannot move easily. And quick as breath, the big snake comes over the top of the rock and hisses at me. We are very close, about one arm's length. This snake I know could tell how much fear I have. I decide to not move a hair. So we stare at each other for a pretty long time. Then I notice, my head is against the giant rock. I think maybe this is a good time to listen to the rock, while standing off the snake. So I sit there, stuck and shaking, staring at the snake, trying to listen to the rock.

"Oh! I hope real hard that no one comes by and sees me! I think I look very foolish, and I am scared half to death! This is what happens, I speak to myself, when a youth is sent to do an old one's job. Tears begin to roll down my cheek. I feel so sorry for myself.

"Then I think I hear sounds inside the rock. I hold my breath. Snake hisses and moves its head a little closer. I hear more sounds. And more. I try to hold myself still from shaking so I can hear the rock. That does not work so good, but the sound gets louder and I can hear it better. I cannot believe this. The rock is really singing to me! So I listen hard, and remember the song real good. Perfect. I sing it out loud to the rock, forgetting about the snake still arched in front of me. The rock likes my singing a lot. I sing several times and notice that snake likes the song too. It smiles at me, and moves away back into its hole.

"This is such a very exciting time for me. I have succeeded! I make myself very happy. Very proud. I think I am pretty hot stuff. When the snake is out of sight I pull myself loose and thank the rock. I leave a present of my necklace for the rock. It is not much of a gift for what the rock gave, but it is the most special thing I have. The rock is happy. I am happy. Snake is happy. I run all the way back home, singing the song. I make a great presentation at the ceremony. Everyone is happy." He stopped talking and looked at me gently.

I wished I had someone to talk to who had also heard the story, someone I could compare notes with. Indeed, Domano was a master storyteller. He had completely captured my attention. I could see the jungle plants and smell the damp floor and flowers. I could almost swear I heard the birds and the people. When the story ended it was as though I returned to the living room of his apartment. I felt confused, and a little surprised to be in Santa Cruz. I think I was disappointed that I couldn't really go to the jungle and stay there as long as I wanted.

Domano patted his belly and said, "Let's go for a little trek on the beach."

There was an easy path near his place down the cliff to the sandy beach. It was empty. We walked barefoot on the edge of the waves not speaking a word. Suddenly I felt watched. I looked up, and standing firmly with her hands on her hips was an old Indian woman in a red dress. She was staring intently at me. I gasped. I had never seen a woman like her before. She was even more forceful and dynamic than Domano had been when I had first seen him on the cliff. The bottoms of my feet tingled. My stomach seemed to be shaking of its own accord. I heard ringing in my ears and felt a now-familiar fear welling up inside me. It was almost as if all of the beach were aimed at her. She had a disarming air of command about her. I had no overt or logical reason to be afraid of her, but she unnerved me to my core. It seemed that here was a woman who could tackle any situation, problem, or adversary, like a tank. She was old, but obviously very strong, quick, and intelligent. In my world women just weren't like that. They were Donna Reed or somebody's anonymous little old gray-haired mother who sat and knitted in a rocking chair all day, sipping on tea and eating prunes.

She challenged my reality, my worth, my accomplishments, and my goals. The sheer possibility of her existence intrigued me, but I didn't want anything to do with her. I didn't dare.

"Ah! Chea!" Domano smiled. "Another piece of your destiny." And she began to walk toward us.

"No!" I choked, my panic increasing.

"Come." He was firm but understanding. "The time to open a new door is here for you. We will only talk briefly. Come. I want you to meet this woman who has been my life companion.

"Come."

3

MEETING DEATH
AND DESTINY

We met again, the three of us, in the Hetakas' apartment two weeks later. I honestly didn't know why I went. They invited me in. I sat down in the same spot as before, on the bench in the sunlight. I was very nervous. I felt that I was in way over my head. Chea stood in the doorway to the kitchen. She was perhaps just under five feet tall, stocky, and about the same age as Domano. Her hair was thick, stark white and pulled back into a roll. She was not cheery and playful like Domano, and I felt peculiarly alarmed by her. She had no expression at all; I couldn't read her. I wondered what she was thinking about me. She just stood motionless, watching me.

She wore a pair of black corduroy slacks, a black sweatshirt with a hood, and sandals. I thought how unusually she was dressed for a woman of her age and background. But after all, this was Santa Cruz in 1974, and one could see just about anything in Santa Cruz in those days.

She smiled at me gently, then came and sat down next to me. I stiffened involuntarily. She was soft spoken, her eyes deep and quiet. She was highly alert but warm and consoling. Even though there was a great deal of strength about her, she was not manly. This was a quality that I had never observed before in a woman. I didn't understand it. And even though I felt I could trust her, I continued to feel an unexplainable alarm in her presence. I wished she weren't there. Domano had excused himself to go to the kitchen to fix me some coffee. "Special dark beans for you, and some sugar, I've got."

"We have much work to do." Chea tried to catch my eyes. I didn't want to look at her. "We will teach you as much as we can, the things our teachers taught to us. They were not from our village. In the beginning we believed them to be white people from the edge of the jungle lands. But later we learned they come from farther away. There were six of them altogether. Three taught Domano in his home village, and three lived in my village and taught me. After a few years we all came together. And that's when Domano and I became companions. This was long ago when we were very young. We will talk more about that later. First I will tell you about our Earth. She is changing. It is the time now that everything becomes different. The very center of our Earth and ourselves is shifting. This brings new knowledge and ways of being. We will teach you these things as they were taught to us." She spoke matter-of-factly, in a rather businesslike way. Her command of the language was much better than Domano's, but she still had a thick accent and a little confusion with syntax from time to time. I had trouble understanding her. I didn't want to listen to her. I was afraid she was going to be the one to do all the talking and teaching, and I wanted Domano to do that. He was light and fun. So, like a child, without consciously realizing it, I tried to ignore her. I hoped that if I did it well enough, she'd go away or disappear. And I wouldn't have to deal with her any longer.

"This will take place in the city. Here." Chea pointed down to the ground. "In town, instead of in the wild lands as we were taught. This is because most of your people now live in cities and this is where the central axis of group shifting is taking place. It is more difficult to learn these things in the city, but if you and your people can't learn them here and maintain control over the shifts, then you will not be able to do it at all."

I didn't want to have to talk to her, but she struck my curiosity too hard. I had to ask, "What happens if we can't do it at all? What does that mean?"

Chea looked at me through just her left eye, like a bird, then said, "That means you have to learn a new way of being, or you will cease to be. Learn how to shift with your planet and solar system or face extinction.

"These traditions we have to pass on to you are learned by the doing. By action. We will tell you, but telling doesn't teach, it only prepares. To truly know a thing, one must live it completely. Through the body. When the body has learned, so has the heart, the inner parts of your being. The last to have the knowing is your thoughts. In your world you are taught that your thoughts are what needs to be taught. It is believed if this part of your mind thinks it knows, then surely that is all that is needed. So you try to teach just your thoughts and pay no attention to the rest of you." I could see her through the corner of my eye, watching me, calculating what she said. I realized then that she was actually quite a bit smaller than me.

Her voice became more animated. "Your thoughts are just that. Your thoughts. They know nothing for themselves. They are just movements and patterns. They are tools of greater, more elusive parts of ourselves. And without training and discipline they are very poor tools. They trick us and tell us that they are the master and the center. And then we spend our lives trapped in their movements and patterns. Hooked like a big fish."

Domano came back in with coffee and cookies and set them on the floor in front of us. I was relieved to have him back in the room. He spoke as he sat down on the other bench with his cup. "In the times passing we lived from here," he said, tapping his abdomen. "In this time, to shift, we must now learn to live from here." He tapped the center of his chest. "From the upper belly, the life of a person is strung from patterns that are two-directional only. They are made only this way or that way. Mine or yours. Black or white. Up or down. Good or evil. It is the habits of our thoughts and their feelings that make us see only in this way. And the foundation of these patterns is fear. Fear makes our cultures animate. It is the on switch, you could say, for all that people do."

Chea brought her legs up, crossing them under her, and pointed to her upper belly. "A world that puts all its attention to this part of its self and ignores its other parts becomes singular in its dimension and eventually will throw itself off balance, as we see in our world has happened. We see a world split into warring opposites, where the undisciplined thoughts are master, and control is elusive, and the pursuit of this control is all-consuming. Only the people don't know any more what it is they are needing to control. They just assume that more control over more and more is what is most advantageous. They are looking so hard outside themselves with the eyes of their warring thoughts, they never notice all of their own self." I didn't want to hear what she was saying. I knew she was right. Our culture was in bad shape. I could hear a real compassion and concern in her voice, even though her face didn't show it. But I didn't see why they were talking about world problems that to me seemed out of our reach to influence.

Then Chea's face softened slightly, and she said, "This makes them afraid. They are afraid of all that is unknown. Afraid of the loss of anything. Afraid of powerlessness. Afraid of pain. Afraid of failure. And most of all they have a fear that has all the other fears inside itself: they fear all death. Within the midst of their imagined annihilation they breathe every breath. Their bodies knowing only this fear and the fleeting divergences that distract them from it. The people of this planet are forgetting how to experience outside the tyrannical habits of their minds.

"It is our tradition we give to you that will lead you to break out of the habits of mind."

"But I know plenty of people who are happy and fulfilled."
I looked over to Domano.

He said softly, "This is just a picture of their masks. I
assure you, what looks like happiness is just a picture for
themselves and all to see that describes their distractions from
the real condition beneath of love confused by pain and fear.
And also, there is a whisper of something else, out of reach.
Something more than what they know, something grand and
exquisite. You know of this.

"Most of them do not pursue this mysterious thing. They
are too lazy and fearful. They try to ignore it. But that just
makes much confusion and pain for them. You are one who
pursues it."

This was beginning to sound far more exotic and mysterious than the studying of tribal cultural and social applications,
and technological historical advancements and variations, or,
heaven forbid, kinship structures.

"Is that what your tradition is going to teach me? To pursue this . . . unknown?"

"One can pursue forever and never catch," Chea said,
imitating running with two fingers going round and round in
front of her. "We teach you how to catch."

"Yes. Catch," Domano added as he mimed a fisherman
reeling in a huge fish, and the fish turns out to be so big it
drags him into the water. As before, he was very funny, and his
actions were performed to perfection. He glugged and choked
on the imaginary water as it splashed over his head, but he
never let go of his "rod" and diligently kept reeling in the line.
I laughed till I could barely breathe and actually had tears on
my face. This was the first time I had seen Chea laugh. I hadn't
expected her to be so unrestrained. She suddenly showed the
same innocence Domano displayed. In the height of his antics
she held her nose with one hand and jumped into Domano's
imaginary ocean, bottom first, and began to splash around in
the "water" with him. She took me completely by surprise. I

had thought she was far too reserved to behave in such a way. I didn't know what to make of either of them. They were both so different from anybody I had ever met before. Domano struggled and choked as though surprised by Chea, and we all laughed and joked for a while before they resumed the lesson. I must admit I had become very intrigued.

Chea was still chuckling as she sat back on the bench, gesturing with her arm. She said, "This is a tradition of action. It will be our way to set you into doing. You will find there will be little need for talking about it. We will always give you ample instruction and explanation. But the reality of learning is the experience of it, not the talking about it. You can ask us anything you want at any time, and we will do what we can to give you understanding.

"We ask only a commitment from you of silence to the outside."

"What do you mean, 'silence to the outside'?" I asked.

"It is our only condition that we ask of you." Chea spoke as though she wanted to make sure I understood. "It is critical or we would not require it. It is that you must not tell anyone about us, or any of the teachings. You must not write down or record anything from any of these sessions. No notes. No letters."

"But how can I remember anything clearly? How can I study without notes, or records, or—something?" I was so surprised at what they said that I felt offended. I prided myself on my intellectual prowess. After all, I had just applied for enrollment as a freshman to the University of California at Santa Cruz. To me studying and learning meant observing, analyzing, discussing, taking notes, practicing, and reviewing. It seemed almost an impossibility that I could accomplish anything under their conditions. I felt cornered and frustrated, as if I were failing before I had begun. I had very little idea what it was they wanted to teach me, but I wanted to learn it, whatever it was. I was coming to like them, even Chea. They had something about them that was special. They were curiously vital and able. And I wanted that.

I sat silently for a time thinking out the consequences of this silence. No notes! No talking! What would I say to my husband? How could I spend whole afternoons with these people and never tell him? He was my best friend. We talked about almost everything. Would I have to lie to him? Or to my kids? "What about my husband?" I asked.

"It is for your benefit we make this condition," Chea said, picking up her cup again. "Right now these teachings are for you. This rule is to help you, not restrict you. For you, our new young friend, talking about learning is a way for you to keep all of your attention locked in the habits of your mind. It is like prison bars for you. And notes as well. What we have to teach you is outside these bars. It is what is beyond the linear." Chea took both my hands. Her face actually showed great concern, and it was as though she were speaking directly into my eyes. "You are not your husband. You have your own death. Your own destiny. You cannot tie yourself to the shadow of another being, to another's mental habits. To learn our ways, you must do this learning for only you. Not anyone else. You must know in your heart that you are accomplishing this thing for you alone."

For me alone. That concept felt odd. If felt scary, selfish, almost sacrilegious. How could they ask such a thing of me? If I had no one in my life it would be easier, it wouldn't make any difference. But to shut my loved ones out, how could I?

Chea's voice got sterner. "How best can you be for your family and community? How best can you be good for them? It is by you making yourself a better person for yourself first. Yes?"

"Yes," I answered unsurely.

"You must swear to yourself first that you do this for you. And then you must commit to us to abide by our conditions of silence, or you will not be able to learn. You think you betray your husband by keeping secrets. You betray only yourself by tying yourself to his shadow."

I was shaking. She was right. For the first time I saw that I had abandoned my own dreams, my destiny, to be a ghost-like builder in someone else's. I was not living the life I had hoped for in my youth, but the life that had been prescribed by a cultural expectation. I mumbled out loud, "How disgusting. Living a lie. And never even noticing!" I disliked myself intensely. I felt very uncomfortable. I had actually betrayed myself, throwing away all my own ideas and hopes as though they were nothing, a child's fantasies, worthless. "My God."

"Yes," Domano said. "It has been that to you, these shadows of your culture, your husband. We will fix you more coffee. You sit in the sunlight and think as long as you need on this commitment."

I looked up at them. They were both staring at me intensely and lovingly. Then they got up and took the tray into the kitchen. I had brought both of my legs up onto the bench and was sitting with them pressed to my chest, with my hands wrapped over my knees and my arms hugging the sides of my legs. I didn't even know when I had moved to get into that position. It occurred to me then just how unconscious I was. My mind fell on old pieces of memories of my ambitions, visions, my views of myself. I was going to be an artist and a scholar. Maybe a musician or a composer. Or I thought I could even write poetry and hobnob with actors, writers, and painters and sip espresso in quaint coffee shops. I planned to travel and explore the ruins of ancient cities, and discuss philosophy and science.

I think I must have been in shock. I sat curled up, shaking and rocking. I never noticed Domano and Chea returning to the room with the fresh coffee and cookies.

Domano stepped up and handed me my coffee. "How best can one be true to oneself? How is this mystery in each of our lives brought to balance? Can people weed through all the desires of their culture to find their own destiny? You knew your destiny was nearby when you saw me on the cliff. You knew your destiny when you were but a girl. Can you see it now?"

I was so pained, crying, grieving for all my abandoned dreams and lost time. I rocked myself and sipped my coffee. I loved my children and my husband so very much. I wouldn't give them up for the world, but they were not my original ambitions. How did it happen? I was not doing a single thing from my old dreams. They were right. I had a littered space in my life where the rest of my destiny should be.

Domano and Chea were so unlike anybody I knew. They were clear, passionate, and self-assured. They had a knowledge I could only guess about. Indeed, they seemed unusually balanced all the time. I wanted that. I wanted that to be my destiny.

I finished my coffee and set the cup back on the tray. The room seemed to be getting overly warm. I was actually beginning to sweat, something I almost never did.

Domano, gently studying me, said, "I will tell you a little story about how things came to be.

"In the beginning of things there had not yet been time to make all things and set all things into doing. In this place, a beginning place for our world, there were, sitting and preparing things that were to come, two very old women. These two were very, very old, and knew much. This was in a time before the Sun lived. It was dark all the time. It was so long ago that it was before death lived, also. Everything was pretty different. One day the old women were talking about light and death for our world. One old woman said she would be happy without light if there would be no death. The other old woman said that if it were not possible to have the one without the other, it was better to have both. Because life without light was unbearable."

Chea had been playing a little clay whistle as Domano was telling me his story. She stopped when he finished and set it down. It was in the shape of a turtle, about four inches long. Her face became expressionless again. "Death," she said, "is the point of change. Everything in our world experiences different forms of change. To be with us means radical change. Is this what you want for yourself? Do you agree with our request?"

"Yes, I want what you have. It frightens me out of my wits, but I still want it. Is it my destiny to be like you? You seem almost . . . unreal."

Chea studied my eyes again. "You will meet your own destiny soon enough. There is only one thing we can guarantee you."

"What is that?" I asked.

"Why, change, of course," she said with a chuckle. "Change is the common denominator in this world. You could say that a change is a death, the movement that pulls you away from one thing and pushes you into another. Movement. We are beings expressing our existence in the midst of tide after tide of movement. If we do not learn how to manipulate ourselves within these currents, we spend our time being tossed about like seaweed in a storm. One can learn to perceive the points of change and use them. This is *ka ta see*. *Tla ikt la ka ta see.* The learning of the ways of balance. This is said to be the dance of the stars, to learn how to not be carried off with the tides, but to keep balance. To dance. To give movement of your choosing."

I was beginning to feel sick. I was sweating profusely, and my head was spinning. "Chea," I said. "I think I'd better go home. I feel kind of sick. If I've got something, I don't want to give it to you guys."

"Why don't you just lie down for a minute," she said. "Rest. You rest a bit before you go drive. I don't think it's such a good idea, you go driving like this."

Domano agreed with her. They reassured me that it was all right for me to rest there, that I would feel better soon. Probably I was catching some bug. Meanwhile, they would tell me about the dance.

"The dance!" Chea's eyes glittered as she sat back against the wall on the bench with every muscle poised, the corners of her mouth just barely turned up. "The dance is joy itself." She seemed to wait for my reaction. "It is our position of connection. Our point of balance. This is our only possession. It is the focused collection of our attention. The centering of the flow of life. The center of the universe. And this is also our point of change. Look at me. It is the being this moment of existing that we are breathing this very instant, to the next instant and breath, and the next. It has no time and location. The point is at the present, you see.

"How much of your attention can you bring to this present? And the next? Where have you scattered all your attention? Can you turn it away from all its preoccupations and bring it here? This is the key. Your power lies in your attention. A change can either be a movement that drains your power or a movement that you can draw power from. It can be of chance, or of your making."

She paused and looked out the window a moment, as though she were fighting for the right words. "This dance, to see it from far away, has nothing to do with struggle or pain, or chauvinism, or maliciousness. It has to do with compassion, spontaneity, beauty, pure passion, materialization, and dematerialization. It is equity and union with all that there is. The dance is from here," and then she spoke passionately, tapping the center of her chest. "From the heart. There is only one thing worth pursuing in this world: The dance. The balance. *Ka ta see.*

"One day your death will catch you. And will you lie down and say, 'Oh, come. Take me. I've been waiting so long for you'? Or will you snivel and whimper for all the things

you never were or did? Or be overcome by the terror of annihilation? I tell you, Kay, that for one who meets his death and
lives again, the world changes. They know what it is to lose
everything. They have felt the very nature of death, and they
know that it is not annihilation but a movement. They sense
the value and uniqueness of our world and cherish it and their
time within it beyond all else. Life itself becomes their
beloved. They gain the ability to turn decisions into power.
How else can one become a shaman but by a rapid and
extreme movement of such force that it breaks one away from
all that went before?"

I felt extremely light headed. Everything was tilting and
spinning. Even though I understood what Chea was saying, I
couldn't hold any words in my head. I was very nauseated and
was about to become sick. "Chea," I said gagging, "Is that
what I'm going to do? Become dead? A shaman?" She seemed
to be prepared for me and had brought a bucket.

"You asked about your destiny. Let your body clean itself.
Don't fight the sickness so. You try to relax a bit. Your body
knows what it needs to do. Right now it is smarter than you
are. Your destiny is close at hand. You must prepare yourself
to meet her. Let your stomach clear itself. And let your mind
clear itself. Don't fight with your thoughts. Let them go. Let
your mind relax with its emptiness, and be free for a moment
from the tyranny of your thoughts. Turn your vision to see the
expanses of this thing we call mind."

After I vomited my nausea subsided somewhat, but my
weakness and incapacity were increasing. I could barely move
my arms. Domano eased my head back onto the bench, and
Chea lifted my legs. I felt as if I were dissolving away into the
air. I followed Chea's instructions to allow my mind to
become empty for the first time in my life. And just as she had
said, I found that there existed there an immeasurable expanse
of mental observance and capacity that has nothing to do with
singular thoughts as sentences. Rather what I found were

profound states of thorough knowing and thorough understanding in the form of complex whole bodies of knowledge, or potentials for extensions of the self beyond all previous boundaries.

I was so weak I had to struggle to speak, "There is something very wrong with me. I'm sick. I'm scared. I see something . . . else . . . "

"Do not try to talk," Chea said. "Save your energy. Just let the words go off their own way. Fear is the only thing hindering you. Don't allow the fear to grow. You cannot turn back now. Let yourself enjoy the stillness in your mind. Observe. Become that which observes."

I tried to get up, but I couldn't move. My legs and arms felt very far away and had a dull, vibrating ache.

Chea brushed the hair back off my forehead. "The world sometimes is a frightening place. Being alive can be terrifying. To dance, you must balance the fear with the ecstasy— experiencing the sheer magnificence of all the endless existence that is so close all around you." She got up and went into the kitchen.

Some time later she leaned over me. "Kay, we have to go. You have an appointment. We know it is hard for you to move, but you have to make an effort. We will help."

They pulled me up, propping me between them and slinging my arms over their shoulders. I was too weak and sick. I couldn't move. They ended up dragging me through the kitchen and toward the back door. Everything was dark and getting darker. I don't remember going through the back door, yet we ended up somewhere outside, going down a dirt path with lots of foliage on the sides. It was dark, nighttime. There was a moon in the sky, making light enough to see. A small clearing was ahead of us, and I could see two shadowy figures at the far edge of it. There was not a thought in my head. I had become completely captivated and awed by the endless expanse of our existence, the way our world, as

34

I knew it, folded into other worlds, overlapping, ebbing, and receding.

We had stopped. They were propping me up, and Chea was slapping my face and calling me. "Kay! Bring your attention here! Kay! Kay! You must meet these two." She pointed down the path to the clearing at the two figures there. "Death and Destiny."

As I reoriented my attention back to my body and the figures ahead, sheer terror completely gripped me. "No! No! No! No!" I kept screaming, trying to make my body work enough to break free and run. I suddenly realized who they were and what my "appointment" was. I vomited again. My body shook involuntarily. I had no strength. I knew then that I was dying. They dragged me by my underarms a few feet closer.

Chea whispered into my left ear, "They are your Death and Destiny. You must honor them as your trusted elders. Know them well in your heart and your dance will always be with perfect intention. Know them here," she stroked me across the top of my forehead, "and you will know your dance among the stars.

"Death is everything. And it is nothing. It ends the old and builds the new and is what weaves this living. In all our making there is unmaking. Death is but the same that helped you here into this world. Death and Destiny come with you here and stalk you all your way back."

We moved a few feet closer. I was so completely overwhelmed by my fear that I had trouble staying conscious. I knew I had only moments left to live. The closer I got to the two figures the sooner I would die. I had no command over my body. Inside I was hysterical, panicked, and flailing. Outside my body did not respond, and I was being dragged into the clearing.

As we approached, I could hear the voice of one of the figures. The sounds were deeply haunting and passionate, like song, but primal. My terror seemed to meld with these sounds. I felt them swelling within me until I could no longer tell if they originated from the figures or from me. I felt as if the sounds were burning inside me.

We reached the far side of the clearing and stood in front of the figures. I could see them clearly now, the song growing in intensity. The figure on the right, as I looked at them, was the singer. She was young and beautiful. She pulled back the hood of her long cloak. Her hair was flowing, her eyes hypnotic and deep like the sea. Her song continued as the figure on the left lifted her arm to slide back the hood of her cloak. She was horror itself. I could hardly breathe. The song grew louder as the horrible one turned her eyes on me and smiled.

She looked like a living corpse. Bone with rotted skin barely hanging on it. There was light in her eyes and quickness in her actions. She held out her hand to me and spoke. "I am your Death."

I was compelled to reach out to her. Domano grabbed my arm and pulled it back. "Don't let her touch you. You are close to your death now. The closer she gets, the closer you are to leaving completely this body and this world. A day will come when she will reach out and you will not be able to slip away. That day she will take you with her. For now, you must listen well, little one."

Death spoke again: "Here is your Destiny who haunts you with the voice of the thrill of deeds portended to be and the daring you will need in your life."

I struggled and choked and yelled out, "Oh my god! What the hell am I doing here?!"

"Quiet yourself. Listen. Listen to her," Domano whispered as he kept me from moving and held his hand over my mouth.

Death spoke once again, the raspy words resounding slowly in the air around us. "I am the revealer, the announcer and describer of cycles, for the mystery of attention is mine. Through me know your equity with all things. Sing your momentum, Stellifa, and live your life to its very fullest. For balance's sake seek wellbeing and harmony with all things, and waste or harm nothing." Then she lowered her head and pulled her hood up until her eyes were hidden. Clouds covered the moon and the clearing darkened.

Domano and Chea helped me back down the path. My hysteria waned, but I was still very weak and sweaty. When we returned to the apartment, Domano went into the living room and began drumming and singing. Chea took me in the bathroom and helped me undress and bathe. Her actions were motherly, but her face was expressionless. The water was cold and brought back my strength and sense of sobriety. We said nothing.

The afternoon was almost gone when I got dressed. It didn't seem possible, but it was still the same day that I had arrived. I stood at the window looking to the west and listening to Domano for a short while. Chea handed me my purse and coat and hushed me with a finger to her lips.

I left without a word and had no contact with them until I returned two weeks later.

4

POWER OF THE SONG

I arrived on schedule. I don't know why. It was a crazy thing to do. I was truly terrified. I didn't trust them, yet I was compelled to go. I had thought about my experiences of the last meeting often during the preceding two weeks. I dreamt incessantly about the figures of Death and Destiny and the haunting of Destiny's song. I had no idea what had happened to me. The more I thought back on it, the less sure I was about any of it. I wondered if I had eaten something that made me get so sick. I couldn't tell if the figures I had seen had been a delirious dream or hypnosis or even somehow real. Maybe I returned to find out if any part of the Hetakas was *really* real, or if I was just jumping to wild conclusions.

I had become disjointed from the familiar. The authenticity of this world was losing its grip. Deep inside me there grew an unlimitedness to the universe. It was not a feeling. It was not a thought. It was a *piece* of me. I could no longer count on the world I used to know.

As I entered their home and we went through the usual amenities, the Hetakas seemed quite cheery and nonchalant, as though nothing out of the ordinary had ever happened. They brought out coffee and little sandwiches. I sat confused and silent.

Finally Domano began to speak. "For us to teach you it so much becomes a matter of words. Ideas are not words. And experiences are not words. So our task becomes leading you to experiences that give you learning. And to do that sometimes we need words. They are slippery, though, just like a water snake. Words can mean many different things to different people. When we describe something we are only correct from one viewpoint. Change the seat of observation and it is no longer completely true. Words are truly a miracle, but are like coyote. They are great tricksters. They can lead you down primrose lane, no?"

His using that old phrase threw me off. I wondered how he ever came across it, and I lost track of what he was saying.

"This is why I say we can not pass on knowingness to you through words. It is only your own personal experience that will make you truly understand a thing. Your being must have interaction in order for you to obtain thorough, true knowing. Our words maybe will help you digest the experience and lead your attention to the next. But with learning from experience, you will come to know how to do all of this without us. To do, learn, and know all by and for yourself. A time will come when you will no longer need us.

"But for right now, you want to know what you did last time. What happened. You tore a little hole in your web and fell off." He chuckled as he mimed with his fingers the tearing of an imaginary web and something unwittingly falling through it. "A little piece of you knows now there is more world than what your habits let you live in."

I thought to myself, at what cost is all this? Will they injure me? Kill me? Are all our lessons going to be like the last? What is the extent of their knowledge? Are there really people who have extraordinary abilities? What on Earth would I do with such a thing in my life? Where would it fit?

But a part of me didn't care where it would fit. It felt free and wild and curious. It wanted the extraordinary.

He leaned forward and said, "You died."

I knew it had felt as if I had died, but I was alive now, so how could I have died? Most likely, I thought, it was hypnosis. The possibility of a drug-induced experience never entered my mind. For me that was a most unfamiliar scenario.

"Your life has changed since the last time you were here," he continued. "You cannot find that world you left. It is because you made a huge movement. You changed. You moved your center all the way off your web." Reassuringly, he said, "You died.

"Everything you were, and everything you knew, and everything you discovered, created your experience of these primal forces. Death is the force in our universe that pulls everything apart. Brings to its end everything. It dissolves. It's the force of change. It is a force. Power. Movement. The world is like a current of a stream or the seas. It pushes in, through and out of 'here,' continually. The force that brings this is the force that causes the birth and death of a thing. As it dies to us it is born to something else. This force flows through the webs, through dimensions. There is knowledge in this force. And as with everything there is consciousness. When something is pushed into a world it has a kind of momentum, an inertia of action. One could say it has a plan. That is its other half—Destiny. This double-edged force is a framework of our world. It does not eliminate free will. It is more correct to say this force is a structure free will expands in. It is a little different kind of intelligence, a consciousness, than people are used to. Every nation of peoples has noticed the actions of this force as 'Deity'. The figures you saw were a personification of this force, this action in our universe.

"If you look at the world in a certain way, all you see is life and its movement—change. Collecting and dispersing. Moving along. When one *knows* this inside it brings great joy and passion. You see, death teaches you about life. Life is the common bond between all things. Death is the movement of life along its way. Death provides dynamic flux. Contained random expansion. Chaos."

He looked at me and laughed. I must have had a very puzzled expression. Not only was this old Indian hard to follow and getting technical but it was his choice of words, they were unnerving. To me, chaos seemed next to complete annihilation. I had read a little Hinduism a few years before that illustrated this concept. It spoke of the breaths of Brahma, describing the universe as coming into existence out of the chaos of Brahma's exhaled breath, and then dissolving into chaos again and being inhaled into oblivion.

He chuckled, "That water snake slipped right out of your fingers already. Breathe. Make peace for yourself. We will always repeat, until you learn. Breathe deeper."

After a moment he shook his head and said, "There is ablaze from the center, the heart of each and all things — life. From galaxies to photons. Life is conscious, intelligent energy that can collect itself into any function or shape. Your scientists break their atom apart, and what do they find? Energy moves around it, in it, forming it. If they look at these energies from one certain view, they would see it is in two halves moving like a dance, together. Then if they moved to a different view, they would see it has five parts, intimately, intricately woven together. And from another, one part only. They are all correct. Pretty crazy stuff, this energy that lives, yes? It collects around inertia to form energy patterns and matter. A person can learn how to collect it, store it, move it. When it collects into something, that is an individual. Its matrix has a unique pulsing, a rhythm, that belongs only to it. It sings to the universe and life pours through it, carrying its little song. It tells everybody around about its existence. This is life energy itself being scattered out as a gift from the heart. An individual's song is its joy. And we share them with each other continually. This is our web."

He moved his arms dramatically, demonstrating what he meant. He was delightfully theatrical. I knew he felt deeply about what he was telling me. I just hoped I could remember it all.

"Death is only what shoves life along its way. It is a doorway to something new. Nothing is annihilated or lost or forgotten. All is carried on to the next place and all experience is shared and remembered. It is a great trick to learn to use this doorway. You must face, confront your death, prepare to die. This changes your place among the webs, gives you courage, shows you how living is a matter of attention."

Domano got up and walked to the window, smiling in his sweet, impish way. "I'll tell you a little story. You will like it. It is a good story.

"It was a fine, sunny day. Bright. And smelling good. There was this place by the spring. Grasses, trees, and birds tweeting all around. You could smell sweet plants in the air. There was living here a fine snake. One day a man came walking through the grasses. Looking at everything, and sniffing and touching. He sat down next to the stream to rest and drink. Snake saw the man and came over to greet him.

"'Hello there, human,' he says.

"'Hello, fine snake.'

"'Welcome to my beautiful home,' says snake.

"'How very good,' says human. 'You live here long, yes?'

"'My mothers before me came here before the trees arrived.'

"'Oh my,' the human says, 'that is a fine history. And this is a fine day!'

"'Then why,' asks snake, 'do you look so sad?'

"'Oh snake, I am just a foolish old man. My years are going to come to an end soon. I do not wish to go. My hospitable friend, death for a human is not easy like for animals and plants. I miss the flowers already. Snake. What is your secret for living so long? Why do you not die?'

"Snake laughs, 'Because I shed my skin.'

"'Teach me, snake. Teach me, please, to shed my skin, so I may live another day.'

"'As you wish, human.'

"Snake took the old human into his care. And through the weeks ahead, taught him to sleep like a snake and peel his skin off. From then on when the man felt his time coming to an end, he would just go to sleep and peel his skin off. And he was happy and no longer afraid."

Chea, who had been silent and still until now, began to hum a disturbing song. It took me a moment to place it. It was the song of the Destiny figure. I jumped involuntarily. While Domano had been talking, I had gradually forgotten my fears. But now I felt very unsafe again, cornered, vulnerable. I wondered what they were going to do. Chea stopped humming and spoke, "How else can humans come to find their own power but by dying to what they were and then to live anew? Only dying can change people enough to allow them to harness their attention and their energy.

"You are too afraid to hear me. Let us go for a walk, down on the boardwalk."

I agreed. It felt safer to me where there were lots of people mingling around. Chea seemed stern and abrupt. I really wanted to understand the Hetakas and trust them, but I was so intimidated, it was hard for me to even say anything to them. I had no idea what questions to ask to get the answers I wanted. And it was extremely difficult for me in general to confront anyone. As we walked along and they talked, I concentrated on working up the nerve to ask them what was really eating at me. Finally I interrupted them and blurted out, "Just tell me straight out. No cosmic stuff, just clear English. What did you do to me on my last visit?" I was so nervous I was shaking, and so was my voice.

They looked at each other and said together, "We pushed you."

43

I was almost in tears with frustration. I just screamed out of control. "No! No! That's not an answer! I don't know what the hell you're talking about! I want to know plainly and clearly, what you two did to make me have that weird experience! I know you caused it. I just want to know what it was!"

Domano, in his kindest and gentlest manner, said, "Here we are at the land of words again."

Chea added, "What we wish to teach you seems extraordinary only because the people of this planet have ignored these pieces of their world. If someone is to learn of them, their attention has to be shaken loose so that they can see what has been ignored. Our teachers called that being shoved off their web. Pushing their center all the way out of the boundaries of what they know. So we say we pushed you."

"You said I died!" I countered.

"Yes," Chea nodded. "Yes. When one's web is changed or one moves that much, one can say there has been a death. The world you used to live in is no longer alive for you, and you are no longer alive in it."

She frightened me. I yelled back at her in disgust, "Chea, that's creepy! I don't want—death stuff! That's all based on—death! That's sick! I don't want anything to do with it!"

She interrupted me, "When we say death we are speaking of a force in nature that moves everything along its way. Not of ghouls, blood, and rotting things. When life moves, it changes. Each move can be called a death."

Domano stepped in front of me, "Or a birth. Maybe you would rather think you were born last time than died." He smiled at me with his gentle eyes. They both looked at me with kindness and compassion. Nothing seemed to fit. Nothing made sense.

Domano looked around and laughed. "Will you go on a ride on that Wild Mouse with me? Too bad it's not open. I like that ride best. That one is the best ride here. You will go when it is open with me, yes?"

I couldn't believe it. "You actually rode on that?" I felt as if I were stuck in the middle of a bad Mel Brooks movie.

He answered, "Lots. It is my favorite. Which one do you like?"

I couldn't answer. How did we get from death to the Wild Mouse? Just then a couple roller skated past us. They were dressed as Raggedy Ann and Andy, and Andy was holding the steering wheel of a car. (Only in Santa Cruz.)

"How about some taffy?" Domano asked with a big grin. "They have chocolate flavor."

I couldn't think. I felt as if all my thoughts and feelings were bombarding me from all directions, and they were all conflicting. I wanted to be afraid and happy and cry and laugh and be confused and understand all at once. My mind couldn't settle on what it was. It was like a circuit overloading. I looked at Domano and then Chea, and all around the beach and boardwalk. And then I began laughing hysterically. I couldn't stop. The whole world looked ridiculously funny. I was completely out of control.

The Hetakas escorted me to a bench where we sat out the duration of my fit of laughter. Domano continued to joke and tease and egg me on. I can't remember laughing that uncontrollably since I was newly adolescent. After I had regained my composure, we continued to walk down the boardwalk.

Between Domano's jokes he spoke for the first time of our place in the world. "You ever think of the Galaxy we live in? Well, it is a fine place! We are citizens of this fine Galaxy. You ever think of that?"

"No," I giggled. I was expecting a joke.

"And our Solar System?" he asked.

I answered, "I had science classes that taught about it—"

He interrupted, "You ever hear about the Great Turtle? Turtle Island? I will tell you about this.

"My people call this place Turtle Island. I read here in

California, some people here think that Turtle Island means this land —America. Just the Americas. This was not so. The native peoples of these Americas long ago knew we were on an island in space. Somebody made a mistake somewhere, they misunderstood. It is the whole planet that is the Turtle who swims through the teaming waters of space. And we ride on her back. That is the old story of our ancestors. Would you like to hear an adventure of turtle?"

I nodded.

"Of course you would," he continued.

"Once upon time. You see? I learned to make it a European story."

That got lots of laughs. He really got into performing when he had an appreciative audience. There was no stopping him. I expected him to continue his joking and playing the rest of the afternoon.

"Once upon a time, there was this really big turtle," he continued. "She lived at sea and liked swimming real far. One day it came her time to birth her young ones. She swam to a warm, sandy beach at the mouth of such a pretty little river. There was a lagoon at this place. Turtle swam and crawled onto the sand, hunting hard for a safe, sunny dune to dig her egg hole in. Finally she finds a place she likes. It is sunny all day and safe from the tides. She is a good mama. She gets the hole just right and lays her eggs. Lots of eggs. And covers them careful like. Then she does something strange. She does not return to the sea. But stays there near the hole of her eggs and watches all things round 'bout. Day after day.

"Finally the day comes that the eggs hatch. All the eggs hatch but one. All the tiny turtles scratch their way across the sand and off into the sea. But mama turtle, she stays on the sand by her hole with the last egg. This egg mama turtle knows is different. And she wipes the sand off from the top of it, making little turtle noises. Sure enough, the last egg starts to crack and hatch. Out from this egg comes a baby human

46

girl. Oh, this is a pretty fantastic deal. Mama turtle picks her up and cares for her as she grows, giving her the name of Laletton. Which means 'Singing Star Girl.'

"Laletton grew strong and curious. Always she swam the oceans with her mother. Always they were together, Laletton riding on her mother's back. Happy. Singing. Her mother taught her well. Laletton dove deep as the dolphins and could catch fish with the best. And she hunts food for her mama too.

"As Laletton grew older, mother turtle knows her daughter needs creatures of her own kind. All things need their own kind. Only mama turtle has not seen any humans on her world. She had been most places on the land and seas, but never did she see one. She knew she gave birth to the first human in the world. So mama turtle thinks it is a good idea that she teach her daughter the Earth magic of bringing birth to things, that as she came of age to be herself a mama she will know what to do.

"They swam the seas and walked the lands and collected just the right plants and soils, bones, twigs, and waters. Laletton learned very well how to put together a good human. She makes many varieties on all the lands. And from her heart she sang to each one the magic on their mouths that brought them to life. When Laletton was done, mama turtle gathered all her turtle family to teach the new humans about living. They grew strong and curious with a great intensity. And everyone was very happy. They have lots of fun.

"When this work was all done, mama turtle taught her humans one more song magic. A song of many harmonies to sing to call down to Earth those peoples of the skies, so she can introduce her grandchildren to their families in the stars, as it should be."

We walked from the end of the boardwalk down onto the sand. Domano took off his sandals and waded through the edge of the water.

"It is good you laugh," Chea said, patting my arm. "The heart needs laughter. Laughter on the webs is like the wind on the trees — it strengthens them and cleans them. There is a resonance that happens even into other worlds. The fibers brighten. We have an effect. Each one of us. So in everything we do we must at the least have laughter. In living it helps you to keep persistent but never obsessive."

"Hurry! Take your shoes off!" Domano insisted. He quickly buckled his sandals together and strung them over his neck. As I took off my shoes and socks he told me to tie them together and do the same, as Chea had also done. Then he grabbed my hand and pulled me into the cold waves and under the pier. I screamed as the water soaked my clothes. He laughed with such enjoyment it was contagious. We ran the whole length of the beach holding onto each other and yelling through the waves.

Back at the Hetakas' apartment they turned on a little heater to dry us out. We all crowded around it in front of the sunny window.

"Everyone hunts for power," Domano said. "Some search for it through control of others. Some look in control of themselves. Some in righteousness. Others in magic. Almost nobody finds its hiding place. Where do you think it is?"

I hesitated. I didn't want to be wrong. My voice was so quiet they could hardly hear me. "In knowledge?"

"You say what has partial truth," he answered. "Without knowledge one might not use fully one's attention or energy. Indeed, one might not ever find it."

"You said everybody hunts for power. Everybody? Even, say, a monk?" I didn't understand what he was talking about.

"Everyone. Everyone seeks for what it takes to keep on going. To be fulfilled. It takes power to find fulfillment. Power to find the next bottle for a drunkard. To hook the big deal. Find god. Be the best. To fit in. To be sad or happy. To escape. It does not matter. They all need power. They all throw it away.

"When you died, we had to shake it loose, so you can collect it in one spot. Like all of us, you grew up learning to scatter it all over every place. Oh. You see now. You find it."

"It's in attention. Isn't it?" I saw it like a flash. I knew I was right.

Domano smiled. "Power is attention. It is everywhere. Centered from us. And centered from everywhere else. It is all there." He pointed all around us. "And without a great shift in how one relates to the world, one will not be able to collect and control it. This is why shamans meet death, monks discipline their minds, Jesus goes into the desert.

"Humans need to start paying attention to their attention."

He leaned his head forward and lowered his voice as though he were telling us a secret that he didn't want anyone else to hear. I thought that was funny, since we three were the only ones in their apartment. "When a person observes the scientist's atomic energy as a single thing, this thing is attention. This is conscious living energy. It focuses and becomes. We learn to focus our attention, our self and we . . . become. We helped you focus your attention in a different way. You stand on a new place on the web. Now you feel unstable, unfamiliar for a short while."

Domano got up and headed for the kitchen. "Who is for a cup of hot coffee? All? And grapes?"

There was an uncomfortable silence when I was sitting alone again with Chea. Thank goodness Domano returned shortly with the full tray. "*Ka ta see* is crucial," he said. "Attention has to be brought into balance. The farther off the center of balance one gets, the greater there is loss of life energy and loss of straight, clear connections to the centers. Then confusion, fear, aloneness, panic. If unchecked — maybe death. One finds the center of balance with their attention. It is all attention, Kay. Now in the time to come you will see where you have put all your attention. And you, piece by piece, will collect it back and set it in balance. Then we will really get to work!"

49

Chea spoke with her mouth still full of grapes, "Balance is a state due to equilibriums. Equity and harmony with the self and all forms. The world looks very different when we learn how to shift and redirect our attention. The unfathomable beauty, the joy, the extraordinary amount and feeling of exchange with other forms. It is a human heritage."

"My god, Chea," I said, surprised. "That's so poetic."

"Life is poetic," she smiled, "with all its gracefulness and passionate depth. The rush and play of loving. The impregnation of daylight. The extravagancy of darkness. It is living poetry."

"Well, I doubt if most people experience it like that," I said.

"That is because they are afraid," she answered. "Humans fear everything. They have spent eons learning how to be afraid. Now they must learn how not to be afraid."

"Why is that?" I turned my side toward the little heater.

"Because they will not gain their balance as long as they are gestating fear." She said the word "gestating" with such an odd emphasis, the impression was one of something slimy and unwholesome growing within its host. "And if they do not learn to balance, they will die. Our species is moving off its center. We are not even interested in equilibriums. Our life energy is seeping away."

"You make it sound like we're purposefully trying to kill ourselves off," I suggested.

"We are," Chea answered, reaching for more grapes.

"That's silly," I said. I was actually being assertive. I confronted her and didn't even realize that I was doing it. "All species have self-preservation instincts. I can't buy it, Chea. How can you say that?"

"Because man's fear is surpassing man's experience of his passion for living."

"What?" I couldn't follow her meaning.

"What humans feel the most of," she answered, "is fear. It has become their dominant motivator, and it is their biggest obstacle."

"To what?" I asked.

"To whatever humans decide to do," she said. "There are basic desires and feelings that motivate all of a person's actions. They are what cause us to think and feel and decide in the way we do. Fear has woven its way deeply into their fabric.

She slipped from squatting to sitting cross-legged in front of the heater. "As living creatures we all have a primary motive that is the basis for all other motives — the desire for experience. We want to experience the sensations of perception and to think and emotionally respond, or ignore it. And it is the nature of humans that our motives bear a hidden agenda of a desire for power. Spun singly or together they are all the color and iner-tia of the fibers of our web. You could say we have two kinds of motives — desires and fears. Desire for creating, communi-cation, knowledge, pleasure, giving and receiving love, and chal-lenge. And fear of death, the unknown or change, powerlessness, pain, loss, and failure. It is fear that generates hate and stress, distrust, guilt, and so forth. Each fear is a form of the other. And they are all a form of the fear of death. We give away our power to them and become their puppets."

"How can you stop such a thing?" I asked.

She seemed to approve of my asking questions and par-ticipating. "To gain mastery of your fear you must take it in hand and resist succumbing to its panic. Keep your control over your attention, and in spite of your fears go ahead and take action. You must walk into and through your fear."

Domano scooted closer to me and said, "The only way to ensure success here is to feel the passion of living to its fullest. This leaves no room for fear to take control. Otherwise you subject yourself repeatedly to fear, until either it wins or you desensitized yourself to it. With passion is how one moves swiftly through fear and eagerly reaches out to the unknown. In fact, it is difficult to do other than reach out."

I must have looked worried. I didn't understand how pas-sion could overcome fear.

"Being alive has a feeling." He nodded his head at me. "A pleasant, stimulating feeling. An excitement that feels at first faint. Then as attention is put on it, it grows. This sensation, this beautiful awareness, is a formidable tool for collecting power. This is what we call passion of living. Fear drowns out this feeling. And nurturing this passion removes the grounds for fear.

"I will give you now your first homework. You are to find this passion feeling. Quiet yourself. Sit alone and watch for it. You will have much inside to distract you. But for ten minutes three times each day, you will do nothing else but hunt passion. Try this now."

"Do I close my eyes?" I asked.

"Yes. I think that will help, but when you are adept you will do it anywhere, anytime."

I closed my eyes and leaned back against the wall, crossing my legs on the bench. I wasn't very sure of what I was supposed to be doing. I sat there and wondered what the pleasant feeling of being alive feels like. And then a barrage of thoughts crowded into my head. I wondered if I needed to go shopping on my way home and if the kid's bus was going to drop them off on time. Should we really repaint the shower? And on and on.

Domano said quietly, "Just let those thoughts drift on away. Don't hold them. What you look for is on the other side of all those thoughts. An exciting feeling of joy."

As I continued to hunt, I began to reflect on times past that I had felt joy, and I remembered occasions as a child when I felt joyful and excited for no apparent reason other than that of being alive. And the memory, the feeling of it came back to me, a happy, adventurous feeling.

After a time Domano began to speak, "The passion is your song. To feel the passion is to feel and know the song that is your own spirit's vibrations. The experience of this is the foundation of *ka ta see*. When you are balanced you will all the time feel that way. But just because you feel this does not mean you are balanced. *Ka ta see* is understanding and controlling your attention. The first task in learning this way is to be able to feel the passion of living at any time. This is of great advantage. It will heal, advise, and comfort you. Fading away the lonely separateness we all have carried. In a child's way years ago you had some knowing of this." They were quite pleased with my initial success and encouraged me not to forget to hunt three times every day.

"When I stopped holding onto my thoughts," I said, "I could watch them come and go like highway traffic. And some of the same ones came up several times." I was excited by my accomplishments, yet more relaxed than I had been all day and a little surprised at how much I was talking. My feelings of intimidation were leaving.

"Yes," said Domano, "yes. We make habits out of our thoughts. We say them many times and don't even notice. As soon as there is a gap. Quick. We pick a favorite thing to think. And fill our mind. We scatter away our power to them. By our thought habits we convince ourselves that our fears and failings and numbness are what it is all about. It is by habit we think, feel, and believe all that we do. And this is what we use to hide the rest of the world."

"What?" I asked. "Hide what rest of the world?"

"The one that people ignore." Domano giggled as if he had something hidden and was trying to tease me with it. "What we pay attention to becomes what we know as ourself and our world. Then we just don't believe the rest. We ignore it."

I looked around the room and outside, not knowing what this "rest of the world" was, wondering if maybe I could see it if I looked in the right place or in the right way.

"Remember," he said, "we perceive our world with all of our senses and more. The world sings its hundreds of millions of songs to us every minute. But our attention is on only what our habits allow us to experience. All the rest of this perception gets tucked away deep in memory somewhere and ignored. See?"

"You mean like ESP, that kind of stuff?" I asked.

"The stuff of spirits, spooks, and dreams," he laughed. "Yes. That is some of it. The songs and harmonies of our universe are so varied. They reach in many directions, in many ways. There are some so different that we perceive and can make no sense of them, and our minds can only pretend there was nothing. We have the ability to collect our attention and aim it in any wanted direction. But it is our habit to be distracted and numbed and take no notice of the greater portion. This is not just the mysterious and unknowable that is ignored but the everyday as well."

I had never before thought about our thinking as an endless habitual barrage of mostly inconsequential thoughts. I had viewed our thoughts and minds as tools that we used fairly well. But today I could see how inefficient we were, and wasteful. It reminded me of several years earlier when I had studied some Zen Buddhist philosophy. The Buddhists talked about emptying the mind of all thoughts and the achievement of Nirvana and Samadhi. I had not been quite sure what they meant by the concepts of emptying, merging, and dissolving, and I had never understood how or why I would empty myself of my thoughts. But today, while in this hunt, I could see how my thoughts worked. I could feel my attraction for them, almost as if they were alive themselves. And I saw or felt something that was being obscured by them.

"Domano," I said. "In Japan they have a religion called Zen Buddhism. They practice mind exercises, too, particularly one about emptying the mind of all the thoughts. I used to think perhaps it wasn't possible, just a wishful dream. But I think now I see how it could happen. Is there any purpose to it? Why would people want to go to that much trouble?"

Chea raised an eyebrow as they glanced at each other.

"You are full of good surprises. We were not going to come to this for a while, but since we have, let's talk on this.

"Our thoughts are part of where we scatter our attention, our power. Each one is part of a pattern group. They are made of our beliefs, experiences, feelings, fears, and hopes, all our motivators, all collected into jumbled patterns. In a way they are alive and conscious. Depending on how much power we give them, they throw into our consciousness the thoughts they are made of. In this way they control our minds and feelings. They crowd up the works, leaving little room or time to anything else the mind might do. It is a good thing to take our power back and free up the mind for better tasks. These pattern groups of thought don't want to give it up, though. They are afraid they will die. After all, they are doing what they've always done, following instructions we gave them from our thoughts. They're trying to take care of us. Only most of their configurations don't even make much sense, they conflict and cause stress. Every time we rethink one of their component thoughts we give away power to them. To stop the flow of habitual thoughts is to collect lost power and take control of your mind and emotions and actions. It is easier to do this if the patterns realize you accept them as a valid but changing piece of your construction and you mean them no harm. You have no war with yourself. You only wish for them to assist you in some other way. War means somebody loses, and in this, balance is dubious. Balance counsels for equilibrium of advantage and total respect. The patterns now become your mentor and shield instead of your dictator. And you become their healer. To empty one's mind of thoughts at will, you can see, is crucial. It has always been taught all over our world to apprentices of hidden knowledge. The apprentice then can learn how to experience and choose action instead of being trapped in reaction."

She patted me on my hand and smiled. "When you hunt for your song, as you find the joy, the passion, don't lose touch of it. Hold on as long as you can. And while you are holding, let the chatter of your thoughts, which are sitting there and coming and going, just drift off as if in a current, until there are none left. And let that be okay. Just your song and you in your awareness, and nothing else."

It sounded difficult, but I was willing to try, especially if they thought I could do it.

"When you can stop your thoughts at will," she said, "you can then choose where you wish to aim your attention, perceiving and experiencing whatever you want. What you knew as your world and yourself will expand in equity and wonder."

Domano stood up and clapped his hands. "It is coffee and tea time again. For you, yes? Dark coffee?"

"Yes, please," I answered. "I'll have to bring you my favorite cookies next time. You'll love them."

"If they are your favorite, I bet we will like them, too," he replied.

"It's getting late. I should be getting back soon."

"Soon," he said. "But first we have a little more. I will get the goodies. Chea will talk fast."

As he went into the kitchen Chea continued, "You think I'm hard to understand now, you wait till I talk fast."

Domano spoke up from the kitchen, "Oh she's a regular jabber mouth, that old Chea." They laughed and I laughed. I was glad for another break from seriousness. They had said so much, I was becoming worried that I wouldn't be able to remember very much of it.

Chea chuckled. "For sure we two old coots will tell you all these things many times. Your job is just to listen as though you know you are going to remember everything. Listen with more than your ears, from inside you."

I nodded and wondered if she could read my thoughts, or if I were just that transparent.

"We have told you all things are living," she said, "in one way or another. That we are all made from energy, and energies come out from us. We can see the bodies of the things around us. But parts of their bodies we do not see. Our eyes are not working in such a way for us to see their innards or the energies that leave their bodies. But you know they have them, yes?"

"Yes," I nodded again.

"We said that there is far more to the world than what you had accepted. The body of each thing extends into many such unseen reaches. It exchanges information and energies for the entire being and passes it along through many eddies and channels. In this way it could be said that these eddies are like sensory organs. But they are also like doorways that we can pass our awareness into. All things in our world can be said to be constructed in this way."

"Things," I interrupted.

"All things," Chea repeated. "Rocks. Dirt. Mountains. Trees. Animals. People. Spirits. Some things have many eddy centers, some only a few. Humans have many that even vary in size. But they ignore their potential and congest them with thought and energy patterns."

"Is this like instincts in animals?" I interrupted again.

"Yes," Domano answered as he returned from the kitchen with the tray. "Only animals aren't so cluttered like people. They pay more attention to this information."

Chea picked up her tea and continued talking. "The eddy centers are connected inside each being by pathways. Most beings have one center, their heart center, and one pathway that is more prominent and central. That is, except makers, keepers, and guardians. They are a kind of entity that lives in several very different worlds at the same time. These are the individuals who, with the entity of our Earth, are most responsible for the building and changing of this planet. They each have only a body made just of energy, even though they will sometimes take the shape of other things."

"Like what?" I was fascinated.

"Like anything," she answered. "Their usual self can be vast but they are centralized as though from only a single heart-brain center. These folks are usually ignored by humans."

"Am I ever going to see one?" I interrupted again. I wasn't sure I completely believed them.

"Yes," Chea answered with just a hint of a smirk. "But now we will tell you about the central eddy. For humans, the one located at your chest. All things in our world have a central, a heart eddy. It is where one's song originates. It is the place of balance and awakening to our entirety. The heart eddy senses clearly and objectively without judgment or fear.

"Through the centuries that humans have existed on our planet they have defined and focused the way they lived according to the nature of each of the larger eddy centers, one at a time. It has long been the era now for concentrating attention on the eddy of the upper belly. This has been the time of mastery of things, control, conquest, analytical thinking, power, chauvinism, hierarchy, the war of opposites. Now we are moving into the era of the heart eddy. We must take our mastery and learn of the passion of living, of our wholeness, of clarity, of how to reach out into the unknown, of peace and balance."

Domano interjected, "I have just the story for you, before it gets too late.

"This one is about two little Indian fishermen. They are one day in a canoe fishing the river. They are not doing so good, so they take the canoe downstream to where the river widens. It is deeper, too. There are many more fish living there. The only trouble is getting the canoe back up the river to their home with all the fish they will catch. In the rainy season, which it was, it is pretty hard to row against the water. And if the rain were to pour heavy it could even sink a canoe. So there they are. Ictla and Humu."

He said their names with such a funny exaggeration, I

thought that perhaps those names were humorous among his people. It was almost as though he were saying, "Curly and Moe," or "Alfalfa and Buckwheat."

"Ictla was young, he had just barely become a man. Humu was his father. Together they worked hard, taking as many fish as they can carry on their backs. This can feed many in their village. It makes very good giving. They take no more, that would be a waste. Besides, it is too hard to carry home.

"The evening comes. It is too late to start back. They tie the canoe upside down in some brush and bend branches around it to make a shelter for the night. And Humu builds a little fire and cooks a fish for their dinner. The rain came heavy but they are fine. In the morning the river is too hard from the rain to travel. So they tie up their fish to their backs and start to walk back to the village. This jungle here is thick and steep. They have to leave the canoe tied to the brush. There is no way to carry it back. Another day they will return and bring the boat back up the river.

"To go this land way they travel over steep and rocky hills. They have to go pretty high up. The rain is worse and worse. It makes their journey most difficult, and they have to stop again. They get worried about their fish now. It needs to get eaten soon. So they decide to go higher into the hills to a village they know and share their fish with them. This village is much closer than home. And that way no waste comes of the fish.

"So as soon as the rain eases some and they can make their way, they set off. Before too long, they get to this village. They have friends there. The people run out to greet them. The children are yelling and laughing. They offer their fish and ask that maybe everyone can join and make a party. Any time these people can have a party they do. Just a little urging, and sure enough. So other folks go to collect some more people and food. Some of the older men come to say welcome and thanks and give gifts in thanks for the fish. Ictla and Humu accept, and then the men all go off by the big fire to talk.

"There was something very different in this village this day. The medicine man says they have found a white man. He is not too old, but he is kind of sick. The medicine man says that his sickness is in his chest. The rest of his body was well. It was the strangest sickness he has ever seen. He had made medicine for him, but maybe his magic wasn't strong enough for the stranger.

"This white man all the time just sits and stares. Never smiles. Never talks. Doesn't eat much. They even send young women over to him to help please him. But he would not have them either. The medicine man called him the living dead man because he was sick with bad spirits that refused to let his soul back in his chest, or let his body die. The people of the village just did not have the heart to kick him out. The forest spirits would take him quick. So they cared for him for a while. Maybe someday he will be OK again. They ask Humu if he has ever seen anything like this man. Humu says no. But it was interesting just the same.

"They had singing and dancing and good eating. The next morning Ictla and Humu leave for their own village. It is an especially good day because the Sun comes out, and the rain stops for a while. It should be quick and easy to catch game and get home soon. So they take stealthy moves through the forest, quietly watching as they go. At a great distance up in the top of the trees there fluttered a pair of large birds. Humu shot at them, but it was far, and he misses. And so they go on, still as in the hunt. Ictla sees on the other side of the vines, so close to him he could touch it, a huge black jaguar. And behind the jaguar a dark cave. He signals his father to look. Poor Ictla is very afraid he is about to be eaten. But this cat does not move. It just stares at Ictla, as if into his heart. They look at each other, not moving for a long time.

"Humu motions Ictla to start to move very slowly away. The jaguar remains perfectly still, except for her eyes, which follow Ictla. Slowly and carefully the men make their way away from the cat and cave.

"A little later the men find monkeys. This is good luck for them. They begin to shoot, when all the monkeys screech and scatter fast, and their shots miss. Then Ictla sees why the monkeys panicked. To his left stood the jaguar. She stared at him and he could feel her breath.

"They ease away again. And again she did not attack. They walk faster now through the jungle, watching for the cat and watching for game. But still no animals in range. Down steep ravines they have to go, pushing and chopping brush aside. And they hear steps off in the bush. Through many vines Ictla sees her again. The jaguar. She follows them. Humu says she is not stalking, just following. Their village is just over the next ravine. It is bad to have a jaguar at the village. Very dangerous, as you can see. So Humu tells his son they have to lead the jaguar away from home. And if she won't go away they must kill her. Not far, just above the village, is a barren hilltop, where they would have a good advantage. This is where they go. Away from the village and up the other side of the ravine.

"They are almost to the clearing. The jaguar is close to their side. They can hear her footsteps on the branches and see her eyes behind the leaves. She talks to them with soft voices from her throat. Humu whispers to his son, 'Behind her. Behind her. The cave follows her!'

"They run into the clearing, heading for the top of the hill. Humu says, 'This is a spirit jaguar, Ictla. We cannot kill this one.'

"As they run to the top of the hill, there, standing in the edge of the clearing, is the sick white man from their neighbor village. He is pale and sullen. Listless. The jaguar comes to the clearing and bends low, stalking around its edge to the far side. It is the white man that is her mark. She pauses, then lunges at his throat. He is down and his life is pouring into the Earth.

She fixes her grip on his neck to carry him off and looks quickly up at Ictla and Humu. Behind her in the bush is the cave. She drags his body easily into its darkness and disappears."

I was surprised once more to find myself in the living room and not out in the wet jungle. My heart was beating fast. And I missed the sounds of that forest in the sudden quiet of the apartment.

"You are tiring and anxious to get home," Chea said, leaning up against a bench. "It's been a long day. But Domano has one more thing quickly to show you first."

He smiled and asked me to sit on the bench with my back against the wall and close my eyes. "This is another homework. First you will do this with us so you can learn it. Breathe slow. Relax yourself. Picture yourself in a little gentle river. The sunlight is bright and warm. The water is cool and nice to you. Sink into the water up to your lips. Feel it move across your skin. On the river edge are many trees blowing in the wind. You can hear bird song, and insects and the water burbling. Breathe in through your nose and smell the plants and soil and water. Dig your toes into the mud on the river bottom. It is soft, slippery. In front of you falls a big leaf. As you breathe in this leaf floats to you. When you breathe out it floats away. Breathe slow and even for a while and watch this leaf come back and forth. And listen to all the sounds of this place. Smell it. Feel it. Keep the images and sensations. Do not let it slip away. Other thoughts just drift off. The water feels soft and fresh. Keep your breath on the leaf and feel with all this, the joy of your song."

He guided me to stay in the vision, uninterrupted for what seemed quite some time. And then he instructed me to repeat it once every night for five minutes. As I got up to go I couldn't help but notice that I felt a relaxed and peaceful excitement. And I thought how odd that was after all the intense range of things I'd felt that day. I picked up my coat, and I agreed to return in three days.

Two days later I was walking up a hill on the university campus, from the lower parking lot, when I experienced an overwhelming grief. I had no reason to be feeling this way, but nonetheless, I felt as though half my body had been ripped off and spit on. There was no one around. I could see up onto the field with the forest and buildings beyond, and behind me the whole view of the meadows and hills all the way down to the water. It was sunny and there were birds and squirrels. It was so clear I could even see the other side of the bay. Yet I was becoming so upset I was almost sick.

I sat down on the dirt and got a hanky out of my bag. I thought of all the different beings the Hetakas had talked about and their songs and experiences. It was then that I realized this pain and grief was not mine. For some reason I did not understand I was experiencing this, but I had not created it. I decided to find out who it was coming from. Domano and Chea had talked a lot about collecting and aiming one's attention. I thought maybe if I could do this and aim it at the grief, I could follow it back to its source.

So I sat there on the hillside concentrating on this pursuit, until all at once I realized I was sitting on it. It was under and around me. The land was the source. It had been bulldozed and graded, torn apart. It grieved for its missing terrain. It wasn't so much angry at the treatment it received as it was sad for its loss and the lack of respect and dignity that it deserves as humankind's cohabitant and equal. It felt to me huge and intelligent with an enormous capacity for compassion. There was a vastness there that I was not able to touch but just sense. I wondered if it could feel or understand me. I wasn't able to tell. I wanted to talk with it. Perhaps I could console it. I thought that if it was as old as it seemed maybe it could teach incredible things about our world.

The fog started to creep in. My time had gone so fast. I wondered what was happening to me. How could such a weird experience seem so normal and real? How could my world change so fast? I was surprised at myself that I had been actually sitting out there for several hours doing that. And what was really odd was that I wanted to stay and keep at it.

I got up to go. A few students were walking over the field toward the parking lot. I quickly looked at my watch. It was time already for me to get back home and meet the school bus.

5

DANCE OF THE
EARTH FIRE SERPENT

When I returned to Domano and Chea's apartment, they had a sack packed and their coats on, ready to go for a little drive.

"Do not remove your coat," Chea said. "Hurry. We are going to drive up the coast. But not for long, we will have you back on time. We have no car, you know, but your van is perfect." They climbed in the back of the VW bus before I could say a thing, Domano stretching across the bench behind the driver's seat and Chea sitting opposite him.

So we headed north around the beach and up Highway 1. It was a windy and sunny day, but not very cold. They opened the windows in the back, and even though it made it a little cool, I too opened my window. It was exciting to feel the brisk air rushing against my face and through my hair. I wondered what this day would bring. I felt enlivened, full of anticipation, but not quite afraid. I realized that I was in an adventure. It was as if I had stepped again into an alien world and must reconcile myself to the unexpected.

"Today marks a good day," Domano said. "Today we help you tune your body to mingle and merge with the forces of the world."

There was an uncomfortable silence. I was hoping he would clarify what that meant. I didn't want to say anything and perhaps influence the direction of the conversation. I wished he would just define what he was talking about. My agitation became apparent when I tried to look at Domano but found it difficult to see him or make eye contact with him because he was sitting directly behind me. I could see only Chea in my rearview mirror. She looked amused at my frustration.

Domano started to kid me. "Oh, this is a pretty big day for you. It's going to be a real hot one. Trust me, you are going to really like this drive." He giggled. He enjoyed teasing me, and it always caught me off guard. I never could think of anything to say. I tried again to see him in the mirror, but he kept shifting around to prevent it. It made me want to pull the car over and stop so that I could turn around and talk with him face to face. He just chuckled all the more.

"You are running on a dime short today?" he asked. "You are not at all afraid. Not even a little. Do you forget your beloved elders so fast?"

His reminder sent a wave through my stomach. Why wasn't I afraid? I had no idea. Logically, I suppose I should have been. I felt as if I had a passport into adventure, but for some reason, I felt safe, as though today real injury couldn't touch me.

"Your mood is too lax," he continued. "Too secure in your ability not to die. You are all curiosity and no alertness. Be curious, yes. But be watchful of Death, always. Your joy has given you access to your inheritance, but don't let its pleasantness distract you from all other possible things. Let it guide you, with alertness that is made of joy and passion, to the next moment. There is always the possibility of surprise and even danger.

"Today we take you before our friend, the spirit who is our planet. This one is going to help you reach out and harmonize with the forces of the world. This, our benefactor, will be the first to show you the merging and absorbing—the dancing of the web. There are other, older ways to tune the body system for this, but they are slow and lack control, and they no longer hold working congruencies for the peoples of this time. We give you a quest that keeps all the control in your hands, with ease and swiftness and great beauty. Since the sinking of the old lands, long ago, few people were able to do this because there were almost no congruencies left in the webs of man for such experiences. But through the centuries the shamans have added their histories and knowledge to the webs of man, until now there is so much congruency, it is easy for one to succeed. A day will come when it will be the way of humans from birth."

"What is it I'll do?" I asked. "What does our planet have to do with dancing?"

"When the time is set, you will request the living energy from our Earth's heart eddy to concentrate and merge with your body from underneath your feet, cleaning open those eddies, those doorways to your energy path. Then slowly she will move all through the body up into each whirling place, cleaning out the old, bringing brightness and expansion, rousing and mixing with your own fiery serpent of the life inside you. You will feel our Earth and know her, and she will know you. Your hearts will touch each other and mix. Your minds will merge. And you can learn to see the universe she knows, and understand her shifting. She can guide you to know others as well. She is our beloved benefactor. And this is the beginning of the dance of the web."

"Whoa. Wait a minute. This doesn't make any sense to me." I had trouble driving and concentrating on what he was saying. I slowed way down and kept trying to turn quickly around to see him talk, something I never learned how to do very well. I ended up swerving slowly down the road with people wildly trying to pass me. "Merge? Is that what you said? What do you mean? How are our two bodies going to merge?"

"From doing this ceremony, you pass through each other. Then the door to our benefactor will always be open. This is making a weaving that allows each of you to send a piece of yourself to the other. To share and give energies that flow to one, on to the other. A gifting. A sharing between beloved friends. A nourishing."

I had to interrupt. "Me? Oh sure. Do you mean me, a person, is going to nourish a planet?" I still couldn't see his face to tell if he was joking again, but I thought he was. I smiled.

He turned around to me and smiled back, "Yes, we can nourish our Earth. We can't always expect that she can just go on to nourish us forever without us returning a like action. People tend not to see it, but we have an effect, each one of us. Balance says everything must move, must flow, and this movement is a circle. A circle that as it returns to its beginning has itself moved and so builds a spiral. Circle after circle that moves on and on. The source is endless. And replenishing comes from letting it move on and filling up with new. Each moment as it moves it carries all the songs it has heard. And all the stories it has lived. And all this is for you to perceive and relish in as you choose.

I glanced back at Chea in my mirror and asked, "Is this what you meant about the poetry of living?"

She nodded, "Yes. The exchanging."

"You mean, is it like talking?" I asked.

"Not exactly. It is more than that, it's . . . " she paused to find the right words. "As he said, merging. Sharing energy and knowledge by passing through each other. There is a union for a brief time. And as these energies move inside a human, they clean out the old and stagnant patterns, everything that is not of balance. They bring what is needed for the shifting of our era."

Domano leaned up over the front seat. "Then we ask our benefactor to help us weave to the Sun. To the heart eddy of this Sun relative of ours. Just as she taught with herself, we mingle and share hearts with this friend, then let these energies flow on through us to the heart of our benefactor. So also, they mingle and share through us.

"Of these two we ask for help to weave to the heart eddy of our Galaxy to interfuse, share, and pass on as before. And these weavings remain always, so we continue to share and nourish one to the other, from heart to heart to heart to heart. Other weavings can be made too. Ask them some day. They will teach you.

"When a human first learns this merging, the energy paths and whirling places are very small and dim. After the Earth has roused you and you have this life flow to move through you, they get very bright. They begin to glow more and more by themselves, and expand. This current moves as you desire it to. The more you let it flow, the more everything in you brightens and expands, and the more the energies gain in volume. A body even collects and uses larger amounts as though literally filled fuller of life. You don't have to be like in a trance to make it move, it can be any time, anywhere. The store. The car. Just desire the flowing life source to be, and it will be. Soon it becomes a habit all the time.

"A day will come when your energy paths will be as wide as your body and even wider. Listen to these new friends. They are very wise and know much healing. They offer you understanding of your entirety and can help you and teach you in ways no human could. They will be your teachers long after we are gone." He paused a moment, moving around in his seat.

I tried to see him in the mirror again. "We change. Is that how someone becomes a shaman? Do we change physically?"

"The physical and the energy portions of our selves," he answered, "are just different parts of a whole. Like a leg and an arm. There isn't a change to see by others, so much as there is a change that is felt. And as the Earth shifts, she adds new tones to her song, and so with the Sun and our Galaxy. And with humans and all our companions on the Earth. The more you share the flowing with these old ones, the stronger your own song will become. And strong you will be in the shifting song, as well. As all in you is expanding and brightening and you move through your world, the flowing pours out of you, touching everything and changing it with the sharing of this shifting song. You see, you affect every single thing that crosses your path."

"Now, wait a minute," I said. I didn't understand why, but for the first time since I was little, with the Hetakas I found myself feeling free and safe enough to be able to confront them more and more, ask questions, interrupt, even contradict. "Stop saying that. It's ridiculous! That's a lot more responsibility than anyone could handle in their whole life!"

"Whether you flow with the shifting song or not," he patted me on the shoulder, "you affect everything you contact. You affect it with your thoughts and feelings and your very nature."

"And I suppose that affects someone else who passes by there next," I snapped. The thought irritated me. How dare someone tell me that I am responsible for my every thought; that my thoughts had the power to hurt someone. How could I ever control all my thoughts and feelings? How could anyone? The idea that something of that nature, something over which we have so little control, could have the power to affect other people seemed very unfair to me. I had to fight off huge pangs of guilt and anger. It just didn't seem right to me, or very plausible. It was nice to think of the nurturing, healing, loving energy of the planet pouring out of one and having a beautiful, harmonizing effect on the world it passed by, but it was hard to deal with, especially the flip side of the coin.

"Of course it affects," Domano answered. "What you leave behind in your passing is recorded there forever. Do not take on the guilt of the world. This is just the nature of things. Accept it. Use it. Work with it. This is not something of judgment. As a person passes by where you were, they are affected by what you left. But it is their choice to grab on to this effect and use it or to let it fade back into a hidden memory. We share our songs and our stories—these thoughts, feelings, experiences—with each other in countless numbers. It is the nature of things that in our world as it is, some of them can be seen as hurtful and like that. It has not been the inclination of humans to notice. But now, change is moving us into a song that does notice. Little by little humans will begin to care about their management of their thoughts and feelings. They will notice the effects. One searches for answers for themselves, questing for themselves, and ends up giving to the whole world in this way, even if they never intended to."

"Oh, I don't know, guys," I shook my head. "I'm the first in line for all that science fiction stuff, and mind moving matter, and telepathy. That's great fun. But it seems kind of overboard to think that every thought is filling the airs like radio and influencing everything. That's really heavy, and ugly."

"Breathe," Domano reassured me. "Find your song and throw away this guilt. It does not belong to you."

"Well, then, if it's true, whose fault is it that the air is so full of harmful thoughts?"

"It is no one's fault. But everyone's responsibility," he answered. "In time, as this river grows within you and others, you will become strong. So as you pass through the thoughts and feelings left behind by the population you will not grab on and resonate with them. All is recorded, but you no longer will get caught up in these currents. Be subject to them like a leaf in wind. Your songs will be strong, as though louder. And with time you will learn to control your thoughts."

I didn't see how. It all seemed like such a wild supposition to me. The world would be chaos, with people behaving any which way, with no real efficiency, a lack of logic, bizarre behaviors, wars. And then it dawned on me. The world *was* pretty much like that.

"Anybody can do this ceremony," he said. "It is easy, simple. One day you will show others. And they will show others. You can even do it by yourself, so long as you know the steps. The effect does not add onto itself, it multiplies. You see, two people who do this is not twice an effect on our world, but more like five times. And three are not like fifteen, but forty. This is the way webs change."

Chea leaned forward and said, "You must not take our word for it! Use what we say only as a possibility and a guide by which you must find all the answers, truths, understandings, the proofs you need. You must investigate and experience to know for yourself."

"But how?" I asked.

"Hunt in this quest we send you on, for your thought groups." She moved into the view of the mirror. "Watch how they are attached to you, stealing your energy, plugging up your body, making stress and sickness. Watch what they do as the old ones rouse everything to wakefulness. In this state of balance they lose their grip on controlling you and peacefully fade into old memory. The self learns what it is to feel life without the strangling hold of this way we have tied ourselves to the world. It is like a weight lifted. Your body learns this and will always work the rest of your life to get back to it.

"Later, after the ceremony, we are so founded on our habits, because we have known nothing else all our lives, that we slowly rebuild and collect them back. But they can never be rebuilt as strong as before. And as you connect again with the fiery current of the old ones, they are burned off again, and each time they have less power over you, until one day they are happily just memory, resources from the past. One knows who they are, knows the moment, and can dance purposefully on the webs."

"This isn't like anything I've ever heard of before." I wanted to pull the car over. It was too distracting to try to drive and listen at the same time. "Is this what shamans do in your tribe?"

"This ceremony, the quest, has no tie to any tradition. Parts of this arousing have been done in various ways around the world. This way does not tie you to any culture. It has none. It connects you, instead, to our old ones through their hearts. This is not an attempt to permanently become one with them, but to merge and share for a while, to awaken and rebuild yourself from their essence, the life source."

They were quiet for a moment as Chea sat back in the seat. Then Domano said suddenly, "We are almost there. Very good. Just a little farther."

"Make sure you give me plenty of warning, now. I don't want us to end up a bunch of road pizzas." We all laughed.

"You will see it," he said. "On the left, just before the artichokes.

"When we arrive, we will teach you how to set the ground for this ceremony. Always the ground should be set for a ceremony. With the mind and heart you arrange the web of your location to reroute distracting currents and patterns. You create an eddy, a vortex to concentrate and magnify the rhythms you desire. One actually is bending the web, detaching and reattaching fibers. Creating movement of a particular nature through and between the webs.

"Each peoples have their own ways to set the ground. Sometimes they sing the change. Others burn herbs. Some ask the spirit friends to do it for them. Some make drawings on the ground, rearrange what is there, often make buildings or special landscaping. Some folks even just think it into change. They all are good ways. They all work, by themselves or mixed together. People fix them into rituals and then forget what it is they are really doing. They get stuck in methods and fashion and will even fight for it. When all they really are doing is making the web help them better. Setting a series of actions in motion, creating efficiency. Of course, the better one can collect one's attention, the more effective they are at setting a ground. It was—"

"Is that it?" I interrupted. "Right there? By that mail box?"

"No. No," he waved his hand. "It's probably the next one.

"Everything concerning a shaman comes about in the moment. The time of the heart. From the heart is the strongest way to work anything, because it has balance on its side. There have been many shamans that have collected their energies and attention in other areas and doorways of their selves to work their medicine. This is fine, it is good work. But actions set in motion always have the flavor of the doorway of their birth. This makes these things have a strong leaning in this way or that way. From the heart they are in the middle. They are born of balance and joy and can not topple themselves over or create a snowball effect of their twist into the world. Action from the heart even leaves a little gift of balance to the maker and the accepter. So for making the most powerful ceremonies, our teachers said, it must come pure from the heart. The potential here has not yet been even noticed by people.

"Do not worry. This will make good sense to you in a short time. Just remember, the heart place is the center, like the center of a wheel, and for this reason it is the most powerful and enduring. And this world web likes to sing with the heart songs. So one gets lots of help."

This was the first time it ever fully occurred to me that I would be participating in actual ceremonies. I found it quite exciting, but I didn't think I had enough background to understand or appreciate what was happening. "How is the merging done? What do I have to do?"

He turned around and leaned over the front seat again. "Living energies within a being have no image or form of their own. They change and move as we think, and they take the form of our thoughts.

"Our planet is a living being with a life and death and destiny of her own. So this is what we do. We will instruct you in every step. We will set the ground and ask her living energies to condense themselves from her heart and take shape into a red, two-headed, fire-breathing serpent that we call Earth Fire Serpent. We ask for this image because the peoples of this planet have long used symbols of serpents and fire to show about the living energies of things. And they now have much congruency within our webs. In truth we could ask for any image that suited us, or no image at all. So you see, congruency makes for efficiency in actions moving on the webs. There are already many patterns constructed on these symbols, and congruency is drawn to them. It is like drinking of a reservoir and using some of its power and understanding that has been collecting there."

I know I wasn't driving perfectly myself, but the traffic in both directions got a bit crazy. An oncoming car was using my lane to pass, even though I was obviously there. I lay on my horn. "Holy shit! Did you see that nut? I almost went off into the ditch!"

Domano scratched the side of his head. "Is that the game they call chicken?"

I laughed. "Yeah. I guess that's the game all right."

"Not bad," he nodded.

I turned around quickly to look at him. What an odd thing to say. "Now, remember, Domano, you're a real sweet little old man. I'm not so sure they go around saying things like that."

"Oh. I'll have to remember!" He laughed. "But it sounds a bit dull to me." We all laughed.

"You know," he continued, "if this image of the serpent is difficult for you and you would rather she took another shape or no shape, this is fine. That is up to you. In your culture the serpent has some pretty bad press. There have been made patterns for that also. And if those congruencies are strong in your mind and uncomfortable, this we understand. This decision is personal. And has no relevance in judgment. This ceremony is for you. And should be suited to you. One picks congruencies to use by one's own nature and needs. This fiery serpent image was picked by our teachers because of its planetwide use for eons. But the truth of this teaching is that we make the images to suit ourselves, and the energies agree to follow. You will feel this principle yourself when you dance the web."

"That image doesn't bother me," I interjected. "I kind of like it. It's intriguing."

"Pull into that little road right down there," Chea said. "Head toward the beach cliff and keep to your right."

"Oh! Thank goodness!" I was delighted that the driving was over. I drove down the dirt road to its end. There were no other cars or people around. Domano and Chea led me to a spot on the cliff that faced southwest. A small fire had been built there not long ago. They told me to hunt for tiny stones, as many as I could stuff in my pockets. One pocket should be for only red stones, the others could be of any color. And I should be sure to take only the stones that wanted to come with me. They would be needed for setting the ground.

The wind was quite brisk here and dusk just a few hours away. Chea removed the big rocks that had surrounded the little fire and smoothed out the ashes with her hands. There were still tiny bits of smoke rising from a few coals.

"Take off your coat and shoes and socks," she said. "Very soon you will not feel any cold." She arranged the ashes so that their outer edge formed a circle. "The first step to set the ground is to pick the location. We have done this for you today because we knew we would not have enough time otherwise.

"You must have a purpose for this ground. The clearer your purpose, the easier it will be for your companions, our relatives on this Earth, to help you. And the more successful you will be. You must ask for their assistance. If you are with respect from your heart, most will help you, and the rest will just ignore you. When we built the fire we asked on your behalf. Next time you will do this on your own."

"How do I do that?"

"You just ask."

"Ask who, how?"

"You just ask all the beings who wish to, to help you. It's as simple as that."

"Oh."

"Don't worry. You will know when the time comes."

This was moving too fast, and I felt that I wasn't catching on to the whole gist of the event. I hoped it would make more sense as we went along.

"Then you arrange the place for your task, using as many congruencies as you desire." She pointed all around the area and then to the cinders. "The circle is a good one to form. It is said that the creator is a circle whose center is everywhere. You will take your tawny rocks and arrange them around the outer edge of these ashes to make a circle. It is like the creator also because it is endless. Every shape has its own power. Every form makes energy patterns. A circle bends the energies from its area inside and out, back onto itself, round and round, and creates a spiral. It can go into the air or down into the ground or both. And it will be either clockwise or counterclockwise. You can let it turn as it will and work with that, or you can intend for the currents to go in the directions that you want. It is easier when you use congruencies to assist you in your building. Now take your little tawny stones, and as you set them down in one direction ask them to help make the spiral move in that direction. For you today let's move counterclockwise and upward. And layer a second set of stones onto those in the same direction and ask that the energies of this next layer move counterclockwise and downward, so that there are two currents. A good strong current will spiral from way down deep into the Earth out to the outer atmospheres.

"Now, while you are placing them, it is time to ask these spirals to help you to balance this place. To bring equity. We are reweaving the web of this cliff in order to help us accomplish a task. We are setting a series of actions in motion. One has to be present of mind to facilitate the action."

"Do I ask out loud?"

"If you wish."

"What do I say?"

"Whatever you want. The list of things one can do to create congruencies is only as short as one's imagination. The only real rule for ceremony and quest is to treat all creation with equity, respect, and gratitude. All other restrictions or additions are cultural or personal.

"We made this fire for you to add to your list, but it is not necessary. It is a harmonic of the fiery nature of the image of the Earth Fire Serpent."

"Oh. I see."

"Now stand in the center of your little circle and close your eyes. You will find for yourself the direction your nature is suited best to. Staying in your circle, turn counterclockwise. And feel, with all of your song, how each direction touches you. As you keep turning you will feel the change with every few degrees. Keep going very slowly, round and round, until you are sure beyond any doubt of the spot that feels the most harmonious and natural."

As I turned I could feel the soft, warm ashes under my feet. A very strong gust of wind moved across the cliff. I could not tell any difference between the directions at first. After turning many times I was able to find the joy of my song. It was the first time I had tried to experience it while doing something else, and I found it very difficult at first. But after a while I was able to reach out with the joy and distinguish a different quality to the nature of all the directions. Some places felt fast, one felt far away, another made me anxious. And one repeatedly felt safe, familiar, and welcoming. I stopped there and opened my eyes. I was facing south.

"Very good," said Domano. "You reached well. Now step out for a moment and take out of the pocket your red rocks. Use these stones to make a drawing inside your circle of a coiled serpent with two heads. Place the two heads where your feet will be as you stand in there and face south."

After I finished the drawing he instructed me in a movement, which he called a dance step, that I was to make during the ceremony. I was to lift my feet almost off the ground one at a time, in a pulling motion, as if I were pulling something up under my feet. I was not to move around or out of the circle. I was to try to keep each foot on its respective serpent head and remain aimed in the southern direction. Domano would be playing a drum to help me maintain the dance.

"Dance in ceremony," he said, "is so beautiful. It involves all of your being to participate with equity in the movement of creation. Take your place.

"Little Stellifa, you breathe so shallow sometimes. That does not feed your life. Breathe slow now and deep, to fill yourself as though your whole body is an empty vessel, leaving no space between breaths. Make this breathing a habit. When we breathe shallow we close down our sensors and remembering. It has its special place, but for this training we need the deep and filling.

"One can do many things with the breath. This is because it is a carrier of songs and stories. It has become a symbol of life songs and experience. It is the thing we take most into our bodies, assimilate at the heart, and send out with bits of our essence in its current."

He began to drum slowly, and I matched my steps to his beat and breathed as deeply as I could. Before long I was stepping and breathing with the drum.

"Close your eyes and relax your throat. Relax your tongue completely. Good.

"Now find your heartbeat," he said. "Let all the rhythms be the same."

Without changing my steps or breathing I turned my attention to my heartbeat, and it was the same. They were all pulsing together. Somehow this didn't surprise me.

Domano's voice sounded slowly in rhythmic phrases like a chant. The rest of the world slowly faded away, and I was my song that danced with the drum.

Follow this beat that goes down through your body
Deep, deep into the Earth.
And call her to come help you.
Beckon the serpent to follow you back.
This is her heartbeat that you dance and breathe
While she rises
And coils under you.
Breathing her flames before her.
Rousing your fire
Telling your body, "Wake up! Wake up! Arise!"
This is why
Fire breath enters your feet
With the coming of the serpent.
Burning away all that went before.

I felt the Earth rising beneath me with a great fire that was hot and bright but caused no pain. The bottoms of my feet felt as though a doorway in them had opened up. It was as though they had awakened from a long sleep and looked around at the world for a challenge. From below, into my feet and up my legs, everything got brighter and brighter. The inside of me was expanding. The serpent breathed and everything was clean and healthy and vibrant. I could feel my song in my feet and I became aware of her song. She was compassion and life itself. She moved up into my knees and thighs, and then into my hips, breathing her fire, cleaning away the stagnant and harmful. And as Domano described in his chant, she continued to rise.

> Up to your belly she spins.
> Her breath is as your breath
> Her heart beat as yours.
> Radiant and sparkling
> Filling all the hidden spaces.
> Listen
> Feel
> Watch
> As she moves in this whirling place.
> See how it differs from the others.
> Each with their shaman doorways.
> Go with her up into your heart.
> She burns away the masks
> Yelling, "Wake up! Come dance with me!"

My whole body was vibrating and warm. I saw parts of me that I didn't know existed. My emotions were high. I felt light and free and so full of life that it spilled out into the world around me. My whole body, especially my heart, continued to expand from the brightness and heat. She spiraled around into everything and up, through my neck, ears, and mouth. As the light grew my ears popped, and I could feel my sinuses open. Then she rose through my eyes into the top of my head and I heard Domano say,

> Listen
> To the sound of the serpent's song
> That goes stirring into every cell.
> She makes people see as the spirits do.
> She breathes and all expands
> Like a bird spreading wings in the ¼ sun.
> Look. She shows you the endless islands beyond.

Go with her,
Soaring above
Into the light like a star.

I seemed to be pushed upward in a current, into a great gentle light that was just above my head. We went farther and farther, through the light and into a void. Domano's voice coached us on and on until finally we reached another, greater, light. We surged into its center. I felt the serpent and myself surrounded by a striking new presence. I wondered what was happening, when I heard Domano's voice again.

Bathe in the heart of our Sun.
Dance together.
Share your songs.
Know each other in this way.

I felt this new presence saturating me with its nourishing, fiery nature. We three moved in harmony together. And I felt myself spiraling with them on through this brightness and into another void. Domano's voice was faint, but we followed it farther and farther into the void. It felt as if it were going to extend forever, when we finally came to yet another, even brighter, light.

I was overwhelmed by the feeling of it. We shot straight into its center, where I met a great being. I knew that we were in the heart of our Galaxy, and then I heard Domano saying it. I wanted to get closer to it, to get to know it better, but it was time for the four of us to return down the path I had come up, back to my body and the Earth. It was an incredible feeling to move at a lightning speed, spiraling down with the three of them, the living energies of our Galaxy, our Sun, and our Earth, through the voids and the lights, and straight through my body into the center of the Earth. They flooded and filled my body and the Earth and then shot spiraling back up the path, flooding the hearts of the Sun and the Galaxy in such a way that currents from the four of us began to flow continuously in both directions.

When I felt this river rushing through me, I knew I was a substantial part of the universe, that each being is indeed significant. It flowed up and down through my whole body and out my arms and hands. I was continuing to expand and grow brighter as these beings healed and awakened me.

I realized then that they, too, were all giving and nourishing one another through my body. We all four gave, and we all benefited. As they flowed on their long course through me I felt a concentration of energy building in my chest. A feeling of compassion and affection for them and all beings became the only thing in my awareness. I felt my heart center expanding, even beyond my body, as it spread the currents of my benefactors and myself out into the world with every beat. And Domano said,

> It is good
> Always giving
> From heart to heart to heart to heart.
> Fuller and fuller with their life you get.
> Spreading beyond your body.
> Unfolding like a great flower of star light
> That glows farther as each petal opens.
> Be this
> Stellifa
> And open your eyes.
> I will drum and you will dance the web.

I continued to dance, looking out into the ocean. The Sun was low in the sky, streaming through the clouds on the horizon. I was overwhelmed with the beauty of these beings and the moment. My body was flushed with the current of the life energies flowing through me. It was electric and vibrating, like a pressure and yet wonderfully peaceful. I felt that I filled even the space beyond my body. I could feel my song strongly.

I knew who I was, confident and satisfied, reaching out to experience life. I was purely in the moment. I could almost literally hear the sounds of my own song. I was euphoric.

This feeling that was my song, I grew to like more and more. I realized that one dances this life alone, yet there was no loneliness in this passion. It was complete, balanced, and full. And there was a place where my song touched everything else. There was a sense of play and self-sufficiency. I thought I would never again feel separated or lonely.

The Earth's song grabbed my attention. It was so grand. I could hear it as well as feel it, even though I could not tell what part of me was perceiving. There were many tones and harmonies within it. Like the tide, I would get close enough to the song to touch it and then move farther away and then close again. Once, for a moment, our songs mixed. I could not tell where my form was. My sense of time was distorted. And I was her song and mine. It was antiquity, compassion, nurturing, beauty, violence, peace, passions. It was ecstasy.

When the Earth's song receded, the song of the Sun took my attention. Again we approached each other in waves, closer and then farther and then closer. This one's song was somehow more complex, concentrated, and profoundly beautiful. As our songs passed through each other, I again lost sense of my humanness. There was extreme intensity, refinement, love. And qualities I have no words for.

On the horizon this new friend sank below the water line into the night, and we drifted apart. With the darkness I began to feel the song of the Milky Way. A sea gull screeched past me, and I could feel its song. As I turned to watch it fly off, I heard the waves on the rocks below and became aware of the song of the ocean. How magnificent they were!

I could sense that we are surrounded by millions upon millions of individual lives, and always touching.

Then with the darkness came the Galaxy's song. The sound of a billion, billion orchestras! We moved closer in waves, and as with the other two, we blended briefly. This one's song had such grandness, calm, and reverence that it filled absolutely everything and had a sense of time that wasn't time any more.

Each song had a living quality distinct to itself. Something that it was pure ecstasy to come in contact with. And as the song of the Galaxy receded, I identified that quality in my own song.

If there is a heaven, then surely this is it. Heaven on Earth. I can see no separation from the garden.

The light was leaving the sky. Domano drummed while Chea instructed me to keep all the energies moving and put the rest of my attention on the bottoms of my feet. She said I should step high, in time with the breath and beat of the Earth, and when she signaled, run along the cliff letting the whirling places in my feet guide me.

She left no time for me to think or become afraid. She signaled, and I was off—running barefoot in the dark on the sea cliff edge to the sound of the beating. My feet were free and daring and knew the Earth beneath them.

6

THE SIX DIRECTIONS

I was being pulled apart. In the next few days my mind jumped back and forth involuntarily to the moments on the cliff. I thought over and over about the experiences. I did not know what they were or what they meant. Sometimes I wasn't even sure they had really happened. They didn't fit into the way I knew the world. In my world humans were supreme, the sovereigns over all, the most important and intelligent creatures in our world. The development and advancement of everything was up to us, and we were coming along just fine with it. We were even reaching out into space, developing phenomenal energy sources, and eliminating diseases. We were in control and going places. Not only did the Earth belong to us to use as we saw fit, but so did the moon, and soon the planets. Humans knew best, and we would someday have all the answers.

My world was knowable, precise, quantitative, predictable, and controllable. And in contrast, the world of the Hetakas was so very strange and exotic. It held a seductive mystery and beauty. What an alluring prospect it was. It tugged at that part of me that would just throw away civilization and disappear into the jungle forever. Part of me wanted that more than anything else. But another part demanded explanations and order, to set practical goals in my life, to take control. How could I exist without the necessities of a real house, a car, and my college education? How could I follow their world and maintain my family that was living in the other world?

I had no answers, only confusion. I was being pulled in half and didn't know how to stop it. I wondered if these worlds could ever be compatible.

All these things that I had experienced, such as feeling the life and intelligence of a grain of sand or a planet, how, I wondered, could that be so? Science flatly denied the possibility, and it didn't fit well into my idea of the world either. So how was it that I had experienced it? I could not deny my own experience, but that didn't help me decide which view was correct. I was certain I had not been drugged or asleep. Perhaps I had been hypnotized, or maybe I was just losing my marbles.

Could one really blend a piece of oneself with another entity and share knowledge and understanding? On the cliff I had felt unmistakably the presence of other individual intelligent beings, like people but different. They were older, inconceivably vaster, full of understanding and compassion. I had experienced, in some mysterious way, views of the world that were completely alien to me yet seemed perfectly valid.

Life was forcing me to confront the conflict, the incongruencies, and try to reconcile them inside myself, but I didn't know how. The only tool I had confidence in using was analysis, and that only made the conflict worse, because nothing was logical, nothing fit. I felt confused, helpless, and very alone.

When I saw the Hetakas again they would not discuss my experiences the way I wanted to. They would not participate with me in my analyzing. They insisted that the ceremony on the cliff was performed to invite the entities of the Earth, the Sun, and the Galaxy to touch me, help me to wake up, heal me, and teach me by merging together pieces of ourselves for a little while.

"I cannot answer any more on this for you," Domano said. "This is a thing you must solve for yourself."

"But how?" I asked. "I don't know what's right anymore. I don't understand what's been happening to me. I can't figure it out, and you won't explain it."

"We helped give you this tool," he answered, "but only you can use it for yourself. Continue the quest for your song. But now, make it for ten minutes, six times a day. Do it sometimes when you are doing other things, like at the store or making laundry. And watch the river leaf each day. These will make you strong. They will pull your attention together.

"If it's answers you want, then relax. Let your benefactors' energies fill yourself and feel them with your song. Let yourself merge with them as they taught you already. They can answer your questions. These old ones are the best of teachers. Calm down. You will understand."

"Why won't you tell me what happened?" I whined like a little three-year-old.

"We have," Chea said. "You are busy being frustrated and won't pay any attention to what we say. A scientific analysis of our planet and star will not show you and let you feel and talk to the living persons who are these celestial spheres. At this time science can only show you a few measurable qualities of their bodies. You know now that there is far more to our Sun than just a hot fire ball, even though you insist on acting like you don't.

"Everything has individual life and intelligence. We radiate this as our signature, our song, from the center of our being. And we radiate our entire histories and our every thought and feeling.

"The world you used to live in is no longer alive for you. Now your world is much vaster and hauntingly mysterious. If you want to learn about this new world, if you want to quest for balance, then start by learning your song. When we hunt our song, we are turning our perception toward our own beingness. And the nature of our beingness *is* perception. It is

88

a feeling of great affection and completeness. Of appreciation and acceptance. And its melodies and nuances are yours alone.

"The stronger you perceive your own song and the more familiar you are with it, then the more balanced you will be and the easier it becomes to reach out with your being to touch and merge with others and truly, clearly know them. Everything that is exchanged is recorded in our beings, adding something new to our songs.

"Allow yourself to feel your song from your heart, throughout your body, at the strength and volume that it really vibrates at. As though your whole body were a tuning fork."

Domano added very reassuringly, "This is as much as anyone could speak about this. We three made the ceremony for this quest. You were very strong and able to merge with the help of our boosting. Now you know what is possible. You have great things to work toward. Stop this fretting." He spoke with all seriousness. "Breathe. Fill your empty vessel with fresh smog. With regular practice of your homeworks, you will have big answers."

He finally cracked a smile as Chea and I laughed. Then he sniffed the air, acting as though he were smelling something remarkably foul. We all laughed hysterically. He said that my mood had been morose, and one should not let that linger. In moments like that, one needs to find something to laugh at.

Through the weeks ahead Domano and Chea avoided discussing the life source ceremony and concentrated on laying out a framework of our world's construction that they called the making of the webs of the world. Between visits I continued to do my "homework assignments," and was becoming a little more proficient all the time. I could easily do the life source practice of letting the Earth's, Sun's, and Galaxy's energies flow through me. It was refreshing and exhilarating. I could feel my strength improving and my aggravation level decreasing. But the communicating and merging aspects of the exercise I had been unable to duplicate since the ceremony on the cliff.

Chea explained to me that on the cliff I had had assistance to amplify my experience, and that I had been extremely fortunate and successful. Now I was on my own. My being had recorded everything it needed and would help me work toward accomplishing this state again in spite of myself. That sounded all well and good but I still felt very unsure about the reality of their world, and perhaps now even of mine.

They were always very careful to say that their explanations and stories were just ways of talking about things that were very difficult to talk about; they were just symbols, and other symbols were used by other people to describe the same things. They warned me not to get stuck to their surface but to search underneath to find their real meaning.

They described the world as having started with the Creator, who was so old and so vast that nobody could guess the Great One's origins or motives, or even understand what it really is. What matters for us now is that the Creator is everywhere we can perceive and imagine and is busy all the time rebuilding and expanding, but never too busy to feel and hear us. We are, like all the rest of existence, the Great One's children, built of its flesh and breath, and part of its very being.

As the Creator continuously fashions our piece of creation, this unexplainable vastness sings, and a part of it separates itself into two polarized individual and intelligent halves. Then, as the two halves interact, they pull themselves into five distinct polarized rhythmic patterns that continually weave the world we know. Each of these is a force and has an intelligence and life of its own.

Our world is in constant motion, changing all the time. Change occurs from the collection of momentum, or inertia, which attracts energies and forces, like a magnet, into condensing according to the nature of the momentum. And momentum is created by attention. This is how we have a part in the continual building of our world. It is with our thoughts and emotions that we humans make our largest contribution.

According to Chea and Domano, the five basic vibrational patterns, or first songs, as they sometimes called them, are the principles around which our world forms itself. They are the foundation of our matter and the foundation of our psyches. Their reflections run deep through all of our cultures. When we contemplate them we compel these forces to play a more active part in our lives.

As the vibrational patterns weave our world they vary in proportions and placement, altering the qualities of the environment, civilizations, and states of consciousness. Every culture has personified them, often to the point of deification. We build huge thought-form complexes around them, hoping to understand them and gain their assistance. These powerful structures are accessed by symbol and thought, releasing long-stored knowledge and energy, and occasionally leading to contact with the being itself. Each of these culturalized thought forms, or myths, provides information on the nature of these entities, our world, and our own potentials. The surface details change from one location to another, not because one myth is more true than the other, but because the people and places are different, with different histories, influences, and needs. All their systems of reference, their symbols, are perfectly valid unto themselves but lose their congruencies, their alikeness that enables them to magnetically attract and connect, when viewed from the perspective of someone else's symbols.

The Hetakas said the influences in our lives are so complex that it is impossible to trace and identify all of them. And there are even many different worlds, and countless varieties of forces and beings that exist among them. We are but one world. And from the view of our world we can perceive, from time to time, other universes and forces drifting close and passing through us, exchanging songs and pieces of momentums.

Through the summer Domano only told me stories describing the nature of each of the five basic rhythmic forces, relating each one to a direction: west, north, east, south, and above. The direction below belongs to the Mother Earth, who is formed, as we are, of the five primary songs. Chea and Domano refused to discuss much about the stories or anything else. I tried repeatedly to get them to answer my questions, but they would only put me off till a later date and then change the subject.

"Today, our young fledgling," Domano said one day, "I will tell you a story about one of these rhythms of our world. I think maybe I will start with the rhythm from the west. But it does not matter which goes first. I just think this is a nice one for today.

"You see, there was once, a long time past, a large, strong woman who lived high in the mountains. One day when she was walking to her hut from the fields, a group of bandits attacked her village. Many of her people are killed or injured. Struggling to run as hard as she can, she gets very close to her home. She hopes maybe she can still save her children. But storming out of her hut comes four men. One carries the head of her husband. And she sees through her broken walls the dead bodies of her son and daughter.

"She gets crazy in the head and jumps screaming and scratching at those men. They laugh and beat her. Then, far from the village, they leave her to die in a rocky cave on the mountainside.

"When she comes awake again it is nighttime, and the sky is full of rain and thunder and lightning. She is very afraid and does not know where she is. She moves deeper into the cave. Then the memory of her children and mate fill her mind. She screams and cries and beats her head on the ground all the night. Her life is now worthless. Why was she not at the hut in time to save them? There must have been some way to stop them. She swells up with great shame and failure. What will become of her? Will the bandits return to kill her? Or will she have to live all her days in grief and shame?

"She can't stop thinking these things and sobbing. There is no sleep for her. Several days pass, but she does not notice. Finally, she hopes it is safe enough to leave the cave. But it is kind of dark. She wanders down many passages but cannot find a way out. After much walking she comes to this large chamber with cracks in the ceiling. Light leaks through there and shines down on a little hidden lake. There lives, she can see, lots of fish in this lake. So by now she has gotten a great thirst and hunger and jumps in the water to wash and drink and catch fish to eat. The water feels good to her body and refreshes her. Now maybe she will survive another day.

"When she has had enough to eat and drink she lay down on the sand and slept until the next Sun. Then she searched out the chamber to find another way out. But there is none. Just the small shaft she entered by. She is afraid to go back through. Maybe she will get badly lost again in the maze and die of thirst in the dark. This is why she thinks to stay in the large chamber by the lake another day and hunt for a way out in there. The little passage will wait for tomorrow.

"As the Sun gets high in the sky it comes through the cracks down onto the lake. She steps to the water again to catch a fish, and she sees her image. It reminds her of her lost babies and mate, and her anger and guilt and grief swell again. She screams and wails. How could things be so wrong? Why didn't she save her family? She did not understand. She thinks she is the worst kind of person. She let them down. She let her village down. Now she wanted to die too. She did not deserve to live. But she was too afraid to let herself die.

"Her sorrow and despair devour her. She does not leave the large cavern. She has nothing to live for and grows to hate her people back home who have their families and village. Why, she thinks, should they have happiness when hers has been torn away? Why should they have people to be with when she has none? Where were they when her babies were murdered? Why did they not stop it? She decided they were more to blame than her. Why did they not come and hunt for her? How dare them all abandon her after the many things she does for all of them. Her mother was the medicine woman and someday she would be, too, and take her mother's place on the council. What do those people think they are going to do without her and her daughter after her? They will get their just reward, she thought. They will regret the day of massacre more than she did.

"The days and the moons come and go, come and go, and she has not left the big cavern. Sometimes now she is filled with remembering of the laughter of her children when they played in the Sun. And the smile of her mate as he touched her. Then her joy turns to great sadness for the loss of it forever.

"Slowly through the days the joyful memories grow, and the sadness gets smaller. She starts to wonder about her people, how are they doing. If her mother lives still. She feels for them and is no longer able to blame them for her tragedy. She can see that life just moves on and they must have their own pains to carry.

"One day when looking in the water at herself, she thinks back on the day of the attack. Then things become clear to her. She sees there truly was nothing she could do to stop the killing and burning, and no way for her to know of it beforehand. She was not to blame. She did what she could. Now she must do her best to stay alive and hunt for a passage out.

"She decides to catch a bunch of fish to carry with her while she hikes out of the cavern to the many passages. And she takes many old fish bones to scatter behind her as she walks so she can return to the lake when she needs.

"For many days she does this searching, making a trail with the bones. But no opening does she find. So she returns to the lake.

"One day while she catches fish for her hunt and remembers the pleasure of her loved ones, she realizes how much she loves living. How good it feels to feel life inside her flesh. She sees her image in the water and thinks, you, myself, are my closest of friends. And she is satisfied.

"Eventually she tracked every passage and could find no opening. Perhaps it fell in on itself, she says. But there must be a way out. She is stubborn, this woman. She thinks maybe she can make one and decides to climb up to the ceiling to make bigger the crack.

"She bangs at this crack for days upon days, breaking away the rock. The cave walls cut her and bruise her. She falls to the floor but still goes back to break the hole wider. The life in her, she thought, is dancing and free, even in her tragedy.

"One morning while she was up in the crevice she sees this light coming from under the water deep inside the lake. It is the Sun that must be shining down a cavern in the lake. It is bright and probably very close to the outside.

"So right then, down she dives. Straight to the light place, and swims hard against the current, and up and out into the Sun.

"What a joy! She is out! She is in the lake that is at the edge of her village, and many of her people are there washing and swimming. She catches her breath and yells with excitement.

"Everyone sees her. They cannot believe it. She just appeared from nowhere, they think. From the dead. They all shout and rush to greet her. How happy everyone is to see each other again."

"That poor woman," I said. "What a horrible life!"

"She did not think so," said Domano.

"That's just because she finally got out of the cave," I answered.

"She gained much more than that. You think on this. The trick with the west is that just when you think you have got it all fixed, you understand so much, this cycle has come to its end. And is ready to begin again.

"You remember now, the stories are congruencies, symbols. They will help you collect your power—your attention.

"Now. No more for today. You get home. We will see you another time soon."

The next story Domano told was of the north. We drove high into the redwood forest and hiked all afternoon through the dense foliage while he talked.

So far I hadn't understood what the story of the west represented. I had tried to draw some correlations between the story and ones I knew from our culture, but with no success. My biggest stumbling block was that I didn't understand the concept of the directions as life components. These ideas, as I had grasped them to date, were completely new and alien to me.

"Domano," I cleverly tried to enroll him in an explanation. "If the directions are aspects of our lives, then what can I do to see the aspect of the west in my life?"

He laughed. "That is very good. Very good question. You will have to wait until you have been introduced to all the directions before you can fit them together. You need to have the whole in order to see the parts. You see?"

Damn. This sort of patience I didn't have. I found it gnawingly frustrating. When I wanted to know something, I wanted to know it right now. But there was nothing I could do about this. I had researched the concepts in the university library and found absolutely nothing. I was forced to wait for the Hetakas' teachings to just trickle in.

Domano patted my back and smiled. "Here now. I will give you another piece. A story of the north.

"A very long time ago there lived this man. His people called him Mud Man. One day he was with his village in a great ceremony. He had a vision, and the omens all fell on him. The medicine man came to him and said, 'Mud Man, you must leave the village and live alone in the wilderness to the north for one year. One cycle of seasons. Remove all things from your body and take nothing. The spirit people have called you. They will help you. Know that this thing you do is for your people. You must leave at once.'

"So Mud Man removed everything from his body, and in his virility stops and looks once upon his people and runs off into the wild lands to the north.

"He paced himself, and when night has fallen he finds many branches to make a bed and covering.

"On the next day he hunts plants to eat and fashions a rope to make a trap. Soon he catches a little animal to eat and makes a knife from a bone. Then it is time to press on, to go farther north.

"He runs for days. He does well. Then one night he hears a little voice calling, 'Mud Man. Mud Man.' He gets up and follows it. Light comes through the bush from the moon. He looks silently through the leaves, pushing them aside. There sits a pregnant woman whose skin was soil and little plants. She was most beautiful. He steps up to her, and she says, 'Mud Man, do you know who I am?'

"He does not know. He is captivated by her and loves her greatly. She says, 'I have come to help you. Do you know what you hunt for?'

"'No,' he says.

"'It is me,' she answers, and smiles at him. He reaches to embrace her and she disappears.

"'Wait! Wait!' he yells, searching the bushes. His heart breaks. 'Wait! Wait! Where did you go? I need you. Please return to me.' He sinks to the ground and sobs. What kind of spirit is this, he thinks, that would steal away with his heart?

"Again he runs, moving farther north, always in his mind to find again that spirit woman. Sometimes he thinks he hears her in his sleep.

"As the days pass by he finds less and less food. Game is scarce, and the waters are bitter. He meets a boy who is lost alone in this wilderness. Mud Man makes him clothes and gives him his food. He will protect him and take him back to his people. They are together for many days, talking, laughing, hunting. They are happy and have a good time together.

"Then one day by a drying river, Mud Man collects wood while the boy gets water. A huge cat jumps out between them. The boy is not afraid. Mud Man comes fast, yelling to protect him, and throws a knife at this cat. The cat steps back but the boy says, 'It is OK, Mud Man. This cat will eat one of us today. You have a task that needs finishing, so I will be his food today. It is fair. He will be food tomorrow.'

"The cat leaped and dragged the boy off before Mud Man could stop them. Mud Man grew heavy with sorrow.

"A familiar voice like music spoke to him from behind. He turns around and there was the spirit woman he searched for.

"'Your sadness is not for the boy. Know that it is for yourself, for your loss of him. He was happy to be the eater and the food. Honor him by honoring his cycle and his choice to gift you life. Follow me, Mud Man. I have many friends for you to meet.'

"She takes him by the hand and as they walk they get smaller, smaller. They get so small they are as small as the ant people she walks up to.

"'Hello, good people,' she says. 'I have a friend here for you to meet.' They all greet each other in the ant way and the ants take them inside their nest village.

"It is huge. So many ants are everywhere busy, but never too busy to be polite. These people are most amazing. Everyone has a job. They are all happy and working together. There are those building up new rooms, and those tearing apart old ones. There are cleaners, food bringers, and food storers. Babies are tended. The young taught. The old and weak allowed to become food. And at the center was the tribe mother. Always pregnant. Always bringing new life.

"Mud Man and the spirit woman stayed with them for many days. The ants feed and care for them and teach Mud Man much about the hidden beauty in the world. They say, 'You are respectful. Come back anytime, Mud Man. You are always welcome. Let us know if we can ever give you help.'

"As they are leaving and walk back into their own world, the spirit woman fades into the air.

"Mud Man says, 'Wait! Do not leave me again. How do I find you? Wait!' He starts thrashing through the brush, calling for her. But he cannot find her. He searches for days and days. Food and water are scarcer, and he grows weak.

"She comes to him in his sleeping and says to him, 'Go to the house of the songbird people. Learn from them. They will help you.' So he goes to them. They welcome him and give him nourishment. He asks if they have seen the spirit woman.

"They say, 'Oh yes. She is here.'

"He looks around all over the place but does not find her. So he thanks them and goes on with his journey.

"His body weakens again, and the spirit woman speaks to him in his sleep, telling him to go to find her friends, the frog people, the deer people, and the monkey people. They care for him, too, and try to help him find the spirit woman. But he only sees fleeting images of her in the land and in his dreams.

"Not knowing what to do, Mud Man returns to the tribal ant mother for help. She says, 'You forget your source, Mud Man. Now you are sick. Look around everywhere. There is the source. And there is the one you seek. She is the mother of all our tribes. Laugh and eat with us of her gifts tonight. Tomorrow return to your people and teach them what you have found.'"

It seemed natural to become part of the story and relate it to the forest around us. I easily saw Mud Man peeking through the branches nearby and the spirit woman fading into the brush in front of him. I was charmed by the view of the ants as a colony of peoplelike beings living in an organized and efficient society. While we were in the middle of the story, it was real to me.

Now I really wanted to ask what the story had to do with the concept of north, but it was futile to try, so I didn't. I just let myself think out loud instead.

"Did Mud Man expect the spirit woman to be his lover?" I looked back and forth between Chea and Domano.

"These are things we cannot answer for you." Domano slowed down and looked at me affectionately and gently. "You must find these answers for yourself. The stories are . . . what they *are*. Sometimes many different things to many people. Through all your life they will continue to teach you.

"Come. We have to walk faster. It is getting late." He pointed to the Sun.

"Yeah." I knew if I didn't hurry now I'd indeed be late, and the school bus would get to our stop long before I got home.

It was two weeks later when Domano told me this particular story of the east. The rain had just subsided, and the Sun was shining through the droplets on the redwood trees like thousands of tiny prisms. We went with Chea to the campus and sat at the tables outside the Stevenson College Coffee Shop and drank hot French roast. There was a chilly breeze that whispered by from time to time, but I didn't mind. I was coming to love these moments together, with Domano clowning and telling stories. I wondered if there would be days in my later life that would be this exciting and fulfilling. I knew that I would always look back on these times as some of the best in my life.

"Now today, you know, I am going to tell you a story about the east. This is a very early story about Serpent Woman. This was the time before the corn and tobacco were planted and the houses had fire to warm them. This is when huge animals and monsters shared the Earth with humans. Living was hard. They had to be very strong to survive.

"One day Serpent Woman was out gathering food. Sun was just rising and making things warm again for another day. She thinks to herself that she is pretty tired of being cold and having to wait for the Sun to arrive to make her warm again. This should not have to be. Why should she and her people always have to suffer?

"'Who is this Sun person?' she thought to herself, 'that he is so warm? His clothes must be like the fire in the mountain. He must be very wise. Maybe he can help me and my people.' She decides to journey and find him. He shares his warmth and light with her whole world every day, so he must be a pretty nice guy.

"She gathers together her things and heads to the east. She meets many strange and wondrous peoples on her journey. She asks them, 'Do you know where Sun's house is built?' Nobody knows. No one has seen it. So she moves on and on. It is very dangerous, and she almost dies many times.

"Finally she comes to a great water. She asks the folks there, 'Do you know where Sun's house is built?'

"'Across the waters,' Turtle says, 'to the east. I am going there. I will take you.'

"They go and go and go for days and days. Then finally land is there. Turtle says, 'His house is there to the east.'

"The Serpent Woman says, 'Have you been there? Have you seen it?'

"Turtle says, 'No. But everyone knows it is down there. Go. You will find it. May good things be for you and your people, Serpent Woman.'

"She thanked Turtle for all her help. Then she walked until she came to some very high mountains covered with lots of snow. Maybe this house of Sun is up there. So up she goes.

"Way high in these mountains she meets Eagle Man. They fall in love, and he tells her where Sun's house is. It is high up in the sky. This is a secret only Eagles know, because only they can fly high enough to see it.

"'Will you take me there?' Serpent Woman asks.

"'No, I cannot,' Eagle Man answers. 'It is too high and too far to carry anyone. Each must fly on their own. I cannot carry you, my wife, but maybe I can teach you to fly so you can go for yourself.'

"'Yes,' she says. 'Yes. This we must do.'

"They work hard every day, and some of Eagle Man's people say, 'Who is she to try to learn to fly? She is a Serpent Woman. Who does she think she is?! These things belong to us!'

"Eagle Man says, 'Do not hinder her with your thoughts. No one hindered you with their thoughts when you were learning flying. So do not hinder another with yours.' Eagle Man's people were shamed and left them alone.

"Many cycles pass and Serpent Woman learns to fly. She and Eagle Man glide through the skies together and can see their whole world beneath them. They are very happy. She is so good at flying that wings begin to grow from her sides. And one day she is ready to travel to Sun's house.

"She says to her husband, 'Will you come with me to ask Sun for some help for our peoples? You are my husband now and I do not wish to be parted from you by distance or deed.'

"He says, of course. He was hoping she would say this.

"The journey was long and very hard. Finally they make it. And Sun says, 'Welcome. Welcome. Come into my humble abode. Let me bring you refreshment. It is good to see you, Eagle Man. It has been a long time. And you, Serpent Woman. This is indeed a special honor. You are the first of your kind to make it here. What can I do for you?'

"She tells Sun of her people and how they suffer, and she asks if there is anything he can do to help them stay warm, to have an easier, safer life.

"Sun said, 'If you want to stay a while, I will teach you many things for your people.'

"So they did. Sun and his people teach them to make fire and tools. How to grow food in the ground and keep animals for milk, clothes, and meat. They learn to make buildings and art. And learn about dance, ritual, and writing.

"Serpent Woman and Eagle Man like it there very much. There is harmony and peace. Good friendships and much knowledge. It is hard for them to leave. But Serpent Woman says, 'We carry things that belong to our people. We must take this to them.'

"And Sun says, 'Please come back again soon. We have great gifts for you and your peoples. There is so much here to share. Teach your people to fly here, too. We have lots of gifts for each of them.'

"Serpent Woman and Eagle Man returned and taught their peoples. And from time to time one of them learned how to fly strong enough to fly to Sun's house. And they always brought back gifts for their peoples from Sun and his people."

Suddenly I noticed that I was in the coffee shop patio, holding my warm cup of coffee. The story was over, and Chea and Domano were smiling. Domano leaned back in his chair and almost tipped it over. I was reluctant to laugh at him. I wasn't quite sure if he had done it on purpose or if it was an accident.

Chea laughed loudly and slapped the table. "You are going to get yourself in trouble yet!" And they both laughed as Domano lifted his feet and, still holding his cup of coffee, rocked the chair back and forth on its back legs. I couldn't help but laugh then.

As much as I didn't want to, I had to go. There was nothing I could do about it. Our time was up again.

"That is all there is for today," Chea stood up and finished her coffee. "We will see you in four days. Monday. On the pier. OK?"

"Yes."

We hugged goodbye and walked our separate ways.

I was enjoying my summer before I became a student at the university. I took the kids to swim in the neighborhood pool at the river, to play at the beaches, and to go on walks through the forest. We even tried to grow a little garden, but the light was so dim and sparse that it grew very badly.

I thought about the stories and the directions, but they were just like most movies to me. They were enjoyable and easy to remember, but I couldn't see any special relationships among them, or between them and my life.

On my next visit with Domano and Chea we walked down on the wharf and sat on the edge with our feet dangling over. It was sunny and hot, and the air smelled of seaweed and salt. People were fishing nearby for crabs, but they had not caught any.

Domano had reserved this afternoon for telling a story of the rhythm of the south. I decided that I was going to thoroughly enjoy the day, the company, and the story and forget about worrying whether the stories had any cosmic significance.

Domano had gotten some fish bait, from where I have no idea, and was tearing it into tiny pieces and throwing them slowly over the pier, one at a time.

"I want to tell you," he said, "about old grandfather Curious Mountain and his little grandson, Summer Wind. Summer Wind was just five years old. And Curious Mountain was very, very old. Probably the oldest man in the village. He was very kind and soft spoken. It is the summer season and grandfather Curious Mountain takes little Summer Wind on a hunting trip. It is hot and bright. The rains had been good that year, so the rivers and springs were full, moving fast.

"The land is blooming in every color. They see the birds building nests. All the animal peoples are birthing and tending their young. The grasses are tall and sweet smelling. Fruit is on the bush.

"Grandfather Curious Mountain teaches Summer Wind how to shoot and sling rocks. He sets targets every morning in the grassy field. Then shows him how to pick materials for tools and weapons. It is important to get everything just right to make a tool that will work well and long. They collect many things needed for their making.

"Then they fix a little trap and catch a rabbit for dinner. Grandfather Curious Mountain teaches him very carefully and slowly each thing that must be done to an animal to make it food. He says that certain parts are always given right away to the spirits and creature relatives as our gift of thanks. This must always be done. If a hunter tried to eat them, he would get sick.

"The old man and the boy make a lot of playing and joking. They chase each other and hide and stalk. Laughing all the time. The boy is very excited at all he sees and learns. The world is new for him. He is little still and his needs and ways are simple, and his vigor great.

"Curious Mountain is a patient man, but he wasn't always. He sees his world with excitement again like his grandson. Now he desires to participate with it. But when he was a young warrior he thought he could conquer and capture it, as young warriors sometimes think.

"'Look at how bold and clever the world is at summertime,' Grandfather says. 'Everybody grows as fast as they can. Sun gets as hot as it can. Everything is working hard and playing hard while they can. They have many children. Always watch around you at these relatives. Now they do their summer dance.

"One day when they were practicing shooting, they see down a ways in a rain gully, the mountain lion is dragging a really big buck down onto the rocky ledge. Then she runs off to bring her children to eat. The deer is safe there. It is pretty hard to get it out. Even she had a rough time to drag it there.

"While she is gone, this coyote who has been watching her sneaks up to the buck and thinks he is going to take it away. First he tries to drag it up the gully wall. He pulls and pulls but can only move it a few feet.

"Then he tries to pull it up from the other direction, but he can only move it a little bit. Still he pulls and pulls. He will not give up, even though this buck is much too big for him. He knocks many rocks over, and under one was a big yellow jacket nest. They are very angry at their house being banged up and they sting and chase coyote. He gets stung all over and finally leaves the deer to go roll in the dirt and the river.

"But this coyote, he is crazy. He still wants this whole buck for himself more than ever. He walks round and round it. Looking. Now he thinks he will pull it down the gully, instead. This gully is pretty rocky and steep. Coyote pulls and drags until the deer is almost off the ledge. Then he braces his feet and gives a big tug, and the buck rolls off the ledge right on top of coyote. They slide a good twenty feet. Coyote is really banged up. He has to struggle hard to get out from under the deer. As he is free, mama mountain lion returns with her children. She is really angry and jumps at this coyote. She does not wish to kill him, just to teach him a lesson and make him leave. She claws him good.

"He still does not want to give up on this buck. He still thinks he has stolen it. He tries to stand his ground.

"Lion whacks him again. This time he almost loses an eye. And the cubs come up and bite his tail and scratch at him.

"Finally he has enough and backs off. He tries to run away but a cub is still hanging by its teeth on his tail. He shakes and bats and growls, running in circles.

"Mama mountain lion roars. Then her and her babies begin eating their dinner and coyote runs far away.

"Grandfather Curious Mountain and Summer Wind laugh and laugh.

"'Come, little one,' says Grandfather, 'We will go now, too, while she is still busy. We do not want her to think we are a problem, too.'

"Summer Wind says, 'Grandfather? Can we come here again?'

"'Yes,' he says, 'If I still walk among the living in the summer to come, I will bring you again.'"

Summer was always a treasured time for me. I liked this story the best so far. We walked slowly around the pier and down onto the beach before we said goodbye and made arrangements to meet again the following week.

It was warm and pleasant with a few clouds streaked high across the sky. I walked slowly with Domano and Chea through downtown Santa Cruz as he told this story of the direction of above. Periodically we would sit on one of the garden benches along Pacific Avenue and watch the people while he continued talking. Everything was sunny and bright and blooming. It almost seemed that the many different people we watched could be part of the story. These were indeed becoming my favorite times.

Domano tipped a nonexistent hat to an elderly woman we passed.

"This is a story about a man and a great city," he began. "His name is Seed Man. And his city is called Tulat. He is very important to his tribe, because he knows the magic of how to speak to the gods. He is one of the five elders of the council of the people.

"For years the people talked of making a great temple city. They think about huge buildings and carvings and altars. They talk and talk. But they never are quite sure how big. Or where should it be? Should it be this way or that way? They cannot make up their minds.

"One day they come to the council. They say they want the council to help them with the city. The council says, 'You the people are the only ones who can decide what you want. You figure out what that is, and then we will help you.'

"Time passed on and finally the people had an idea for how this city could be. They returned to the council and said, 'This is how we want our city. Will you help us?'

"The council says, 'Seed Man is the builder. He knows these things. You counsel with him until you make a plan. Then we can all rally our peoples to join together to build your great temple city.'

"Everyone was very excited. Their dream finally is coming to be. And maybe, they think, many of the people will live long enough to see it happen if they work strong and hard.

"Seed Man worked a long time with the people, making plans for each and every part of the work. How the roads, the courts, and buildings will lay out. How each place is to be used. What kind of stones and materials should be used. Where the little houses would be and how they come together. They talk about crops, water, waste, laws. And the air and fires. Where they will get all these things. Who is to do which work. The people had no idea how much it would take to create their dream. But they will not give up. Not now. It is too clear in their minds and their hearts.

"When the land is all plotted out and the central temple begun, the people put up their little houses and fields where they belonged and moved into the city they were building. Year after year the people work, following Seed Man's plans. A generation passed. And another, and another. Fathers gave their work to their sons. The dream continued.

"The day came when Seed Man's plan was finished. And the people were very proud! Now they have a great sacred temple city to live in, that people will come from far away to visit, trade, and worship in. This was good. They prosper and are happy. Many generations pass.

"One day some people say they think there should be another temple in the city for the newcomers, a temple of their own ancestors and traditions. It would be fair. Good for the city. Good for the people. Everyone thinks long on this. There is much talk. Then they go to Seed Man at the council. They say, 'The people want to add this new temple to the city. Can you help us?'

"Everyone talks long and hard. Most of the people want to build, but a few say no. They want to stick to the old plan of their ancestors.

"Seed Man says to them, 'A city is alive. And all living things must change with time. This is the law. Decide what you want.'

"Eventually they agree to add the new temple. So then there is a place for different peoples to worship as to their own custom. They work a long time, as before making the plan in every detail with Seed Man.

"When it was ready, the council collected its peoples together to build this new project. It all went well. It was a good thing.

"Generations passed, and the city prospered. More and more people came. And now more and more people stayed. The district for living places became crowded. New fields were planted. The water wells were getting low. Struggles and strife broke out among the people.

"The people went to the council to seek help. They wanted Seed Man to make a plan for them to stop the fighting.

"Seed Man said, 'What were you thinking to begin fighting? I can make you a hundred plans, but until you are again one-minded they are but feathers in the wind.'

"The people did not understand Seed Man's words, and they got angry at him and stormed out of the temple.

"The fighting got worse. The people became divided and war broke out from time to time. Life went on but trade was less. The waters grew worse. Crops failed. There was theft and senseless destruction.

"Then one day a great war flared in the city. Family against family. Friend against friend. Until nothing was left but the ruins of stone and the giant statues on top of the center temple of four council elders in a row, with a statue of Seed Man standing behind them."

Now the stories of the directions were complete, and the summer was almost at its end. I would be starting at the university in a few weeks. I was becoming nervous and anxious about how well I would do and how well I could still manage the kids and the home.

I thought now that I was going to be in town for my classes regularly every week, it would be much easier to see the Hetakas. The "homework" I had to do for them was so minimal that I didn't feel it was a problem at all.

As I left the Hetakas by the Old Theatre on Walnut Avenue, I assumed that certainly they would explain the details and meanings of the directions and the stories at our next meeting. As I drove out of town I thought about the story of Tulat and the people we saw on the mall and wondered if it was a true story about some ancient city far away.

7

THE EYES OF THE HEART

The factor of silence was beginning to take a toll on me. There was so much that I wanted to share, so much I wanted to write down to ensure that I wouldn't forget. Part of my regular routine was telling or reading stories to my kids in the evenings, and it felt very uncomfortable, even unfair, not to be able to tell some of Domano's stories to the kids.

It was becoming increasingly difficult not to talk about the teachings, especially with my husband. Occasionally I'd forget myself and slip, and then hope I had said something that didn't sound suspicious. It was starting to feel like a cloak and dagger adventure, but I couldn't decide whether I felt excited or guilty. I could not understand the reason for the silence rule, and I wondered if I would ever adjust.

In the summer months it had been particularly difficult to find free time. We had only one car. My husband was a student, and during the school year I would put the kids on the school bus and drive into town with him. That gave me several hours three or four days a week with the car to take care of errands and see the Hetakas. But summertime meant the whole family was home every day.

I was becoming increasingly stressed out. I could not see the line between being true to oneself and being true to one's loved ones. I felt that anything that I did for only myself was an infringement on my family and that I was being untrue to them. This created a tearing apart within me between the guilt and the feelings of extreme creativity and self-assurance that were part of the quest for one's song. How could something that felt that beautiful, peaceful, strengthening, and even sacred be at all negative to anyone?

I couldn't believe I was actually doing something that I did not share with any of my family, and that frightened me. I didn't want this to become something that would grow between us. Nor did I want my new knowledge to be separated from the rest of my life. I wanted desperately to find a way to integrate what I was learning and still abide by what I perceived as my commitments to my family and my teachers.

Domano, Chea, and I were walking around the campus just days before the fall quarter was to begin, when I decided to ask them about my conflict. "It is not our traditions that make you feel this way," Chea answered. "It is the silence that bothers you. You believe that you must only do things that benefit your family, even if they are damaging to you. You see motherhood and being a wife as never doing a thing that is just for yourself. You have been told that this is wrong, selfish. That you must sacrifice everything for your loved ones, even your self-worth, your health, strength, clarity, your very passion. Anything. You not only tie yourself to their shadows, you make yourself their slave and floor mat."

"Oh, really! Chea!" I said. "That's kind of heavy, don't you think?"

"No," she answered flatly. "Why do you think you feel so bad? Because your Cheerios lost their crunch? You are not the only woman who feels this. It is this era. This culture. Women of this time have lost social acceptance to become their potential and share that with their children and their race. When a people impair their women they show the same indignity toward Mother Earth. They cripple them both and set the stage for their own extinction.

"You are just disobeying your lifelong instructions for a woman of your culture. That is your guilt." She seemed solemn, but then smiled approvingly, and motioned for us to walk across the street to Crown College. "Indian peoples say, each person as an individual has the responsibility to live at the house of each direction, or as some peoples say, travel around the medicine wheel and learn the way the world looks from each direction. To gain the gifts of each of the first songs as best they can.

"Each person is born with her own abilities, her potentials, which are a resonation of one or sometimes two of the first songs. Each gift is different. It is up to us to find and develop it. But then we do not have to stop there. For *ka ta see* one never stops traveling the circle and bringing into oneself and one's life, the endless knowledge and gifts of the directions and our world."

Chea drew a circle on the ground, notched each direction, and ran the stick around and around the circle. Then, poking the center, she said it was like the axle of the wheel. It was the place where all directions meet, a place where the Creator's influence can easily be perceived. It represents the heart of a thing and is in the place of complete equity and balance. The heart of an individual life form is the center of its world. She said that all things can be found within us from this place — the patterns, forces, and deities, the polarized halves of creation, the Creator, our connection to all other forces. Everything can be perceived and connected to in the heart.

"As I have said many times," she moved her hands from her abdomen to her chest as though she were lifting something heavy, "our race is shifting the framework of its activity from the mastery and control that centers at the belly to the equity and balance of the heart. In the past, things were once of such a way that action based from the belly was bringing a balance. But as things change, a point is reached when a new orientation and expansion is desired to maintain balance. Then the shifting begins. Each being developing and shifting according to its gifts.

"For us humans in this shifting we need to learn to become brothers and sisters to each other and to all the other forms, as well."

As we walked we came down from Crown College into the central courtyard of Cowell College and sat on the wall. Chea pointed out to me chalk marks she and Domano had made around the court. They were four circles about three feet in diameter placed at all the cardinal points, and one in the center. She said they were marks where they had set the ground for something special for me that day.

I immediately felt a wake of anxiety in my stomach, and the bottoms of my feet began to tingle.

"You mean right here?" I asked. "With all these people walking around?" I began to feel painfully self-conscious. I wondered what they had in mind, but I found it too difficult to ask. The old familiar fear was beginning to swell inside me. I was breathing in short, shallow breaths. I could no longer hear the passersby or the birds.

Domano spoke softly. "Calm down. Breathe deep and fill yourself. There need be no fear here. Bring quiet to your mind, and find your song. This is simple what we do here today. Breathe."

I tried to breathe deeply and still my thoughts, but the fear overran all my efforts. It was a horse run away with its cart—me. Domano and Chea had to sit on either side of me holding onto my arms and speaking softly into my ears at the same time to calm me down and prevent me from hyperventilating and causing a scene. I was quite disoriented and have no recollection of what they said.

Eventually I was able to proceed with their plan. No one took any notice of us or my weird behavior, they were all much too involved in their own dramas to be aware of mine. Needless to say, that was a great relief to me. I was a shy and strongly private person. I found public displays distasteful and dreaded ever making any of my own.

They waited until I could at least clear my mind of most of its thoughts and feelings before having me sit cross-legged inside the circle on the west side of the courtyard.

"Sit," Chea instructed. "Face the east. Keep yourself calm and clear. All you are to do is observe. The drama will unfold in front of you. Pay attention to the way you observe it. How you feel about it. The kind of thoughts you have while you sit here." She sat down a few feet to my left and Domano then sat a few feet to my right.

My vision got slightly unclear and fainter. Then a second image superimposed onto the view of the courtyard. It was a forest scene where the redwood trees met the field to the south of the court and overlooked the bay. There were four Native American men there in the summer dress of the local tribe of at least two to three hundred years ago.

Each scene was transparent and equal in dominance and clarity. Each seemed as valid as the other. I was able to perceive them both with several senses—hearing, smelling, and seeing. I was amazed and couldn't even begin to guess what I was seeing or how. I felt nervous but completely fascinated.

The men were coming up to a deer they had just shot. The man in front who approached the deer first bent down tenderly at its side and stroked its head while the deer took its last breath. He seemed sad at the death of this animal, and I, too, felt very concerned for the deer.

The other men approached and took things out of little bags that were strapped to their waists. Two of them held knives. They said a few things to the deer as though honoring it greatly. Then they all quietly sang as they moved the body around and cut out its entrails. One man dug a shallow hole, while the first man held the organs and then, with tears on his face, placed them in the hole.

They collected a few thick branches to make a carrying device, and when their work and their song was completed they carried the deer off downhill through the field.

I was taken with their caring and tenderness, the way death was so natural to them, and their seeming desire to minimize the deer's pain. I wondered if I could kill and cut an animal as efficiently as they did, even if it were necessary. I questioned my own unsteady beliefs about nonviolence and vegetarianism, and the validity and proper place they should have in my life.

"Step out of the circle, Kay," Chea said, helping me up. "Come to the circle over in the north."

As I rose and walked to the north side of the court, the historical vision faded and the courtyard resumed its natural appearance.

We stood next to the circle at the north side for a few minutes, just watching the passersby, until Chea felt it was time for me to enter the circle and sit down. They instructed me to breathe deeply and just watch.

The view of the court shifted, as it had done before, becoming two separate scenes overlapping like two photographic films laid on top of each other.

The second picture was the same forest scene that I had viewed in the west circle, only I was viewing it from a different angle. I began to breathe heavily. The same group of Indians came walking up the field and into the trees to retrieve the deer they had shot, just as before.

I could not understand how this could be. Everything was replaying as though it were a rerun of a holographic film. I was unable to breathe deeply any longer and was taking very quick, shallow breaths again.

"What is this?" I gasped. "How's this possible? How are you doing this?"

Domano and Chea quickly moved in close on either side of me and began to whisper simultaneously into my ears. My feet tingled, and fear was again rapidly overtaking my awareness.

By the time the leader of the party bent over the deer and stroked its head, I was becoming calm enough to observe the scene and my reactions to it. I was quiet, but tense with adrenaline.

While the deer was still alive it made no attempt to escape its fate. In fact, it almost seemed as though it gave into it willingly and graciously. The leader looked into its eyes as one would look into the eyes of an old friend. There was an understanding between them. And although I did not know his language, he appeared to thank the deer for giving itself to his people.

The rest of the men approached, the last two taking their knives from their sides while the other two carefully removed herbs from their bags. The first man scattered his herbs around the ground, and the second man held his in his hand while speaking to the deer. Then, as they all surrounded it and began to roll it over, he stuffed his handful of herbs into the deer's mouth as though he were feeding it.

I felt very strongly that all five of them, the four men and the deer, formed some kind of a team, and that there had been no violence in this entire interaction. A sense of dignity and honor surrounded them.

The men sang together to the deer as they cut it open and removed its entrails. The hole was dug quickly, and the first man took the organs and placed them there as one would place a gift under a Christmas tree. He mumbled something and scattered a few more herbs around the hole. Then with clear, quick intent they found branches and formed their device to carry the deer back down the field.

There was no remorse or guilt. There was honor and grief as one would show for a family member who had passed on. The men seemed grateful to both the deer and the surrounding area. I respected all of them, but I did not understand them.

Chea had me rise again and walk around the courtyard to the east side. I was shaking, and I felt very self-conscious. Reality wasn't supposed to be like this. The vision faded, as before, into the busy college scene. They had me breathe deeply for a few moments before sitting inside the eastern circle. Chea sat again on my left and Domano to my right.

This time I knew what to expect, and although it felt very disjointing, I didn't become fearful. The second picture appeared and became as clear and strong as before, and it was, as I anticipated, the same scene, viewed from around the courtyard. I was in awe of this whole process and experience. No one but the three of us seemed to be able to see it. I kept wondering how on Earth such a thing could be possible.

The hunting party hiked up the field and into the forest toward the dying deer. The other men waited with reverence while the first man approached the still-living deer and bent down to stroke its head. As he spoke to the deer he raised his head and hand very slightly, as if to gesture a connection to something above, or beyond. And as the last breath left it, he seemed to follow with his eyes something that rose up into the trees.

The other men acknowledged the change and stepped up to the deer, careful never to walk around the head of the animal on the east side. They took out their knives and stood on either side of its hindquarters, while the first two men carefully removed the herbs from their bags.

The first hunter slowly and deliberately scattered his herbs around the area, with an attitude of appreciation to everything that was there. The second man, while holding his herbs in his hand and speaking, gestured toward the deer, then toward the trees where the first man had looked, and then quickly up and around the sky. He seemed to be offering the herbs as a gift and asking something of the deer. There was a sense of sharing and camaraderie. He placed the herbs into the deer's mouth and closed it, as though he were tenderly feeding it its favorite food for the last time.

As the men rolled the deer over and sang to it, I felt as if this were going to be the last earthly contact they would have with one another. And it seemed to me, as they periodically raised their knives in a swooping gesture, that their song not only honored the beast but requested that it return somehow. In one sense there was sadness that this animal would no longer wander the fields and forest, but in another sense there was gladness for this change in its reality. It seemed a paradox to me.

They removed the entrails and dug the hole as before. The first man placed them respectfully. Each man seemed to be aware of his job, and they all worked together as though they had done this hundreds of times. They gathered their sticks and carried the deer out of the trees and down the field, talking among themselves.

Chea again instructed me to stand and walk around the court, this time to the circle in the south. I focused my attention on the college students. They didn't seem to be reacting to me as if I were doing anything out of the ordinary, which, again, was a relief. I had actually forgotten where I was for a while and had been completely unaware of them.

After a few moments I stepped into the south circle and we all sat down again. The view split and I heard steps behind me and turned to see the four hunters walking up the hill. While three of them passed by on either side of me, one walked right through me. I made a noise involuntarily, but no one in either scene took any notice of me.

The men confidently walked up to the deer, the leader bending down and quickly stroking its head to ease its transition. The last two men were young, strong, and handsome. They moved up next to the deer as they reached for their knives. They seemed very skilled and knowledgeable. I was impressed with their dexterity and prowess.

They made me happy and aware of my song. I again felt the desire to forsake modern life and escape to the forest. The day was fairly hot, and the sunlight rippled in patterns on their skin. The men were all sweating and had a restrained excitement about them. The bounty of the forest was theirs to share. They were successful.

The second man placed his handful of herbs into the deer's mouth, speaking in his own language as if to say, "Here, eat. We share our food with you. Enjoy for one last time, my old friend." They rolled the body over, removed the innards with speed and skill, and placed them into the hole. The carrying device was constructed, and they picked up the deer with ease. Their song was the same song, but now it seemed to be a happy one, almost of celebration.

They walked not two inches away from me with the deer. I bent aside so as to not be in their way, forgetting for a moment that I wasn't in their world. I watched them walk down the field toward the bay. They laughed and talked quietly with one another. They made me feel very excited by life, as if I could accomplish anything if I wanted to.

Chea had me get up and step out of the circle, then pointed to the balcony on one of the buildings. We walked up to where she had indicated, and there was another circle of chalk drawn on the floor. After a moment she told me to enter it, that it was for the direction above.

I did not sit down this time. The three of us stood leaning against the railing looking out into the court. My vision shifted smoothly. I could see the hunting party hiking up the field from the south and the deer through the trees below me.

Everything happened as before, except I could see a much more extended view. I felt that this was just one piece in a much larger set of events. I could see how this hunt had been organized ahead of time, following a set of procedures and techniques that had been repeated for centuries.

When the deer died, I saw a wispy, shimmering shape rise from the deer's chest and head and float into the low branches of the tree above them. It was two-legged and looked vaguely like a combination between a deer and a man. It was curious and attentive, looking carefully at each of the hunters. As the first hunter watched the shape rise, light streaked between them. And as the second man placed the herbs in the deer's mouth, the spirit deer took a special interest and moved closer. Light flashed between the second man, the deer's body, and the spirit deer's mouth.

The men lifted the deer when all was finished, and the leader looked back at the spirit deer in a gesture of invitation to join them. Keeping a distance, the spirit deer slowly followed them down the field toward their village.

We watched them disappear in the distance. Below us the entrails glowed in the open shallow hole, and light shapes and beams shot to and from them.

Chea instructed me to step out of the circle. My vision returned to normal as we walked down to the center of the court. I was tense. It felt good to stretch out the muscles on my neck and shoulders.

Chea pointed to the central circle on the ground and touched my chest with her other hand. "This place represents the center of a world, the axis pole. If you quiet your thoughts when you go into this place, you will be able to perceive the meeting and dancing of all these forces." She made a sweeping gesture around the courtyard, and she and Domano both smiled gently at me.

I emptied my mind as best I could and sat down in the center circle. I was facing south. The second image appeared as before, and I could see the hunting party approaching from the field. They were the heroes, the adventurers, risking perhaps everything in order to find sustenance for themselves and their people. The leader of the band stepped out in front of the others just as before and knelt down at the deer's side to stroke its head. They were just a few feet to my right. I could see the leader's eyes. There was some connection between his eyes and heart and the eyes and heart of the deer. They all shone with light as he spoke so gently to the animal.

Somehow I knew things from this light. The heart was their meeting place. There was no judgment, no war there. Life overfilled it until the very last second.

I thought I recognized the expansion of the mind that I had experienced when I met Death and Destiny. I could feel them nearby, but there was no fear. There was a feeling of something huge having opened up, and a uniting, of what, exactly, I could not say. My anxieties melted away, and I was delightfully curious about everything I could perceive.

The light from the hunter and the deer spread outward to everything in the area. The excitement increased. I became aware of the songs of the things around me. There was mind and emotion and intuition. I could no longer hear the haranguing barrage of my own thoughts, they had drifted away. I felt free of them, free to explore beyond them.

I wondered what all this was that I perceived. What kind of an experience was this? How could there be two worlds? It was so real, so complete. I had not consumed anything during this visit with the Hetakas, so I could not be having a chemically induced hallucination. Besides, they had told me on several occasions before that that was strictly not their way. So what, I wondered, were they doing to make this possible? Whatever it was, I felt accepting, excited, and intensely curious, but with no anxiety or presupposition. I wanted to know all the answers, but I did not care what they were.

Everything throughout my chest and arms warmed up. I could feel the air, as it rushed in and pushed my lungs outward, taking something of me with it on its journey back out into the world. I knew that the leader and the deer also felt the air swelling their own chests.

What a beautiful camaraderie they had. The leader spoke. They understood each other perfectly. There was asking, offering, and acceptance with dignity and honor.

The deer, while staring at the leader, let go of its last breath. Its light rose up and was in the shape of the two-legged deer. It was very alert and agile and with caring and curiosity studied each man there.

How many eons and eons back has this very process been repeated on our world? Has it been repeated on other worlds? Who were these people? Did they worry about the right and wrong of killing? Did they take their survival with gratitude or demand? Who were their gods? Just how different and similar were we? Did they know the same primary forces that I was trying to learn about? I wanted to ask for their help, to have them tell me what were the gifts of these directions.

The three other men approached the deer, and a new awareness entered my mind. I saw a relationship between the life source ceremony I'd had on the beach cliff and the rhythm of the north, and another between the quest for passion and the south. Death was associated with the west. The east was related to the expansion and control of the mind. And above was hard to grasp, it had to do with the unfoldment of things.

I was elated. I didn't know how I knew, but I was sure that I was correct. I could tell that the pursuit of a direction not only provides information on that direction but can eventually lead one to the other directions as well. I found them all there in the center. This seemed to be a kind of shortcut to their understanding. There in the center one keeps one's feet on the Earth and can quickly explore the whole circle and the above as well, yet their influences remain balanced.

When one journeys out to the edge of the circle in only one direction, it's a little like living in a light of only one color instead of the whole spectrum. There isn't anything good, bad, or preferable about this, just different.

As I looked around me I thought I understood a little about what the Hetakas had said about the previous eras of humans and how they were oriented around the predominant qualities of different body areas. There also seemed to be some kind of connection between body areas and the directions. For example, the heart area and the center place of the directions relate to the era we are now moving into in the end of this century, the belly area relates to the south and our ending era, the hips to the west, the feet to the north, the throat to the east, and the upper part of the head to the above.

It occurred to me then that along with the gifts there were also less desirable expressions of a direction and an era. The era we are ending now seemed to be a very good example. We've accomplished and mastered a great deal, but we have also expressed much greed, treachery, pessimism, depression, and destruction. I wondered what a society would look like that was oriented to the south but expressed the gifts instead of the concentration of the less desirable qualities. Would they be a people who know their song and love all living things with excitement and respect? In this dying era have there been a people such as this somewhere on our planet? I wondered what forces in our culture made it develop the way it did instead of into this other possible formation.

Oddly enough, I felt no judgment of these societies, just a boundless curiosity. Of all the possible ways we could have been, what molded us as we are? Have our own choices really brought us to this place in time? Without a doubt it looked to be so from here. But I knew that when I left this circle my chattering mind would have a hard time believing it.

What peculiar creatures we are to argue habitually with ourselves, even after finding proof for a theory. We'll even continue to contradict and confuse ourselves right to our graves. That struck me as being quite funny, and I laughed out loud.

What an odd state of mind I was in. I could see things so clearly and from a much broader perspective. I viewed things in ways that had never occurred to me before.

As the leader of the hunting band scattered his herbs all around the area, mumbling his customary phrases, I looked around in each direction with him. And again my mind was flooded with new ideas and perceptions.

When I turned to the north, I could see the glowing energies from the earth and the sky flowing through me, the men, and all the things and creatures there. As I thought about it, this energy increased in volume as it flowed through me. I could feel my body literally taking on and holding more of it than it had held before, as though my cells were soaking up the flow like hungry little sponges. And then, as before, I could see and feel this glowing spreading outward from each of our forms to the surrounding area. It twinkled and shimmered, whipping around at all speeds and in all colors.

I knew that somehow the ceremony on the beach cliff had sensitized me toward observing and increasing these energy flows. I didn't yet understand this, but I knew there was a connection. I felt vitalized and healthy, as if I had regained a state of wellbeing that I had lost somewhere along the line, and then added even more onto that. There was an air of inevitability about it, as though sooner or later, as a human being, I would experience this restoration.

I looked back at the deer. The second man was feeding his handful of herbs into its mouth. I felt a strong wave of emotion. The spirit deer moved in closer and the energies flowed between its heart and mouth, the man's heart, and the deer's body. The energy was filled with the ecstasy of their songs and the caring and concern and wonder they had for each other.

I focused on the south. My own identity and song became foremost in my mind. I had been taught as a child that the thing that should be the most precious to me in my life was the Creator. I had accepted this idea until after my meeting with Death and Destiny and the experience of almost dying. Then I had started to feel that the most beloved thing in my life was my livingness. It felt like a contradiction at first. But at that moment, sitting there in the center circle, I saw distinctly that our closest connection with and awareness of the Creator is through our life, our own conscious livingness.

I thought perhaps I was beginning to understand the words of Death. My outlook changed instantly of how one might live one's life and prioritize one's activities. It put the pursuit of ideals and dreams into a whole new perspective. What else is there to do in life but to follow one's muse, one's passions? How better to feel life and learn of it and the Creator?

The different factions of my life that had seemed so desperately separate from each other, and none of which I was willing to give up, appeared much more cohesive and integratable. Each activity and pursuit seemed almost part of the others. I didn't need to try to draw some kind of line or barrier between my spirituality and my child rearing or my education. They could all be parts of the same thing. They didn't have to feel as though they were all at war with one another inside me. They could actually work together, each activity benefiting the other. I could find my sense of joy in each one.

I shared the wonder and excitement of those men in the forest. How easy it was, I thought, to have the passion of one's song and the life source energies. The real trick was in the sustaining of them: the continued discipline of controlling one's attention that would allow these abilities to grow. It felt to me that if one's song is the foundation, then the life source energy is the fuel of *ka ta see.*

Something moved in the bushes to my left. I turned to see what it was. There was a large bird rustling in the trees, watching the hunters. In my world two young women were walking through the courtyard just under where the bird sat. One of them said to the other, "Oh, man! I can't believe you! Come out of your bubble, man. Wake up! That dude's a real jerk!" Then the bird looked straight at me. How strange it seemed that these layers of time were almost choreographed together.

The word *bubble* stuck in my mind. We all seemed to be stuck in a restraining field of our ideas and fears, something that we refrain from leaving or looking beyond, something by which we prejudge everything.

I wanted to break out of mine right then, to see what was left without it. Was it a smaller or larger world?

I knew that this was the place, in the center, to do it, to learn how to live without those veils, those cages. One would find here the strength, courage, understanding, and sustenance to accomplish it, to see from the heart.

I was so excited and happy. I had finally started to understand the meaning of habits and habitual mind chatter, and what one would achieve from stopping all the chatter in one's mind. It was a key to the cage door.

How different would the world look? Would my kids look any different to me? Or my goals and ambitions?

The hunters were rolling the deer's body over and beginning to cut its entrails out. I was so close this time I could see every detail, but it didn't make me sick. I actually found it extraordinarily fascinating.

They offered the organs as before, and the lights of the energies moved all around. I saw that this was one of the methods they used for seeking the friendship, the patronage of the spirits. Because the spirits weren't encumbered by our veils, knowledge and assistance from them was by far clearer than and superior to that gained from another human. I thought how incredibly rich and extensive these men's lives must have been.

They all seemed satisfied with their solicitations and gathered up the branches to build their carrying device. They strapped the deer up and headed down the hill. And again they laughed and talked quietly. I wondered what they would think of our world if they could see it. Would they be impressed or disappointed?

The lights quivered all around the entrails, when Chea distracted my attention and helped me out of the circle. She had me move quickly straight to the west. The second scene was still perfectly clear. It was confusing. I wasn't completely sure where to step or what I was going to run into. I almost stepped in the offering of entrails and jumped over the image in order not to disturb it.

We picked up speed to a jog as we ran around the buildings to the west of the courtyard, then across the street and into the woods west of the Crown College complex.

Chea was running on my left, and Domano was to my right. I was still disoriented. My vision was drifting in and out of three or four different scenes all at once. They would appear and disappear, become dominant, and then fade to a whisper and back again. I didn't know which one I was in.

Domano and Chea kept telling me to run and not stop. I was running faster than they were and kept getting farther ahead of them. I had no idea what was happening or what to expect. My disorientation made me increasingly frightened. I felt a tremendous tightness in my stomach and was beginning to feel nauseated. I hated feeling scared half to death and completely in the dark about what was happening. And most of all I hated being nauseated and vomiting.

My anxiety multiplied. I was becoming very confused and could not tell which world was mine. I tried to dodge everything but kept tripping and running into branches and tree trunks. I couldn't handle it any longer and burst into tears.

I yelled back at Domano, "Why are we doing this? What's happening? I can't do this anymore. Make it stop. Please! Make it stop."

"Keep running, Kay. You must go in spite of your fear."

I slowed down. "No! I don't know where I am. This scares me. What are you doing to me?"

"Keep going!" he yelled. "Do not stop. Do not stop! Grab that fear and go!"

I tried to keep going, but with all my crying and the scenes around me shifting and fading, I ran straight into a huge redwood tree and fell down. Domano and Chea yanked me up and shoved me forward, yelling at me to keep running.

"Why are we running?" I said, sobbing and out of breath. "Where are we running to?"

They didn't answer; they just kept waving me on urgently. I felt like a motor being revved higher and higher. It was as if my very bones and flesh had begun resonating at an ever-increasing rate, set toward explosion. My fear grew. Thoughts of things that I had ever been afraid of rushed my mind over and over. I couldn't tell what I was seeing. The sounds of each world I viewed and of our own running through the brush faded away and returned repeatedly, leaving a caustic pressure in my ears.

There was something vile around me. I felt as if I were being separated from Domano and Chea and from all that was familiar. I loathed everything, including myself, and suspected that I had been treacherously betrayed.

I stopped and looked back, but I could not see them.

I panicked. "No! No! Stop!" I quit running and just stood there clenched and screaming as loud as I could until my voice went hoarse, "No! No! No!"

I caught glimpses of Domano and Chea from time to time, as the layers of scenes faded out and back. They were standing several feet away to either side, calmly speaking to me, but I couldn't hear them. I was seriously nauseated and completely out of control.

Back in the center circle in the courtyard I had been so happy and excited. I didn't understand why this had to happen or what it was. I felt cheated, violated.

The hoarser my voice got, the steadier the visual layers around me became. The sounds leveled out and my ears popped. All at once there was just the normal scene of the forest with Domano and Chea standing there staring at me. The massive fear and anger just dissipated, and I found myself clenching every muscle as hard as I could and trying to scream.

Domano and Chea were stone-faced. It was very odd. The storm of hysteria left as quickly and mysteriously as it had arrived. I felt ridiculous standing out there in the middle of nowhere with my fists in the air and my mouth wide open. It struck me as very funny. I couldn't keep their solemn mood. I tried not to laugh, but that only made me laugh harder. They became even more solemn, and by then I was on the ground laughing to tears. Finally Domano cracked a little giggle. They looked at each other and he did a riotous imitation of me stomping, clenched and screaming. We did some serious joking and laughed for a long time.

I cannot describe how glad and relieved I was to be back in the normal world, experiencing and feeling normal things. I could not express my feelings or questions. I was too involved in relishing my normalness.

I thought to myself then that I would never again complain of the common, ordinary, boring things in everyday life. At that moment they looked like heaven to me.

Domano said as we lay back on the ferns and grasses, "When you were in the circle at the center, back there, you started to see with the eyes of the heart. When you left that circle, you were attacked by all your old habits and thoughts and fears that have kept you from seeing in this way, because you have not yet developed the gifts of the north and east.

"From the heart one perceives clearly, with no hindrance or judgment. There is curiosity and compassion and equity there. The gifts from all the directions together make the eyes of the heart.

"To gain this, one need only to begin by pursuing one's joy. The gift of the south. It is good to start the journey of the circle there, because the joy, the song, is the creation of the heart. Each direction can lead you to the center. But the south is the easiest. Like a shortcut.

"The things that stop this journey, to the directions, to the center, these are the things that people in your world have called evil and demons.

"They are of what we have created. Now each person fights their own Armageddon to throw the devil at last out of power and into the far away. This is the war within. The surrendering."

"What happened?" I interrupted. "Trying to remember it all, even now, it's all jumbled. What happened to me?"

"When you see through the eyes of the heart," Domano answered, "you feel and remember. But when you choose to see through fear and habit, all your power is sucked away by them. And then you cannot find the strength or will to look and remember beyond them. These eyes of the heart are always perceiving. But it takes strong intent and power to remember it, to look at the world in this way. Sometimes it can be like having two different memories of a single time.

· "When you left the circle, you returned to your old way to look at the world. Through your habits and fears. They jumped on you to get things back to normal. To get their power back. You were caught between the two ways of being for a while. Like a little war."

"Is that why we were running?" I asked. "To get away from the habits?"

"No," Chea smiled. "You cannot run away from them." They both chuckled and glanced at each other. "We ran to get you as far away from people as possible before you started screaming."

"What?" I asked. "You knew I would . . . ?" It took me a second, but then the whole picture dawned on me. The image of me flipping out completely in front of hundreds of people on campus struck me as even funnier than standing in the woods screaming at two deadpan-faced old folks. I laughed so hard I popped off the waist button on my jeans.

Domano teased me again, "Yeah. We had a real hard time to make you move very fast. You almost didn't get far enough away." He laughed and mimicked someone waving their hands in the air spastically, screaming and rolling their eyes.

Chea laughed as if she knew all about being flipped out. Even though I still found her unnerving and often avoided directly talking to her or looking at her, I couldn't help but notice how warm her laughter and joking was. Her cheeks were flushed with color and her eyes sparkled with life. Even after all this time I found her unreachable, and it was not by her fault but by my own intimidation.

Today I was a bit more able to observe her, even though I tried in my own mind to keep it from a distance. I had been avoiding her so intensely that she could have been wallpaper for all I cared. She had not been like a real person to me. I suppose I had felt that if I ignored her enough, she'd disappear and I wouldn't have to deal with her.

But today I saw the movement of her aging skin, her body breathing, and moisture in her eyes and mouth. I couldn't deny her existence any longer. Domano was so extroverted, talkative, and animated. He had charisma coming out his ears. It was easy to relate to him. Chea was so solemn and quiet by comparison. I had never met a woman before who had no superficial social behaviors. She was like raw power, just parked there next to you. I had no way to relate to her but to be afraid.

Laughing together put her in a more human perspective for me. I was feeling considerably more relaxed. We were so very different. I didn't understand her at all, but she seemed to understand me and my problems.

The laughing cleared my head and stomach and relieved my tension. When I finally stopped, my questions about the courtyard stampeded into my mind like a herd of wild horses.

"What were all the scenes back there?" I asked. "How did they keep repeating? How did you do all that?"

Domano smiled gently and patted my knee. "They were just memories of a thing past that were held by that place."

"But it kept repeating," I insisted. "How did you make it do that?"

"Shh," he put his finger to his lips. "Try not to talk on this just yet. Including to yourself. Work on remembering all you can, but no talking about it. We will talk all you want on another day.

"Look at the Sun. You see how late it is. You must get back to your house to meet your children."

"But I want—" I tried to ask again about the courtyard, but they both interrupted me as they stood up to go.

We headed back toward the campus and Domano mimed someone riding a small bicycle through the dense forest. He ran along with his knees bent, moving them in a circular motion as though he were pedaling, holding his arms out in front as if grabbing onto handle bars. He'd pedal hard up inclines and rapidly out of control on a decline, jolting over bumps and logs. He'd sing along, then bulge his eyes and give a wide-mouthed yelp at the sign of the slightest possibility of danger.

As usual, his performance was superb and very funny. We laughed all the way back down the hill to my car.

"Try not to talk to yourself on these things," Domano said leaning in through my car window. "Concentrate on the life source stream that flows in you from our benefactors. And quest for your song. Before our next meeting, this is most especially important. And work on freeing your mind from its chatter in these matters. Do the best you can. You will need to be strong with these things on the next time we meet!"

They both smiled at me in their sweet way and waved as I drove out of the parking lot and headed down the hill. My thoughts turned toward home. What was it that I was going to pick up for dinner? I couldn't remember. And there was something I was supposed to do for my little girl. I couldn't remember that, either.

The drive was long. Perhaps I'd remember before I passed the last store. I was forgetting more things like that lately and slipping behind in my housekeeping. I didn't know how to explain myself. I suppose sometimes I seemed pretty flaky. Usually I would feel quite guilty, but today I had so much to reflect on and I was so exhilarated that I didn't feel the least bit of guilt.

Then I realized what Domano had said to me as I was driving off. I played it back in my head like a tape. He said to concentrate and do all my quests as best I could—"You will need to be strong with these things on the next time we meet!"

He had never before given me last-minute instructions or reminders. He had even sounded a little urgent. I wondered what he meant, what they had planned for me for the next week. What would I have to be strong for? I started to feel nervous. What if it was something dangerous?

Just then, I realized I was past the last store, almost home. I remembered that I was going to go to the kid's school and pick up some materials from my daughter's teacher. But it was too late now. Everyone would be gone.

Now I felt guilty. And exhilarated. And foolish. And spacy. And scared. My stomach turned into a sick knot. My temples throbbed. I pulled the car over, stopping close to the creek. I got out and sat on a rock near the edge, trying not to think or feel, and just stared into the water passing by.

8

KEEPERS OF THE WIND

One of the most disconcerting things in life has got to be losing control of your environment, your world. The more I tried to maintain it, the less I had. So during the next week I heeded Domano's words and practiced as often as I could remember, no matter where I was. Although I knew I had a choice to stop the teachings at any time, it felt as if it was too late for that. The genie was out of the bottle, and now it seemed the most sensible thing to do would be to learn how to live with and utilize it.

The day of our meeting came. I drove into town with my husband and took the car over to the Hetakas. Domano had said to do the best I could, and I had. Now I would find out if it was good enough.

They greeted me in their usual polite manner. Chea was wearing the same red dress that she'd had on when I first met her. It gave me a wave of anxiety in my stomach. She smiled sweetly and patted my back. I sat down in the middle of my usual bench by the window, trying to take up as much room as possible so that neither of them would sit down next to me. It worked. They sat together on the other bench.

Domano smiled as if he had a wonderful surprise for me. "Today you prepare for a great task. This will be your first quest to meet a keeper spirit."

"A what?" I asked.

Chea shook her head and smiled. "There are many kinds of life forms on our planet. The ones who assist our Earth in the evolving of her lands, waters, and airs are called by our teachers the makers, keepers, and guardians. We spoke of them before. Now you will meet one." She seemed so excited for me, like a parent whose child is about to encounter a new task or phase in life. My stomach felt another wave of anxiety.

"They are vast creatures and span many worlds." She was more enthusiastic than I had ever seen her. "Each has its own history and its own song. You will learn to identify them by the feeling and sound of their songs.

"It is often the case when you befriend one of these, and many other kinds of beings, or as some peoples say, spirits, they will ask you to protect their work and race. This is a good thing, but remember never to promise something to a being that you may not actually be able to follow through on."

"What happens if you can't?" I asked.

"It creates a great deal of imbalance," she answered, "and weakens your ability to interact with these beings in a worthwhile way."

Domano added, "There is also a danger to become dependent on them. Like a crutch."

"And sometimes they will visit you," Chea said, "even in your dreams. When they have befriended you, they will tell you things, warn you, protect your home, and teach you about extraordinary things. Sometimes they will give healing, if that is what you seek.

"They will add to the song of your history in a most dramatic way, because they are in the middle of the shifting and sing that song louder than any other."

Domano jumped up. "It is so sunny and beautiful today. Let's not waste this. We can talk outside. Yes? To the boardwalk?"

"Yes," Chea and I said together.

We walked down the beach shore road toward the little bridge that spans the San Lorenzo River to the boardwalk. The traffic was heavy for a weekday. I could hear people laughing and playing on the beach nearby, and a rhythmic chorus of screams from the Giant Dipper.

It felt so good to be in the Sun. My house up in the redwood forest tended to be quite dark most of the time, and I was beginning to treasure the moments I spent in town, where I could be in the open sunlight.

"Just like with people," Chea said, "you have different sorts of friendships with other life forms. The first is less personal. You acknowledge them and speak or maybe even listen to them, but from a distance. Then a closer friendship will have you touching one another with emotions and mind and if you can get very still, intuition. This is a good friendship, very personal and beneficial. Shamans often have many such spirit helpers in this way."

Domano added, with a sparkle of enticement in his eyes, "The most important relationships are the ones of interfusion, bonding. Where two life forms merge together for a little time, as you have with our benefactor the Earth. Your hearts have passed through each other. This is the quest we work for."

Just then a car screeched around the corner and honked at us to get out of the way, almost hitting Domano. He rapidly scooted about four feet, his hands waving in the air, with his eyes bulging and his mouth open as wide as he could get it. He was teasing me again about my screaming fit on our last visit. People were watching and I got embarrassed. I wanted to tell him to stop, but I just couldn't muster up the nerve. I put my hand over my face instead and laughed.

"Don't pay any attention to him," Chea laughed. "He is just a show-off. I will tell you about questing.

"All quests for befriending a spirit mentor must come from the heart. This is the only way to guarantee that there will be no danger. You must be in the present as completely as you can. Your act of pursuing contact must be final. There can be no turning back. No wishy-washy requests. This entire action must be deliberate, prepared for, and performed without judgment."

"Danger?" I interrupted.

"Only for the reckless." She was trying to be consoling. "Once you have made the decision to quest, you must pay attention to everything around you. Let the life source flow constantly, and feel your environment with your song. Try to notice as many of the life forms about you as you can, and what they are doing. Every detail is significant. They are telling you something. And remember, time passes differently to the spirits. Don't let that throw you off."

Once we got on the boardwalk Domano wandered off a bit and started playing a peekaboo game with a little boy who was hiding from his parents. He was about ten years old, face full of freckles, and bright flame-red hair. This kid looked as if he made mischief his primary occupation. He reminded me of the kind of kid, when I was in grade school, that was avoided at all costs, because if he didn't beat you up, he'd humiliate you in an even more awful way.

His parents were walking slowly down the middle of the boardwalk calling for him, sounding like the kind of parents who would never dream of disciplining their child. The place was quite crowded, especially for a weekday. Junior ducked behind a pillar near one of the booths. He was sure his stealth allowed him to evade everyone's notice.

Domano crept up to the other side of the pillar and slowly peeked around with a big smirk on his face. The boy was quite shocked that someone had caught and beaten him at his own game. He tried to ignore Domano and remain still in his hiding place. Domano pulled back.

When the parents were about level with the pillar, he again peeked around at the boy, who didn't know whether to stay hidden there and take the chance of having his location given away by this old man or to run for it. He was noticeably disturbed.

I must admit, I was delighted to see this little bully get outsmarted. I started to laugh, but Chea motioned me not to bring attention to them. We moved a few feet over, where we could observe perfectly without being obvious. She turned to me and bubbled over with a subdued girlish giggle.

I had never seen her do that before. It felt very personal to me. Finally she was interacting with me as one woman to another. I didn't know who was more interesting to watch, Chea or the boy and Domano.

"He'll have that little boy ready to swear off pranks for the rest of his life," Chea said, still giggling. "But now I need to help you prepare for questing."

"But what if I get hurt?"

She ignored my question. "It is important to feel your song as strongly as you can and reach out from your heart. Touch the entire place with it as it is pushed outward by the energies flowing through you like a great river. This is how one maintains safety always.

"Each one of our energy centers is an information collector that specializes, just like the senses specialize. And they give the information they have in their own flavored way. As you are reaching out, collect all your attention on perceiving what is there. When you touch with your song you use every sense and center."

"But that sounds extremely difficult," I interrupted.

"You will have to stop your thoughts from chattering. That is how it is done. First find your song, then let it reach out with the flow of the life source. These two together will help you clear away the chatter. Try this now."

"There's all these people," I objected.

"They won't notice a thing. I promise. You will not look any different.

"Go ahead."

At first it seemed a little like patting my head and rubbing my stomach at the same time. But after a little while I got the hang of it. Then it was very easy to let go of my thoughts. They just wandered off as if the current had washed them away.

"Now reach out to feel this place," Chea said. "Observe all you can."

It was disorienting. It reminded me of being in the center circle at the Cowell courtyard, but this time there was just one world to observe. It looked so very precious and special. The colors looked brighter and deeper, and the smells were more inviting. I saw bugs, birds, the sky, all the people. It felt as if I were visiting an alien world and viewing it for the first time. The farther out I reached, the more I could sense the individualness of each person as they passed. The warmth of the day was a miracle; I felt like a battery recharging in the sunlight.

"This is pretty good." Chea touched my arm. "You are doing fine. You let go of your thoughts easily this time, but do not get sidetracked by euphoria. Use it like fuel.

"Now, this is important. You must remember these steps for whenever you quest: feel your song; let go of your thoughts; let the energies flow; be aware of the expansion of the mind; feel, observe, and reach out from the heart; and set the ground where you are by saturating it with the current as it flows through you while you are observing. This will put you in the center, in balance, *ka ta see.*"

Just then we were dive-bombed by the little red headed bully. He had made a break for it, and darted between us, blasting his way down the boardwalk, weaving in and out of the crowd. His father caught a glimpse of him and turned without much enthusiasm to follow him.

Domano whipped by even faster than the boy and managed to get in front of him without the boy noticing. Chea tugged my arm to hurry and catch up. As nonchalantly as possible, we scurried down the walkway to watch the action.

Domano had guessed exactly where the boy would attempt to hide next, and he slipped in nearby unnoticed. The boy was all the way behind his little gate partition when he finally saw Domano grinning from ear to ear. The little brute jumped a couple of feet. Domano clapped his hands and laughed heartily, and the boy was off and running again. His parents both saw him and jogged through the crowd this time, yelling for him.

The look on that little guy's face was sheer astonishment. He didn't seem afraid, he just became completely determined to win at his game. He made a dash for the stairs that go down to the beach, and his parents snatched him. He looked around in all directions for his mysterious adversary and seemed a bit embarrassed to find that Domano had been watching his entire capture. Domano gave him a slight and noble nod.

Junior was intrigued. I could hear his wheels churning away, plotting his next escapade, hoping to outfox both his parents and Domano. Dad bribed him momentarily away with a ride on one of those upside-down stomach-shaking machines. When they were out of sight Domano returned.

He was all smiles. "Let's you and us go on this Wild Mouse ride. It is my favorite. Come. We can all ride. It's fun." He waved and waved for me to follow him. "It's fun. Come on."

"Oh no," I answered. "You two go ahead. I'll wait. I'll be fine. Go ahead." I remembered going on the Wild Mouse years ago. It was not my idea of fun at all. I thought I probably had lost a couple of years off my life on that thing.

"You have no need for being fearful," Domano said. "We will be there with you."

He didn't seem to understand. That's what made it really scary. I didn't quite trust them to not do something weird that would endanger me or at the least scare me half to death.

"Oh, please?" he asked. "I will pay. My treat. This is the best ride here. The best ride. Come on. Yes?"

"You are becoming overwhelmed by your thoughts and fears," Chea said. "You no longer feel your song and let the current flow. Can you tell? Your whole sight is now controlled by your old fearful habits. It has changed the world you can see at this moment. Where are the bright colors? The joy? The marvel of each person? The curiosity? Is this not true?"

I didn't want to admit it, but she was right. I was amazed at how complete and rapid the shift in my awareness had been. I had noticed my thoughts leaving before, but this was the first time I had ever actually noticed them engulfing and literally capturing me, completely taking over my mood, my intentions, the entire way the the world looked to me.

"Can you find your song again?" Chea gently asked.

The completeness and scope of the control our thoughts maintained on our race was staggering. Not in my wildest dreams had I ever guessed the real extent to their power over us. I thought, "then cometh the devil and taketh away the Word. . . . "

Domano imitated a little fly buzzing around with his fingers, and flew them right into my open mouth.

"I was just practicing to be a Venus fly trap when I grow up," I said, laughing at both our jokes.

They thought my response was very funny.

"You see now for sure," Domano said softly, "how important a thought is. This is why when we quest, we strive to let them leave us. For *ka ta see,* the dance of balance, we have to retrieve all our power that has been thrown away to them. To take and keep control of all of our awareness.

"Will you take a ride with me now?"

My curiosity was returning. Even though I knew I did not like the ride, and I was afraid of it and what the Hetakas might do, I wanted to see what was being offered, what was on the other side of my cage.

"Sure," I answered. "Why not? You'll notify my next of kin, of course?"

We got in line. There was going to be a wait. Nobody said anything.

We waited for a good ten minutes, and still no one had said a thing. That made me nervous. Domano had a little closed-mouth smile and he fidgeted back and forth on his feet, clenching and unclenching his hands. His behavior was one of boredom and anxiousness. I had never seen him act like that before, or show those kinds of feelings. Something was off. I was hoping very hard that it wasn't going to be another traumatic lesson, the kind that was like a football tackle with me at the bottom of the pile.

Then I noticed a toddler nearby who was quite interested in Domano's actions. She stared intently at him, then turned and looked with equal intent at her father. The two men were performing the exact same actions. Domano was mimicking the father perfectly. Nobody had noticed but the toddler and Chea, and finally me.

I turned away from the father as discreetly as I could and laughed. Domano had performed his act so well that I had believed he was engrossed in real boredom and anxiety.

"When a person sees with their habits," Domano said, "instead of with their heart, it is easy to trick them, to show the thoughts just what they need to see in order to believe."

The line started to move again. We would get on this time. Domano grabbed my hand and rushed up to the front seat of the car. Chea got into the second seat. We buckled in and he told me to hold onto the handles in front as though they were my fear itself, to ride my fear and use the energy from it. He said that I should never give up my mind to fear, that we can't progress as individuals or as a race until we overcome this, our greatest obstacle.

"It is only fear," he continued, "that makes these pursuits dangerous. They are not so by themselves. It's our terror that brings the hands of Death so close."

Chea leaned forward, "The very nature of makers, keepers, and guardians is so much different than ours. To us they seem very alien. When humans meet one for a first time the strangeness of their being makes waves of fear in us. They do not mean to do this, usually, but it is our natural response to a form so bizarre, so vast. A human senses how they sit on a place like a doorway to a thousand worlds. Their power is inconceivable."

"They are not the same thing," Domano added, "as animal or plant spirits. They are the most intense beings on this planet next to our benefactor herself. They . . . "

The car was off. I thought to myself, "Oh God! I wish I hadn't done this!"

All that talk about fear, and I could easily see myself flying off that death trap, head first. I was scared inside and out. I tried to keep hold of my fear, to not let it control my decisions or actions, but in truth, I was in a hopeless state. I held onto the bar so tightly my hands hurt. And then, with absolutely no control whatsoever, no matter how badly I didn't want to give into it, a hearty scream came barreling out of my throat.

Domano bounced in his seat, relaxed and smiling, having a great old time. He yelled to me, "See? I told you so. Best ride here!"

Seeing his lack of fear, and his ability to enjoy even this moment, eased my tension a little. It helped me see again that my terror was only my personal response, and that I didn't have to be consumed that way.

That realization lasted until the next hairpin turn, where my screaming reached at least to bloodcurdling level. I thought, "Well, I failed that little exam. Guess I won't have to be meeting any big spirits this time."

I thought the ride would last forever. What I wanted most in life right then was to get off that thing.

It finally ended. I couldn't get out of it fast enough.

Domano said, clapping his hands, "Let's go again! Get in line quick. Let us go. Come!"

I was speechless. My knees were literally shaking. I had always thought that phrase was just a joke, a figure of speech, but my knees were actually very weak and of their own accord, wobbling. I hadn't thought to cover or tie up my hair before we took off. It occurred to me then that it must have been all ratted up, sticking out in the air like the wild woman's from Borneo.

"Come!" Domano said eagerly, like a little kid.

"This is just like with a keeper. You will be real afraid the first time, but less and less each time after. You will see." And with a great boyish energy and exuberance, he said, "Come!"

"Can I rest?" I asked. "I think I want to go puke somewhere."

They thought that was a great joke. I was dead serious. Where did they get all that stamina? I was in my prime, my mid-twenties, and I was outdone by a couple of antiques.

Chea giggled, "Laugh. Come. Let yourself have some fun. Life can be short. You don't want to hide under the bed and miss it all, do you?"

I looked up. "Yes." My knees were still shaking. If meeting a keeper was going to be like that ride, then I could do without it in my life. Easily. I walked over to a bench and sat down.

They came and sat down next to me.

"Watch these people here with this ride," Domano leaned over and spoke. "Look how many there are. Folks like to get close to their death. It makes them feel the thrill of living. When death is close, the excitement for living rises. Humans get intensely aware of it. Watch them."

I didn't want to watch them. I wanted to go home. I wanted a hair brush, but I didn't even have my purse with me.

I tried to run my fingers through my hair to pull out some of the tangles. It was at least as bad as I had imagined. I was glad I couldn't see it.

I watched the people halfheartedly. I couldn't tell anything special about them. They all just looked like a bunch of loud party goers to me.

"Let's watch in line." Domano jumped up, pulling my hand. He even had more persistence than my kids.

"Oh, all right," I said, "but this is the last. The very last time."

I watched but still didn't see what he was talking about. Most of the people just seemed wide-eyed and noisier as they left the ride.

We got on in the front seat again, with Chea behind. Domano motioned for me to grip the bar in front, and off we went. Again my anxiety registered in a category all its own. How the hell did I let myself get talked into this a second time? Man, what a nitwit! My pulse and blood pressure must have tripled. I was miserable and terrorized, and I refused to notice if there was any reduction in my fear response. If the rest of my studying with them was going to have to be like this, I quit. On the spot.

"There. You see?" Domano said as the car stopped. "You are going to be in fine shape for your questing tonight."

"Tonight?!" I was stunned. "You mean nighttime? Dark? Today's nighttime? That's, that's, so soon. I need more . . . "

"Come sit down with me," Chea interrupted and laughed. "You really are a mess. You gave in to fear with very little provocation. Tonight you must hold your own or you could die."

"But really, Chea, don't you think this is too soon? I don't know how to do any of those things. I'm just beginning. Can't we do it later, say, next year?"

"You'll be fine," she said, still chuckling.

"Fine?!" I was starting to get louder. "You just said I could die! That doesn't sound very fine to me."

"People are always a little apprehensive the first time."

"No," I said. "I can't. I just can't."

"It is time," she got very firm. "There is nothing that can change that. She is waiting for you. Even if you do not go out tonight and meet her in the forest, she will come to you. She will burst into your house and introduce herself to you.

"Listen to me. This is dangerous, yes, because you have so much fear. And she can squish you like a tiny bug at any moment. But chances are she won't do that."

"Chances are?" I interrupted again. "Why take the chance? I think, just like a big old alligator or a tiger, I think we should just leave them be in their own home, unbothered. We should just leave them alone.

"Chea, if they're that dangerous, why the hell rile them up?"

Chea didn't answer.

"Oh, God!" I was getting desperate. "I can see by that look on your faces that you're not going to budge. Are you?"

"It is not our decision," Domano said. "*She* has decided."

My stomach felt as if I had eaten rocks for breakfast. "I think I want to go puke somewhere."

"Come, come," Domano chuckled. "Stop acting like such a . . . what's your word? Wootsie? You are much stronger than you like to think."

"Have you listened to our instructions?" Chea chuckled. "It would be a good idea to know what to do."

"Well," I said, "perhaps you could repeat them. Just to make sure."

"Just to make sure," they said together, nodding. They went through the process again and had me repeat it this time.

"We are going to meet tonight," Chea continued, "on the mountaintop just above your house. You will start this process when you leave the house and find your way up the hill observing in that way."

"Where on the hill will you be? It's a long ridge," I said.

"As you observe," Domano said, "you will tell where we have been, where we are."

I laughed. I thought he was teasing me again.

"This task is not difficult." He wasn't smiling. "You will see. It is important to trust yourself."

"What time?" I asked.

"After dark, and you have put the kids to bed," Chea answered.

"Just 'after dark,'" I said. "That's pretty nebulous. How are we ever going to cross paths? One of us could be wandering around up there a long time waiting around."

"You worry too much," Domano said. "You will know when the time is correct. Trust in yourself. Look back at all you have done. All you have learned."

"How on Earth am I going to know how to find you?" I asked. "Just out of the blue?"

Domano smiled enthusiastically, tapping his heart. "You will know. You will have feelings of certainty."

At least he felt confident. It just didn't make sense to me that I would all of a sudden know for sure when and where to meet them.

Domano turned around quickly. The little red headed bully was stealthily making the slip from his parents again. Domano laughed with delight.

"You will pardon me for a minute?" he asked and hurried off in the direction of the boy. Chea and I looked at each other, smiled, and followed Domano as quickly as we could.

This promised to be quite entertaining. At first I couldn't even see Domano. Chea was moving through the crowd very rapidly, and I was having a hard time keeping up with her. I got blocked off by a huge group of young mothers snailing along with their strollers. They couldn't have slowed me down better if they had planned it.

I was trying to catch up to Chea when I saw the boy's father searching for him in the same direction. I looked around for signs of Domano or the boy. Suddenly I was grabbed from behind. It was Chea. How she got behind me I'll never know. I had been looking at her in the other direction just a second before.

She pointed to a small hole in the front of one of the booths made by a loose plank in the paneling. I could see the toe of a small tennis shoe just inside. Someone was throwing pieces of wrapped taffy, one at a time, into the opening at the boy. I looked around, but with all the people I couldn't see where they were coming from.

After a minute the taffy came whizzing back out again. And back in. And then back out. Then nothing.

The boy impatiently poked his nose out the hole to scout the area. He didn't seem to be able to see whoever was there throwing the candy. Thinking the coast was clear, he stepped out and turned smack into Domano, who had been hiding until the last second behind a rather large man.

The little guy was beside himself with excitement to have a real playmate at a game that he treasured. He shrieked with surprise and took off running again. Domano was close behind, using the people of the crowd as cover. The boy kept turning his head around as he ran to see if he was being followed. He looked convinced that he had lost Domano and his father.

Then Domano picked up speed, weaved his way around to the front of the boy, and came out into his path just as the boy turned his head to the rear to check for pursuers. Again he ran right into Domano who, grinning ear to ear, quickly slipped a leaf into the boy's front shirt pocket and then disappeared into the crowd.

The boy accepted the challenge. He was not going to be outdone and began searching through the crowd for Domano, looking in all directions and being very alert.

We followed at a discreet distance. The boy was still not aware of our connection to his adversary. Periodically we could see Domano. He stayed within six feet of the boy, hiding behind the crowd and pieces of architecture. Occasionally he'd throw a piece of taffy, hitting the boy in the chest, and then scurry off in a different direction.

Just when the boy thought he was about to win, he spotted his parents and made a mad dash for cover. Domano purposefully bumped into the father and distracted his attention.

I was amazed by the ease and agility with which Domano was able to stalk through the crowd as though they were trees in the jungle, and yet remain nonchalant enough to not look odd and attract attention.

Chea tapped my arm. "We will follow slowly. There is more that you need to learn for the quest."

"Oh." I was disappointed. I had hoped they had forgotten about the quest.

"When you get to the spot, you will saturate it so that you and the land will become familiar with each other. Be careful what you think.

"Then you clearly ask of this wind keeper for the contact. You state exactly what kind of interaction you seek."

"Do I say this out loud?" I asked.

"If you want to," Chea answered. "It is not necessary. Many spirits like the sound of the human voice. But your clarity and purpose are what is important. Your one mindedness. That is what matters to the spirits."

"Do I have to fast?" I interrupted.

"Do what fast?" she asked.

"No. Fast. Quit eating or stop some other activity in order to perform this?"

"It is not necessary for most things. But if it makes you more comfortable, then do it. I do not recommend stuffing yourself just before, you would probably lose it. The body, especially the stomach, has to be in a state of passiveness, relaxation. Not overworked. It has to be relaxed enough to help the mind stop its chatter. You do not want the body to be attracting your attention. For you I think light nibbling would be good. Nutritious things. No junk, or sugar.

"One never consumes alcohol or drugs before ceremonies or questing. I can tell you for sure the spirits do not like this. It makes humans ugly to them."

"But what about tobacco or that stuff Amazon people use that they blow up the nose, or peyote cactus, or sacred mushrooms?"

"Tobacco by itself, if it is not abused, is fine. It does not make the human ugly. But your cigarettes have things that are mixed in that are most harmful. And when a person smokes too much of this, it acts like drugs. Weakens the body, drugs the mind. It makes humans ugly to some spirits.

"The other things you mentioned, they are sacred unto themselves. They each have their own process and rules and are never mixed with any other procedures. When used in these ancient ways, the ways that were given to people eons ago by the spirits for specific reasons, then the human is helped. But if they are taken outside those limits then they become harmful and will make you ugly and sick. Do you understand this?"

"Yes. Except in Europe and I think in some other places, alcohol has been used as a sacrament. Like mass. And in the drunken rites of Bacchus of Rome. What's that? Why there, and not here with this?"

"That was a different thing. A different purpose and time. Different symbols. In mass, it is not always alcohol that has been used. The actual substance is not the issue, it is the symbol, the connecting, the shifting of awareness.

151

"In the drunken celebration the purpose became not to contact and commune with the spirits but to honor the nature of play and laughter and plenty, and to connect to parts of the self that have become stifled, crippled, and out of balance by drowning out the stress and disheveling the thoughts. The process was considered sacred to them. Remember, that was a whole different time and people. What worked then could have drawbacks now."

"I would think so."

"Each people," she continued, "have their own ways of collecting their attention back to their center and communicating with the spirits and the Creator. Each should be honored for itself and never held in judgment. A person will not find all traditions equally easy to grasp or succeed in. One that will be suited to you and easy for you will be difficult for another. And so on.

"We are all different from each other, individuals. We need different things. It is good that there are so many different ways."

"So, what if I'm standing there," I asked, "and I request this contact, and nothing happens?"

"You repeat it and reach outward with your awareness. Watch for the spirit to come. It will. Trust. And be patient."

"But what if it never comes? What if it refuses?"

"You will know," she answered. "Then you respectfully retreat, and try again another time. Don't be stressed. Leave the anxiousness behind. Things work on a different time scale here. Let it be OK, one way or the other. There is no failure possible. One just performs the actions of one's quest the best one can. What comes of it just does. That's all."

"I'm scared, Chea."

"I know. It is to be expected. Just be easy on yourself."

"I don't know how."

"Of course you do. Breathe. Relax. You will be in the middle of your song when you request. You will see.

"After you request, you watch with your whole being for

this wind keeper to come. She will approach and come very close to you, observing. She will test you. And you must stay steadfast and resolute. Keep in your center and open your arms to the sides, standing as tall as you can. And open your whole self, like an empty vessel.

"Reach out with your song and touch this being. It will move into your awareness, your beingness. As it fills you and you fill it, your beingnesses will mix. Your hearts will touch and merge together. You will know the mind and heart of this one, and she will know you.

"Then it will be time to ask her her name or calling sound. It might be a simple sound, or it could be a song or a picture. Or several things. These are not to be shared with others unless she requests that of you.

"Ask whatever questions you want to, or request for favors. Don't get upset if you forget to ask. You can contact this new friend anytime again that you want to. When once you have merged with a spirit, they are your intimate friend, like your closest family, for the rest of your life."

"Can one alienate them?" I asked. "End the friendship, so to speak?"

"Yes, by betraying them. Dishonoring them. But I can't imagine why anyone would want to do such a thing. They are the best and most loyal friends, helpers, and teachers a human could have."

"But how will I know if I have actually merged, and I'm not just fooling myself?"

"There will be no doubt in your mind whatsoever. You will know absolutely. If you have doubts, then you only touched the spirit with your song. Then you should try again. If not on that occasion, then at another time.

"Sometimes this is all that will happen, and there will never be a merging with this one. Accept this. Be grateful for the kind of friendship that was offered. Honor it. Make use of it. They will always be great and loyal friends."

153

"Then what's the difference? Why bother with the merging?" I asked.

"Because what is exchanged is so far greater. Knowledge that can be found no other way. Love and understanding. And a continued ability to speak clearly to each other with your thoughts and feelings.

"There is no real way to explain the degree and quality of exchange. It has to be experienced."

Chea and I both caught sight of Domano throwing taffy pieces, one at a time, and then catching them as they were being thrown back. Occasionally he'd duck behind someone in the crowd and let them get pelted with the candy.

"Chea," I asked, "is this merging something that I will be doing a lot?"

"At first, for now, you will bond with only this particular wind spirit. Then, when the time is right, we will tell you to pursue and merge with other wind spirits, one at a time. This is a long process. And after you have learned enough we will teach you to merge with other kinds of spirits, makers, and keepers.

"But one must be very cautious. There are many beings and thought forms, and with some of them it would be better if you did not spend time communicating with them."

"Why? Are they dangerous? How dangerous? This isn't something that's going to be like some horror movie, is it?" She had a knack for unsettling me just as I would get a bit at ease about a new situation and trauma.

"First," Chea smiled and shook her head, "you need to be able to tell the difference between thought forms and spirits. One doesn't want to open oneself up to an average thought form. These days they are products of imbalance. You don't want to add that to yourself.

"And second, one needs to be strong and well prepared for these things. You can't just run out and try to become intimate with spirits. One must prepare for each kind, and each encounter."

I walked over to the rail and looked to the ocean. "You mean that these things are really dangerous. I could get seriously hurt or killed. Don't you?"

Chea walked up next to me and patted my arm. "Of course. All life is dangerous. You do not drive a car without proper preparation. Same with this knowledge. Humans have made themselves very weak through the centuries. On lands long destroyed, these used to be common practices. Now it is time for these things and the strength and balance to return. Only this time there will eventually be even more."

She smiled and looked at me with great caring and tenderness. "I would not ask of you to do something that you were not ready for. We would not allow you to take that kind of risk."

"Oh, Chea. I don't feel ready at all! Why do you think I'm ready for this?"

"Because," she smiled, "you can use all the gifts of the directions at once and put yourself in the center. The gifts have made you stronger."

"But I can only just barely do that. I'm not very good either, at any of them."

Chea laughed. "You are very good at your song. You always have been, even long before we met you. The song pulls you straight into your heart place, where, if you can stay there long enough, the other gifts begin to unfold. Is it not how it has been for you?"

"I don't know," I answered. "What did you mean about spirits that I shouldn't talk to?"

I didn't know what was funny about that, but Chea really laughed. "It is the thoughts of other people that you should not be wasting time talking to. As for spirits, some are better for talking to than others. Some are greatly concerned with the affairs of humans. And some do not want to be bothered. They are all our companions here. Or as the Sioux say, they are all our relatives.

"In time you will learn more about which ones are the friendliest and approachable, and what kind of help they can offer."

"Oh Chea," I whined. "It's almost time for me to go pick up my husband. I think we should wait on this quest thing. Where's Domano? I should know more about this. Be more prepared. This is crazy. This really scares me."

She looked me straight in the eye. "Good. You will conduct yourself with the proper respect and alertness. Ah! Here he is."

Domano bounced up to us. "It is time to get back. Yes? Come. We will talk about tonight on the way to your car."

When I picked up my husband at the university, he wanted to know what had happened to my hair. I had forgotten about it. I told him I had been down at the beach, and it had gotten quite windy.

That night it was hard to listen to the kids. All I could think about was the impending quest. I was very frightened, but at the same time I was intrigued and curious. I felt honored and special to be able to participate in such an unusual and primitive experience. I wondered how many people outside the remotest tribes ever had an opportunity like this.

I fixed everyone's dinner and tried to act normal, but I was so nervous and excited I could hardly eat. And I barely remembered what anyone said from one minute to the next.

Finally, it was time to put the kids to bed. My husband had gone to his study in the back of the house. The kids were picking up on my anxiety and were being very difficult. Just when I thought they were asleep and I could go outside, one of them would pop out of their room and want attention.

After what seemed like an interminably long time, the kids fell asleep. I double-checked them and got my coat, then quietly slipped outside.

I wasn't sure if it was the proper time to go, but it was a good opportunity—perhaps my only one. So off I went.

There was no moon, and the redwood forest was very dark. Every branch and little noise scared me half out of my skin. I stopped and tried to recount all the steps I was to take. Then I remembered that I was supposed to walk from my center by putting my attention on my song and the other directions all at once. Now that I was under pressure to do this, it seemed especially difficult.

After a while I was able to get my song and the energies going somewhat, but it was impossible to stop my thoughts, let alone feel the expansion of the mind. I stumbled along up the hill, trying to maintain what centering awareness I had and not be so frightened.

I heard a huge roaring rustle through the top of the trees not far away. I could hear it moving from my left around behind me and off into the distance. I shivered involuntarily. I could feel that it was alive and intelligent, and that it was looking for me.

I tried desperately to regain my song and the flow. And as I walked on I began to feel the things around me. The forest was full of strange and beautiful life.

Then everything stopped. It was completely still. I could hear the roar of the wind moving in the top of just one tree at a time, charging through the forest straight at me. My breath stopped. Her strength and power were indeed inconceivable. She stayed in the treetops and whipped right over me. I could tell that she recognized me.

I kept struggling with my song while I scrambled as fast as I could to the hilltop to find Chea and Domano. When I got to the top they were not there. I must have picked the wrong part of the ridge.

They had said I would be able to tell where they had been and where they currently were. I tried to calm myself and get to my center, so that perhaps I could accomplish this divining act. But I felt nothing that seemed to indicate that the Hetakas were nearby.

The sounds of the forest grew very intense. I was terrified. I couldn't stop my thoughts or my fear. I stood still and worked on my song and flowing for a moment. Everything went silent again except the distant rustling of the wind in the trees. She came from my right this time and circled all the way around me. I could feel the edge of her blowing on my face and in my hair. I didn't know why, but I followed her.

She was different than I had expected. She was very much an independent thing from the usual breeze that blew up the hillside from the west. She had an intense wind that was concentrated into an area of a few cubic yards and moved at all different speeds and in any direction, in spite of the prevailing breeze or without it. She even stood in one place, blowing intensely, for many minutes at a time. She would go up and down in the trees, move in curves or straight lines and angles, or double back on herself.

As I followed her she would go ahead of me a short distance, then stop and wait for me to catch up. It was difficult to hike through this area at night. The foliage was dense and the ground was quite steep in places. It was so dark that I could barely make out the brush in front of me. I was getting scratched and jabbed, and I stumbled often.

I couldn't believe that I was actually doing this, scurrying through the forest in the middle of the night to a clandestine meeting with shamans and spirits. I had never thought of my studies and meetings with the Hetakas quite like this before. I was in the adventure, but now it was completely exotic and wholly real. I was excited, even thrilled, to be a part of this, yet I was terrified to the core.

I never thought of trying to back out at this point. It was as though there were no place to back out to. There was only forward.

I could feel the nearness of Death, as though she was just on the other side of the wind keeper. Everything was extraordinarily intense. My awareness of my song increased, and with it I was able to observe the surroundings with greater clarity. I became aware of the immense possibilities of experience in our lives on this planet. I don't think I had ever felt more alive.

I followed the wind into a small area where there was no brush. Domano and Chea were there. They didn't seem surprised at all that I had found them. But I was quite surprised and relieved to see them.

Chea took my hand. "Go through each of the steps. Perceive with all parts of yourself. You must proceed with great respect and gratitude. Do not let fear take over. You must grab onto it. And above all, keep control of yourself and your decisions. Allow the fear to accompany you if it must. It might even assist you in ways you cannot yet guess.

"Remember. You only spread your arms and open yourself like an empty vessel at the last moment before you merge, when you know you are ready and you have asked for what you want."

Domano touched my arm and smiled. "Trust in yourself. You are ready."

They smiled tenderly at me and stepped backward into the edge of the clearing.

"Wait! Wait!" I screamed. "You can't leave! Where are you going?" I rushed after them.

"We cannot stay," Chea said, trying to calm me down. "This is something you must do all by yourself. It is between you and the wind keeper. We must leave now. Calm yourself. Breathe deeply and maintain your song. Quickly. You must get back to your center."

They stepped back a few more steps and they were gone. They just became part of the darkness, and I could no longer find them.

"Wait! Wait!" I continued to scream. "I can't do this alone. I'm scared. Please don't go! Oh no! Wait!"

I searched through the bushes but could not find them. Suddenly, everything became perfectly silent. The wind was about to return. I ran to the center of the clearing and began struggling to regain my awareness of my song and perform the necessary steps.

She came storming up the hill in the tops of the redwoods and dove down into the clearing, striking me from the left and knocking me off balance. I could feel her intention. She was not malicious, but her strength was alarming. I could tell that she was curious about me. She was an inquisitive, thinking creature. It was obvious what she had to offer me. I could not understand what I had to offer that would interest her.

She took off back down the hill until I couldn't hear her any longer. The normal breeze remained. A night bird sang nearby, and the frogs croaked again. I stood listening and waiting for an unbearably long time. My fear escalated. I wondered if she was going to return, or if I should leave.

I tried to find my song and stay in my center as best I could, but I was so jumpy everything distracted me. Everything frightened me.

Then I heard her rustling sound again, coming straight up the hill and stopping just outside the clearing. I could feel her watching me. Death stood behind her. I was so frightened I could barely breathe. In my mind I could hear Chea saying to take fear by the hand, to go ahead in spite of it and with it. I became utterly determined to hold my center and reach out with my song, no matter how fearful I got.

She moved up in front of me. I could feel her breath on my face, in my hair. I stated my request, opened my arms, and reached out as an empty vessel. My song was strong. I could feel the life of everything around me. There was a gentle glow on the dirt and trees. I was extremely joyful and afraid at the same time.

There was no doubt in my mind that the wind keeper could kill me at any time, more easily than we would squash an ant. But I knew she wouldn't. If I were to die, it would be of my own fear or carelessness.

As she moved in closer I could feel the nature of her being. She was unlike anything I had ever experienced or imagined. She was extremely intelligent, compassionate, and curious. She had a special interest in humans and their development. The degree of her power and energy was shocking to my system. I could feel inside her, her connections to other worlds, other dimensions.

That alienness about her was what evoked the most fear in me. I could not put my finger on what it was exactly. When I thought about it, it made no sense. But the feeling of her was so very different that it startled me beyond reason.

She moved in closer. Our breath mixed. I knew that she was loving and cared for the life of this planet and those that lived on her with all of her own existence.

And then she was all around and blowing straight through me. There was light everywhere. She knew me well and I knew much about her. I could feel her surging through me like an electrical current. She was one of many like her that controlled the atmospheres at different locations. She was not a god, just a living being whose task seems quite formidable to us.

I could see her history. She was ancient like the Earth. She had seen the dinosaurs and the lands shift. And she will be here long after we are gone.

I came to know her song and share her life energies, and she mine. We would be friends for the rest of my life. I knew

I could count on her for help, that she would hear me, no matter where I was, and I would hear her.

Our songs separated. She was moving away into the treetops. I realized that I was shaking all over. Inside I was ecstatic and wanted another contact, but my body had been dangerously exhausted by my fear. I was forced to retreat and stumble my way back through the forest to my home. I could sense her periodically, rustling in the trees, following.

9

THE MEDICINE SONGS

I was eager to get back to Domano and Chea to tell them about my experiences with the wind keeper. I went over to their apartment several days ahead of our appointment time, but no one was there. I knocked and knocked and called out. I even went over to the beach and looked, but with no luck.

I expected them to be there. I was so anxious to talk about my success. I had so much to say and many questions. This thoroughly frustrated me. I decided to go to the boardwalk and hunt for them.

I walked its length twice but did not see them. Then I thought to check the downtown mall. I spent the rest of my time going up and down the streets and into their favorite coffee shops, but they were just not to be found. This was the first time I had had to go home empty-handed, and I thought I would bust.

The next day I came into town with my husband again. I decided I'd wander around the campus before class and check all the coffee shops and the library to see if I could find them.

On my way to the library, as I was walking down the path through the trees, I felt the presence of something familiar. There was no reason for this—no sounds, smells, nothing to see. It was just a knowing. It was the feeling of the wind keeper. It felt as though she was greeting me.

I stopped and looked around. I was glad to meet her again. Since our first meeting on the mountain, this was the third time she had come to me. The other two were up in the hills by my house.

She rustled then in the treetops above me. It was her. I had no doubt. Then she swooped down around me and nuzzled up against me. I got a strong picture in my mind of the Stevenson College Coffee Shop. I didn't know why, but I felt compelled to go there, so I turned around and headed back to the east side of campus.

When I walked in, there were Chea and Domano sitting by the window. They waved me over. I couldn't believe it. I hadn't really expected to find them on campus that day even though I was looking for them. I noticed the coincidence between my seeing the cafe in my mind and being compelled to go there, but I didn't understand its significance.

"Hello, hello," Domano said with his big grin. "Come, sit. Join us."

"You look well today," Chea added.

"My god!" I answered. "I can't believe you're here! The weirdest things have been happening. I've been wanting to see you two so bad! Boy, do I have a lot to tell you!"

"Yes," Domano laughed. "You sure do."

"I did it," I continued in a low voice, bobbing up and down in my seat like a five-year-old. "I actually did it! I merged with it! Her. What is it anyway? It? She? He?"

Chea laughed at me. "They are not like that, actually. Perhaps the best answer is all three. We say she, because these grandparents seem a little more female than anything else. But that is just our way. Call them how you feel, now that you have met one."

"Yeah," I nodded, "'she' does seem to fit a little better. Why do you say 'grandparent'?"

"It is a word among our people that shows great respect and kinship," Chea answered. "It honors and yet speaks of familiarity, closeness."

"You mean like a nickname?" I asked.

They both laughed. Domano added, "Yes. A name of affection. Only in our culture, this nickname is the greatest respect."

"Ah!" I said. "I don't think that there's an American equivalent."

"No," answered Domano.

"Well," I continued, "I don't know what I thought was going to happen, but we talked. Only we didn't talk. I mean speak. Can you believe it? She was as curious about me as I was about her.

"When I really think about the quest, though, I still find it so hard to believe. I stood there and had a conversation with nothing. Only I know there was something there. It thinks and feels, but it's not alive like we are. It's so frustrating, I can't prove any of it. I can't even analyze it."

Domano leaned back in his seat and chuckled. "No, I guess you can't. Your science makes it hard for you and for your people, too. But she is as real as anything, only overlooked. To deal with her, a person must use all the senses.

"If she does not live, then how can she tell you to come to us here?"

"But," I answered, "I didn't have any idea that you would be here. It was a complete surprise."

"Why did you come?" he asked.

"I just thought about the coffee shop and I felt like I wanted to be here more than the library. I was compelled. But I never thought you guys would be here."

"You were hunting for us," he asked. "No?"

"Well, yes," I said.

"She answered you. She came to your call for a search," he said, "and hunted us for you. She told you where you needed to come. But you just did not hear all her message. You thought it was your own thoughts."

I interrupted. "But how could I tell the difference? How can I know? One thought is just like another. It's just in there."

"This is what experience gives to you. Thought is full of the song of its maker," Domano answered. "Now you train yourself to watch for this."

"But how?" I asked.

"By knowing your own song well, you can tell right off the product of another thing. When this keeper approached you, you knew her thoughts and feelings. You knew they were hers, not yours. This is true?"

I nodded.

"They were of her voice, you see," he added. "Can you remember how they were different from your own? The voice? The feel? Their direction?"

I had to stop and think. As I recalled the experience, it was difficult to remember something that I had not paid attention to, but I thought I recognized what he was saying.

"You think on this," he said. "I will go get you some French roast."

"Oh, thanks," I reached in my pocket. "Here's some change. Ah, coffee sounds perfect."

There was a long line. A class must have just gotten out. It was going to take him a while. So there I was alone with Chea again. She was very quiet that day. Even after all those months, I still didn't know how to read her.

She said nothing. Her face was unexpressive and calm. The silence was getting to me, so I struggled to find a question for her.

"Chea," I asked, "did the wind keeper really talk to me?"

"Of course," she said, scooting her chair closer. "She has told you many things already. Unfortunately, in the beginning, it is always a little like pearls to the swine, until we can learn to pay attention and become more sensitized. They talk, but we cannot hear. Then, little by little, we begin to hear."

"Tell me. How are your babies?"

"Well, my big babies. They're fine. They like their school and the forest. I don't think they've caught my craziness yet. I think I've been irritating my husband more, though. With my school, the kids, the house, and this, too, I just never get all the cleaning and errands done. I cook whatever is the quickest and easiest. And I'm either too busy or too tired to do anything fun."

"Poor fellow. He was not counting on his world changing, too. He'll recover." She laughed lightly and caringly. "You will need patience with each other.

"Ah. Coffee, at last."

Domano served us all and sat down. I noticed then that it was almost always he who got up to make coffee and snacks or go to the counter at a cafe to order. In my relationship that was usually my job. I didn't quite know what to think about that, but it was curious.

Domano sipped his coffee. "I'll tell you about the wind keepers. I will tell you a story about them.

"This is another good story, of course." We laughed. "The Sun is peeking through onto our table. We have fine coffee. There is good music. What do they call this music?"

"It's reggae," I answered, "from islands in the Caribbean. It's really nice, isn't it?"

"Yes," he said. "It is good for this story. You relax. And enjoy.

"This was long ago. In forgotten times. The land I speak of is now below the waters.

"There was a richness in the soil of this valley. Fields were heavy with harvest, and the forest was full. There lived a gentle people there, liking the ease of things and pleasantness. It was their custom to summon together a whole village or two for collecting crops. All the people came, old, babies, men, women. All of them.

"Only this time a runner must take this message to a third village far up in the mountains. They hoped for their help, too. Nature was sharing great riches with them, more than they can work. A harvest this big did not happen often. But these folks liked to share, if they can. The people of this mountain village, they were very friendly folks, but far enough away that it makes it hard to visit. So they do not. Only for special events.

"It was many years now since their last visit. The runner man was just a little boy. He is very excited to go. To see. He makes himself ready and gets instructions from his elders.

"The trip was long but not too hard. This young man was strong, with good health, and fast. He goes to the chief first. They talk a long time. The chief brings in foods and drinks for the runner.

"And when the chief is satisfied she calls together all the village elders. It is for them to decide whether to go down into the valley, and how many go. There are many things to consider.

"They all counsel for several days. People of the village come forward and speak what they think. Then it is decided. More than half the village will go. The others will stay behind to tend to things.

"This will be most exciting for these folks. They get supplies together and leave for the valley. It is hard for such a big group to travel down the mountains. They go slow. Two weeks pass. The runner hopes they are not taking too long and get there too late. He urges for more speed.

"As they arrive, the valley people are just starting the harvest. The mountain people set their camp and go to join the village people in the fields.

"It was a very happy time for everyone. A reunion of old friends and family members. And meeting of many new friends.

"Among the valley people there was a young woman named Pula. She was strong and clever and pretty like the blossoms of a flower. She was of marrying age and was curious if there would come any young men that would please her. She worked in all the fields to make sure she meets all the men.

"There was one man there, when she first saw him and he smiles at her, she feels herself shake inside. And she wants to know him.

"He was Manaol. Young, strong. A very honest man. He too was thinking maybe this is a good place to find his wife. When he saw Pula in the field, he quick grabbed the big gathering basket to where she was and collected the harvest from her bag.

"She smiles at him a long time. He is nervous. He is afraid she will not care for him, and he stumbles on roots. But she does not notice.

"He is called away by an elder to help with carrying. He is so beside himself by the nearness of Pula, he forgets to say goodbye, or where to see her later. He walks off, smiling a lot, looking at her, not where he walks. And he trips again.

"Later at night he talks with his uncle concerning this woman. They talk about finding her and their families sharing a meal. They all must meet, get to know each other, before the families can decide on a marriage. This affects them all.

"Manaol and his uncle go visit around the village and camp. They come to the home of Pula and her mother and aunts. Manaol's uncle brings many foods and a fine meeting meal was fixed. It was a good introduction. And many more meals could follow.

"During the next days, Pula and Manaol worked in the same fields so they would pass by each other several times through the day. At meals, more friends and family came each time. And great friendships grew and deepened. The day would come soon when harvest was done and the mountain people would have to leave for their home. The families must decide now if there is to be a marriage.

"Pula and Manaol want each other more than anything else. But they will abide by the decision of their families. Late each night they sneak out of the village to meet secretly. They are very in love, and Manaol sings songs of passion to Pula and chases her in the moonlight.

"The day before the mountain people leave, their families decide the young couple should marry, but not until Manaol finishes his commitment to his elders. They will marry at the next summer's end. One circle of seasons. This means Manaol must leave Pula and return to the mountains. In winter there is no passage between. No messages or visits can be taken.

"This is the best decision. One has no choice but to honor commitments. Then they both will be free to live their own lives. He will return with his family in one year to marry and remain in the valley.

"The parting was hard for everyone. But the lovers most. Pula could not bear to see him walk away. She cried off into the woods. Manaol called for her, but she would not show herself. He trailed behind his people looking between the trees, singing his songs for her.

"She listened to them and followed by the road in the forest till the cliffs begin, and he disappeared around the mountain.

"For Pula and Manaol the year passes slow. The winter is long and harsh. Each lives in the dreams of the other. They remember the time together and prepare for their joining.

"Pula's grandmother was a medicine woman. In this year she takes Pula to live with her, to teach her the ways of their ancestors. She learns about marriage and birth and how to live with the spirit people.

"This grandmother introduces her to a wind spirit of their mountains. Pula spends much time learning to be a friend with the spirit, and hear her voice when she speaks.

"One day Pula cries for Manaol. The wind spirit, she wraps around Pula to comfort her. Pula says, if only I could see him, hear him. The wind spirit says she will go into the mountains and find Manaol and return to show her how he is.

Pula does not understand, but she agrees, hoping she will hear news of her love.

"When this wind spirit comes back and surrounds Pula, Pula sees Manaol in his village. Hears his voice as he speaks to his uncles. She is filled with excitement. She asks the wind spirit to carry a picture of her to Manaol. The wind says he has not learned to hear her. He may not understand. Pula pleaded until the wind said she would try.

"So up into the mountains goes the wind spirit. She tries and tries to get Manaol's attention, to make him see the picture of Pula she carries in her heart. But he does not notice. She brushed up against him, again and again. Called his name. Wrapped around him and blew in his face. Yelled in his ears. She even came roaring at him and almost blow him over. She yelled, 'Pula loves you. Pula sends a picture for you to see.' But he still did not hear.

"As she gave up and started to leave the mountains, he sat down on a rock and sighed. And says, 'Oh, if only I could see my Pula again.'

"She stopped and looked at him close. But he did not understand her message. His heart only heard a little echo of the name of his beloved, and it made him pine for her.

"The wind spirit returned to Pula and told her everything. Pula cried and called her grandmother to help her.

"Grandmother was clever. She knew a way for this wind to carry the lover's dreams over long distances. She taught Pula how to make fibers from her heart. How to send them on her voice to the wind spirit to carry to Manaol.

"Pula practiced all the time. She learned how to make these fibers and send them on songs of desire for her beloved.

"One day while Manaol was hunting for wood, he hears Pula's voice singing to him on the wind. He thought, 'This is the magic of the old grandmother. I like it. Wind. Carry this song of my heart back to Pula.'

171

"He sang beautiful. Songs of impatient love. And the wind spirit carried their heart's desire back and forth till the flowers came in summer.

"Then Pula prepared for her wedding and her new home. The weather was good. In one moon's time Manaol and his family will come and she will begin her new life. She is dizzy with excitement.

"In the mountain village, Manaol completes his commitments. He does not want to wait for the appointed time. He wants to leave for the valley right away and plans with his family to go now and then meet them in one moon's time in the valley. This is fine. He says his many farewells to his village and heads off.

"In the high pass of the mountains the weather changes. It is late afternoon. Clouds collect, and it gets colder. Manaol hurries. But he is very high up. It is long to the foothills, a day or two away. He knows he is going to be stuck in the storm. But it is summer, and this should not be too cold or harsh. It would be good now to set up a camp. And he hunts around for a good place and firewood.

"When his camp is set it has gotten even colder. Snow actually is falling. He needs lots more wood for the night. He hikes around and gathers. It is a rocky place. On his way with his load back to his camp, the rocks roll underneath him, and he falls into a little crevice. Rocks, big rocks, fall on top of him.

"He cannot move. Try as he does, the rocks are too many and too heavy. The snow falls harder and night comes.

"The wind spirit friend of Pula's finds Manaol. She tries to have her wind spirit relatives blow the storm away from him until he can get free. They agree to stay away from the crevice, but they will not leave the mountain pass. The storm is there to stay for a while.

"Now Pula's friend rushes down into the valley village. She shakes Pula awake with a dream of her Manaol trapped in the snow. Pula jumps up with a scream. 'Grandmother!

Grandmother! Wake up! Manaol is trapped in the snow. He is on the high pass. The wind has told me. We must go. Oh Grandmother, help me!'

"Pula is beside herself. She fears to lose her beloved Manaol. She cries and cries. Grandmother knows she speaks the truth and goes to wake the warriors of their family to make the journey and rescue him. They must hurry, for he will be dead soon.

"Grandmother is too old to go. She tells the warriors to take Pula. Pula will guide them as the wind spirit guides her.

"They leave before sunrise packed up for snow. They reach the cliffs by dawn. They can see this weather is pretty bad up high. But Pula pushes them on, faster and faster. They reach the pass by nightfall. But she only lets them rest a short time. Then she tied the men and horses and herself together on a line. And she leads them in the darkness through the long pass. The men were afraid, but Pula says her spirit friend will guide them safely.

"The snow was bitter cold. And deep. And drifted like great waves on the ocean. But they keep moving.

"As the Sun began to rise, the storm broke. Clouds pulled apart. Everything sparkled fresh. Then Pula recognizes the place she saw in her dream. The wind spirit took her to the crevice.

"Manaol was almost buried by the snow and rocks. But he lived. They set to freeing him as fast as they could and wrapped him and Pula together in furs on a stretcher. She would bring warmth back to his body.

"Now they head down out of the snow, to make camp and rest.

"Manaol recovers. And in twenty days his family arrives for the wedding feast. Everyone has lots of fun. Everyone is happy. And Manaol and Pula begin their life together."

I looked up at Domano. He was smiling. The Sun was shining through the cafe window, and I heard the reggae music again. It was as though the world of the coffee shop had just started up again at the end of the story. I had been, as every time before, thoroughly captivated by Domano.

"How do you do that?" I asked. "How do you get me so completely involved in your stories, to the point of excluding everything else? Nobody else does that to me. No lectures, not even the TV. The movies sometimes, if it's an exceptional one. But that's in a dark theater. It's set up to get you completely involved, to forget the rest of the world. But you're just talking. Do you do something to me?"

Domano laughed. "It is about time you asked. Haven't you thought this a little peculiar before?"

Chea and I laughed. "Well, yeah. Sort of," I answered. "I was never quite sure. I mean . . . "

Chea chuckled, "You do like to get confused, don't you? It gives your mind something to work on. Something to fidget back and forth about."

We all laughed. Put that way, my inner debates sounded humorous and silly. But she was right. I loved them, and if I didn't have one readily available, I'd make one.

"It has to do with the energy centers in our body," Chea said. "And how we use them to make fibers. Like Pula sent on her breath.

"We all make fibers, tiny energy threads, from all over our bodies, all the time. We send them out to the world. They are the radiations we make, our songs and stories. With concentration we can make them consciously, from the energy center we wish, and send them out.

"But there is a special way to send them, to combine them with the fibers of the mouth and send them out on our breath with our sound. Our teachers called this singing and speaking the fibers."

"But," I interrupted, "how did you get me to see and feel the environment of the story?"

Chea rubbed her thumb and first finger together as she moved her hand outward from her chest, as if she were feeling and pulling on a thread from her sweatshirt and said, "By thinking, seeing, and feeling the environment ourselves and making the fibers in our hearts out of that. Then we sent them to your eyes and ears and heart. Sometimes to your nose and mouth, or your skin. Sometimes to a specific energy center. Each place on your body handles information in its own way. So to have you experience the effect of Pula being shaken loose from her sleeping, he sent them to your belly. You jolted. You felt the surprise, the shock, the danger.

"When he wanted to have you swoon to their love play, he sent them to you heart. That was very easy. You really know about this swooning stuff. You sure like to do that an awful lot." She giggled and tapped my arm.

It was unusual for her to tease me. I liked it. She was doing her best to show that she accepted me, and that was comforting.

She took my hand and said, "To learn this you have to come to understand your energy centers. We want you to do another homework. If the weather is good you should do this outside, on the ground. If you really want to get fancy about it, make yourself a dirt painting, in a circle, of the Earth Fire Serpent all coiled up. Then sit down on it and face your direction.

"Call her into yourself and let the energies flow hard through you and do their cleaning and mending. And when you feel ready, pick a center and take all of your attention there. Observe it. Feel it. Learn its peculiarities. How it deals with the world and your body. Then you must look at the world through this doorway. Stay there and observe all you can.

"Do this for each one. At least once every day."

"Where am I going to find the time to do all that?" I complained. "Do I do my other tasks, too?"

She set her coffee down, "It shouldn't take you that long. You can be anywhere, where you can afford to concentrate. Not driving. You are not required to make the drawing of a serpent. It is just a very good congruency. Keep it simple if you would rather."

Domano added, "You could do good for yourself to imagine the drawing, if you choose. And yes, always do your other homeworks, too."

"How long do I stay observing a center?" I asked.

"As long as you can," Chea answered.

"But what if I get interrupted?" I complained. "I don't even know where the centers are. This sounds like more than I should be trying. Are you sure I ought to do this?"

Domano smiled. "Didn't have enough confusion and stress for you, huh? Would you like us to help you make some more?"

I had to laugh. I was doing it again and working myself into a tizzy. I was afraid of the exercise, but I had no real reason to be. I looked around the cafe. No one was paying any attention to us. The music took my tension away. I really liked this new reggae. It pulled me back to a peaceful mood.

Chea giggled, "What you need is another Wild Mouse ride."

I didn't know if she was serious or not. I laughed. "You just want to see me throw up again, that's all. You have no pity for me."

"That is 'cause you hog it all," Domano said with a big openmouthed laugh. He slapped the table and we all laughed.

"I think maybe we should tell you where to look for the energy centers," said Chea. "That will make you feel better. This exercise is an easy trick to do with your attention. You will learn much.

"When you understand how each center filters and concentrates on different kinds of information and different ways of collecting the same information, then you will know much on the arts of human communication. You will know what is needed to sing and speak the fibers."

"OK," I said. "How often? Will I always do it, like my other homework?"

"Oh no," Chea answered. "Just two weeks. Until we meet next time. You will need to do this just once each day. And try to concentrate for as long as you can at each center.

"It is time to go now, so let's hurry.

"The places to look for the vortexes are below the feet. There is one there. It moves a lot. Then the ones you know on the bottoms of each foot. In each knee. And four in the hips and—"

I interrupted again, "How am I going to remember all this? I have to write it down!"

"No," Chea answered firmly. "Listen like you will remember. Expect yourself to. And you will.

"The hips have two larger ones on top of each other, and a smaller one to either side of them. The small ones move a great deal, often outside the body. But these four usually work in a similar way, in conjunction.

"Then the upper belly has three. One large in the middle and two smaller on the sides. They move, too. The heart you are knowing quite well, but observe there also. The hands are remarkable. They expand and shrink and move all around, even into other realms. Above the heart in the mouth and ears and throat is the next. Then the eyes. This one can move a great deal, too. It sometimes expands itself into the center at the top of the head. And they work together. Then there is one above the head.

"That should do it. It is time to go now. We will see you at our apartment in two weeks.

"You have done well. We are proud of you. You know that. Until then." They rose and headed for the door.

"Wait! Wait!" I said anxiously, following them. "That's it? That's all? Aren't you going to tell me what the centers are like? What they do?"

"No," Chea answered as they were walking out the door.

"But how can I do this?" I whined. "I don't know anything about this. You've got to tell me something about them."

They kept walking slowly toward the field.

Chea smiled and shook her head. "Calm yourself. No one can tell you that. Each person is an individual and uses their own centers in different ways. Some people even are missing some that are common to most humans. And a few others have extra ones.

"We can tell you very basically what their general nature is most likely to be, such as the heart being compassionate and without judgment. But the rest you must find for yourself. I am sorry, but this is the nature of things.

"Learning requires work and determination." She smiled and chuckled, "You have worked yourself up again. Treat yourself to some patience.

"There is your young mate. You will be late for your class. We must go. In two weeks then."

That evening at home I took a walk out into the forest to try my new homework. I wondered how I was going to "paint" the Earth Fire Serpent in the dirt. I couldn't use a different-colored soil, because it was all the same color out there.

Finally I decided to clear away the leaves from an area big enough for me to sit in, and I drew a circle around the edge with a stick. Then I laid leaves inside to make the pattern of the coiled serpent. It seemed OK, so I sat down and began the exercise.

I was concentrating well, when my daughter came up to me. She had been hunting all over for me and was wondering what on Earth I was doing all the way out there in the forest sitting in the dirt.

I told her that I liked the forest and enjoyed just being alone with it sometimes. She said she understood. She liked to do that sometimes, too.

As we walked back to the house and discussed the latest trauma of the school lunches, I realized I was going to have to rethink my homework plan and figure out a way to do it when I couldn't be interrupted. That didn't leave me much opportunity. But by snatching half an hour here and fifteen minutes there, I managed.

It was a windy day, sunny and still warm. I finished my classes and rushed over to the Hetakas' apartment. Only Domano was there. Everything was as usual, except all the drums were down, and there were a number of clay whistles on the floor by the abalone shell.

"Some French roast, yes?" Domano asked.

"Yes," I answered. "And I brought you some other flavors to try. There's Espresso, Mocha Java, and Sumatran."

"Thank you," he said. "You are always of good heart. You go ahead, sit. I'll fix this and be with you."

I sat on the floor by the whistles to examine them. There was the turtle that I had seen before, a braid of two snakes, a llama, a pregnant monkey, a guinea pig, a jaguar, a squirrel, a deer, and a bird of prey. And there were two humanized forms: a bird and a jaguar. They were beautiful, worked in a simple primitive style that I could not recognize at the time but months later identified in the library as typical pre-Columbian art of the central Andes.

"Are these all whistles, Domano?"

"Yes," he answered from the kitchen.

"Where did you get them? Did you guys make them?"

"No. We found them in the Andes." He brought the coffee in and set it down. "They are beautiful, yes? The sounds they make are specific. Each whistle helps one's attention to collect. To focus on a different energy center."

"How do they do that?" I asked.

"Each center sings our song in its own way. Like its own harmony, you could say. When we make a form of these

179

sounds in music, we make ourselves use that center. The old ones of the Andes knew this. They made a fine art of it. What do you think?"

"Amazing," I answered. "Can I touch them?"

"Yes. Enjoy them," he smiled. "Try one. Blow on it. It is fine. You will not hurt it."

I picked up the bird of prey and examined it. The mouthpiece was located in the bird's open beak, and four tiny holes were scattered on its back. It was made of reddish fired clay, and had a modest sheen on most of the surface from burnishing.

I was sure that his reference to the old ones meant that these art works were hundreds of years old, priceless relics of antiquity. I wondered how they managed to acquire them, who made them, and how they were used.

"How old are these?" I asked as I set the bird down for fear of breaking it.

Domano looked at me and smiled as if he were teasing. "Oh, about twenty years."

"But you said they were old."

"I said the old ones knew the art. The secrets have been passed down through the long years. These whistles here are the same. We bought them from an old man who often sat at market in a little mountain village."

"In the Andes?" I asked.

"Yes," he answered. "In the Andes. In Peru."

"How were they used? I mean, do you know the ancient cultural applications?"

Domano laughed. "The what?"

"You know. Did they have special ceremonies or anything like that around these things? Were they common or restricted to the priests?"

"Priests kept them." He reached down and picked up the snakes. "They were used for teaching the new priests. Sometimes on great occasions several would be played from the temple to the people. But this was rare. This was all very long ago."

"Before the Spaniards, I'll bet."

"Yes," he said.

"They're so fragile looking. What an incredible treasure this is. I didn't know you guys had stuff like this. They're magnificent! You should put them out where you can enjoy them."

"They are to be concealed until the time of use," he replied.

"But why?" I asked. "They were just sitting in the marketplace when you found them."

"The old man who had them sat at market. Not the whistles. You be more attentive as you listen. You make too many assumptions, young one. Listen with your ears open and empty, not so full of ideas." He smiled.

"Oh," I said. "But why do they have to be concealed?"

"Because there are things that lose their power if they become common. These were sacred to those old ones. It is not their time yet to be public. When things are open to many, they catch the eyes and thoughts of those people. These are not always the best of thoughts. Then this thing would sing with all those thoughts as well as its original song. You see?"

"You mean like contaminate it? Like cooties?" I asked.

Domano laughed and put the snakes down. "Yes. Like cooties. Only this is serious. This is for real. When one has an object that is for using or gaining power, this is most serious. You must take great care of it. Protect it. Or it will no longer be able to work for you. If you are real stupid with it, you could even cause yourself harm.

"Pick one up. Go ahead. Blow on it and tell me, where in your body do you feel it?"

I picked the jaguar. It was highly stylized. All the whistles' finger holes were placed irregularly down the front of their bodies, each in a different pattern. The jaguar was the largest of the collection.

I blew on it and moved my fingers over the holes. I was expecting a piercingly high pitch, but the sound was actually about mid-range. As I played around with it I noticed a sensation in my chest, a warm buzzing. For no logical reason I found myself feeling great compassion and affection for these sounds and the jaguar whistle.

"You see," said Domano. "They pull you right to the spot they are made for. Which center do you think?"

I had no idea. I didn't know what I was looking for. I stopped playing and just looked at Domano for some clue. He was acting as if I had the answer.

"You are thinking your answer away," he said. "Play again. Stop your thinking chatter and just put your attention to these sounds and your body. Most of you knows the answer, it is just your thoughts that do not know yet. Let your body teach it to them. They will like it. Play. Go ahead."

I played again, emptying my mind of its chatter and trying to feel just the sound and my body. Again my chest warmed up and felt very stimulated, and the feeling of great affection returned. I searched through the rest of my body for any sensations that were out of the ordinary. There were none, just the sensations in my chest.

I was very excited. I finally understood what they had been telling me about the feeling of stimulating and concentrating on an energy center. Now the feelings I had been having with the latest homework made sense.

"It's the heart, huh?" I said.

"Yes," he answered. "As attention goes to them, they have more energy. They sing louder. Expand. Brighten."

"Yeah," I nodded.

"Hand me the jaguar," he said. "I'll play, you feel. Memorize this feeling. This song."

I sat back against the bench and closed my eyes, listening and feeling. After a time he picked up another whistle and played it. The sensations in my chest ceased and were replaced by warm vibrations in my throat, mouth, and ears. I felt a keen desire to paint and work with music again, even to sing.

He blew on each whistle and each time I felt a different area of my body resonate with the sounds. The most unusual were the sensations from the centers below my feet and above my head. They were definitely outside my body, yet I could feel them. It was similar to having something vibrate just a few inches from the skin. I could feel it like an echo effect in my feet and scalp.

The sounds of each whistle produced not only physical sensations but also profound emotional and thought responses. I felt my song intensely, and if I observed carefully, I could detect a slight variation at each location, like the adding of another chord of notes or shade of color.

"I will blow this deer," he said. "Sing with it. Perceive everything you can as you make these same sounds."

Domano played a little tune and repeated it over and over. Again my neck, mouth, and ears vibrated with the sounds. I picked up on the song quickly and sang along. It felt very fulfilling, and we were having a great time.

He stopped. "Now you are using the center at your mouth. You are sending energies and fibers out from here helter-skelter in all directions. I want you to collect all of it into one fiber of energy, weave it. Send it to me right here." He touched his left ear. "Yes?"

"How do I do that?" I asked.

"Feel it. Will it," he answered. "It is easy. Just imagine this. Like pretend." He looked like a kid himself, his eyes sparkling with a big, innocent, excited smile.

"Pretend, huh," I said. "I don't think I understand."

"Just try it," he answered. "Close your eyes, and sing with me while I play. Make the fibers go out on your breath."

I was very unsure about what I was to do. It didn't make much sense to me, but I closed my eyes to try anyway.

"How will I know if I've done it?" I asked.

"I will tell you," he answered, and began to play the whistle.

183

After about ten minutes he stopped. "You are letting your mind scatter. Think only of the neck and mouth, and how they feel. And send this feeling on your breath to me in the form of a fiber. A thread."

We tried again. And again, and again. I think that hours must have passed before I was finally able to do it correctly. When I was successful I could almost physically feel the fiber spinning out of my throat and mouth. It was surprising just how much attention it took to create and sustain it.

Domano was adamant about me being very careful when practicing the making of these fibers. Whatever I had on my mind or feelings would be woven into the fibers and would impact on whoever or whatever I sent them to. It could never influence other people to do anything they did not want to do, but it could cause an alteration of mood. For this reason, Domano said, we must use caution and respect for others and be perfectly sure and clear in what we create and give to others.

"Among my people and teachers," he said, "this is the art of the storytelling and singing shaman, the *kala keh nah seh.* They build a stage. The listeners are the willing audience, and the shaman enriches their lives. Shares of himself in this way. It is a kind of healing. The backdrop and sound effects, they are his illusions."

The back door opened and Chea came in. She had a little bag of coffee beans.

"Should I make coffee for anyone?" she asked.

Domano and I answered in unison, "Yes."

"I have a little story for you. While we wait for coffee." Domano said.

"This was in the time when our world was not yet finished. It still looked like the Spider-Creator's web in many places. Lots of the animals and plants had not been put in the world yet. Spider-Creator and her helpers were fixing humans together.

"The helpers make the humans so they can talk like the animals, with their minds and the movements of their webs. This seemed fine. But the old human woman was not pleased.

"She says to Spider-Creator, 'How can my people ever find the many wonders of your webs? They will be happy and content to stay forever in these fields and forests with the beast brothers. They will have no challenge. They will never know beyond the beauty of the day in the field.'

"She knew these things because she was one of the firstborn and traveled very far with the helpers and Spider-Creator.

"'Well,' said Spider-Creator, 'I seek to please and fulfill you. I want good things for you because you are my daughter. What do you want for your people?'

"The old woman said, 'Look at them. They have all they could want. They will never roam to the edge of your webs to find your secrets. Take speech from them. Make them work to find how to talk.'

"And one of the helpers said, 'If we do this, the humans will not know they have any friends. They will surely be sad and could all die.'

"And the old woman said, 'And if you do not, who on Earth will be moved to search the heavens to find you?'

"Spider-Creator said, 'You are both right. How will you keep them from dying?'

"The helpers said, 'The old woman will keep her speech and knowledge. She will go back among them and tell them of all the many wonders at the ends of the world so that they never forget to strive. She will remind them of how they used to talk and how they will learn to talk again.'

"This is how the first shaman came to be."

Chea came in with the coffee.

"You look well, Kay," she said. "How is your family?"

"Oh, they're fine," I answered. "I was wondering if you were going to be here. How are you today?"

185

"I am well," she answered. "We must drink up our coffee so we can finish teaching you about the singing of fibers."

Chea was eager to show me the details of this art and started to explain as soon as I got my cup. "So far you have made fibers from your mouth. This is good. Now Domano will play the jaguar, and I will play the deer, and you will feel your heart and your throat. In the same way as before, make a fiber from this feeling in your heart. Sing and send it up your throat. It will weave together with the fibers of your mouth as you send it out to its destination. It will be of the qualities of both the heart and the mouth.

"Try it now, make the energies flow through you, and as soon as you finish your coffee, sing."

Domano began playing the jaguar while I was still sipping. I had the same sensations in my chest as before.

This time it was relatively easy to make a fiber and send it up and out my mouth. It seemed natural and produced a tremendous feeling of affection and creative satisfaction. It was exciting. I was creating and giving a great gift of affection and inspiration. There was no sense of depletion, as though the source were bottomless and I could do this forever.

"Very good, Kay," Domano said. "Can you see what this means?"

"I don't understand," I answered.

"Can you take this a further step?" Chea asked. "What comes next?"

I had no idea. Suddenly, I felt very thick-headed and stupid.

"Haven't you wondered," asked Chea, "about the possibility of making fibers from the other centers as well?"

The thought had only briefly occurred to me, but when she asked me about it, a flood of possible combinations of fibers and their directions and uses poured into my head. The possibilities were enormous, and each would produce a different effect.

"It takes practice," Domano said. "You practice this. It is an art."

"The strongest effect," said Chea, "is achieved when heart fibers are added to whatever else you weave. The heart is the most powerful. And the world is moving into the time of the heart, so it likes to resonate with it. It is like pushing a wagon downhill instead of uphill."

"I felt like I was giving something," I said.

"You were," Chea answered. "Whenever we communicate with another, we are giving them of our living energy. When you give a fiber, you are giving a tremendous concentration of living energy that can accumulate."

"Do other shamans use this art in their healing ceremonies?" I asked.

They both smiled.

"Yes. You are catching on," Chea said, tapping my arm and giggling. "Let us go out while there is still Sun. Where do you want to walk?"

I looked up out the window. "Oh. The beach. I want to walk in the water."

"OK," Chea said, clapping her hands. "The beach. Shoes off, everybody!"

We all scrambled to get our shoes off as fast as we could.

"Last one out the door is a rotted egg," yelled Domano. He laughed so hard he could hardly get his shoes off, and Chea beat both of us out the door.

When we got to the beach I rolled up my pant legs and walked in the water. It was biting cold, but I walked through the waves anyway.

"You practice on these fibers," Domano said. "We will work more on them later.

"This is a good time for a different kind of story."

"You should tell her about the Woosai," Chea interrupted.

"The Woosai, Mama?" he asked.

"Woosai. The Woosai, Papa," she answered completely straight faced.

I had to laugh. The mama–papa address was so completely out of character for them that it was like a jolt that plopped me back into the present.

"But Mama," he complained.

Still laughing I asked, "What's a Woosai?"

They looked at each other and laughed.

"'They' are a people," Domano answered, "much like us. They had many wars."

"They're all dead?" I asked.

"Oh no," he answered. "They are prosperous now, and at peace for many centuries. But once they almost killed their whole home."

"Where are they," I asked. "Do they have some other name? I don't think I've ever heard of them. What's their location?"

They glanced at each other and smiled.

"It does not matter," Domano said, "Their story is what is of value."

"But," I said, "it sounds like it would be very important to know where that kind of destruction occurred. Who those people were? How they did it? Why, don't you want to tell me?"

"Oh," he answered, shaking his head and smiling. Chea laughed.

"You see," he continued, "Their lands were desert lands and jungle. No other kind of place. The Woosai of the desert, long ago, they had a great hatred and suspicion of the jungle people. The jungle people did not trust the desert folks, either. Generation after generation they made war on each other. They stole property. Destroyed crop lands to starve their enemy. They did every horrible thing you could imagine to each other to fill their fears and greed."

"Are these people in Brazil? South America somewhere?" I interrupted. "Or Africa?"

"Oh, their land is far away," he continued. "Each side thought they were superior. They had religions that talked about peace and life, but they did not really listen to them. They broke the laws of their gods and spirits to get what they want.

"They thought they had very little in common with each other. They did not understand each other. Their governments were different. And their laws and beliefs and their houses and clothes. Their hatred was great. They wanted to make slaves of each other and their land.

"They did not care about the life of the nature around them, either. They killed it in their greed and hatred. They poisoned their soil and waters. Burnt their houses. Cut the jungles.

"In their heat to kill each other they killed millions and millions of animals and plants. The balance was shoved farther and farther away.

"The weather changed. No rains fell in the jungle. Winds blew the soils away. They tried to force the skies to make clouds and rain with their machines."

"Oh!" I interrupted again. "This must be Atlantis!"

"No," he answered. "This is a people whose home is on another land."

"But how come I don't know about them? Is it Lemuria?" I was becoming frustrated.

"Another land," he said again. "Another planet."

"Oh." I was disappointed. I had thought he was telling me a true story. Now it seemed obvious to me that he had made this one up.

"That is why I did not think it was best to tell you. Now you do not want to believe this story."

"How could it be true?" I asked. "How could we know such a story about another planet when we don't even know if there is any life out there at all? I'm sure it's a great story. I want to hear it. I love science fiction." I kicked a big wad of seaweed into the water.

"This is a story that our teachers told to us," Chea answered. "They told us that it was completely true. These Woosai live on a planet with two bright Suns and one very weak Sun. They have two Moons in their sky. There is one large land mass and the rest is ocean. It seems funny to us that their land takes only the shape of desert and jungle. And nothing else. But our teachers said that our planet is special to have so many kinds of lands and climates."

It sounded nice enough, but it was very hard to swallow as true. I couldn't see how they would know such information.

"There are many things in the scheme of existence," Chea continued, "that you do not know yet. Look what you have learned already. Do not make a judgment. Just hold what you hear and see as pieces to a great puzzle. Someday they will all fit in place. But not if you judge them now and throw the pieces away."

I nodded and Domano and I simultaneously jumped onto the incoming wave.

"OK," I answered. "I choose to neither believe or disbelieve. I'll give the Woosai the benefit of the doubt, until I can know for sure." That was easily said, but hard to carry out. I wanted to not make a judgment, to just observe and listen and store the data untainted, for another day, but this was very difficult. In spite of my effort I still wholly disbelieved the story.

"If they did not kill each other, they enslaved," Domano continued. "They were much worse than humans. After many centuries there was almost no jungle left. No crop lands. No water. Almost no animals. Or Woosai. Each blamed the other. Even the rain was now a poison.

"One day the last Woosai were foraging in the trees. They saw each other in their machines and plotted to kill.

"But they finally saw that they would all die forever if they did not help each other rebuild their forests. There would be nothing to keep their children alive. There would be no grandchildren.

"It was difficult. There was no trust. But a truce they made. Their death forced them to work together. They saw for the first time the life they had killed on their planet.

"A new world would have to be built. Their survival meant nursing the planet, together. It took every bit of knowledge and technology they had. It took three of their centuries. Many generations. All thinking of only one thing now: to make their world stay alive.

"They found in each other many things alike. Even though their language was different and details of their religions were different, they discovered underneath the same ideas. That the most important thing to them was life. Life for their children. And life for their planet home.

"Three centuries! All almost dead. They had great remorse. The value of each tiny life they learned. Their religion became one of serving and honoring all life and its many balances. They became masters of ecology.

"Now it is many centuries past. They have a great jungle on their planet again and a desert, with cities in both. Their huts are still the same as hundreds of centuries ago, made from plants and mud and rocks. They each keep and honor many ancient customs.

"They are a people who believe in the intelligence in all life. They are like shamans and talk to their planet's spirits and life forms. Yet they have something we would not expect. They are also masters of technology and space travel. They use no machines or fuels that will hurt their world. They have no rolling cars. They use no wheels on the ground. But they have many flying machines that are fueled by water.

"They have cities in space and fly back and forth with many other races from other worlds. The Woosai teach the others about ecology and their clay that they make into crystal sheets with metal that does not break or melt. They sell them fabric made from the plants and bugs in the jungle that has no weave. They buy and learn many things from them too.

191

"The Woosai are peculiar to us. In their little huts they have no art, no decoration. Nor on their fabric or bodies. They wear very little because their planet is warm. They have big open spaces on their huts, but no doors or windows. When the winds blow the sands or the bugs have hatched, they make an invisible wall with their machine inside.

"This machine lets them talk to others far away like a phone, or send for a ship or supplies. They do not have any machines for just entertainment. They would think our TVs to be very strange.

"They live in close family and village groups. They very often sing and make stories, music, dance, and theater for each other. They are very spontaneous. But what is strange is they have no costumes, no props, no theater building. No artworks but what is live and active in front of them. No books. No paper. They memorize everything. Teaching is given live in the group and with the machines in the huts.

"In the jungle, they cook over fire outside in the common place. They have lights, but they do not use them. In the desert, they cook their foods in a group building together. They use a machine, though.

"They all must put their water through another great machine before they can use it. It is poison to this day since the wars. In the desert there is little rain, but one does not stay out in it without harm. In the jungle the rain is frequent and they are able to move freely out in it.

"In the northern desert there are great high mountains. But no one lives up in them or goes there often, because these mountains belong to the mountain spirits, who are not big on sharing.

"The Woosai are a happy people. They enjoy simple pleasures and being together on their planet. Even though they have space travel, they like their home best and do not leave easily. Many races come there to study in their wild lands, and they must follow all the many strict laws of ecology and peace.

"They have lots of ritual and ceremony. Their knowledge is stored in huge computer places in underground structures in the foothills of the desert. Their machines in the huts and that they wear on their necks and wrists connect them like radio or phone. For a people who have no painting and sculpturing, they seem to put it into the writing, the pictographs, considered by many to be the most beautiful writing anywhere."

I had picked up a string of seaweed bulbs and was popping them as we walked back through the edge of the cold waves. The wind was coming up, and it felt wonderfully free and refreshing blowing in my face and through my hair.

"The Woosai," Domano continued, "are fiercely individuals. Even on the cities and ships in space they wear their native dress and tie their long hair according to family style. Wherever they go, they will not break their laws of nature's balance or cause harm to others. Even to their own death."

"Does this story mean that we, here, are going to keep on polluting and warring until there's nothing left?" I asked.

"This is one thing that happened," he answered. "One people's story. This does not mean we here will all destroy ourselves or become shaman-astronauts. That was their choice. We also have the whole of the universe to pick our future from." And he tossed up a handful of sand that arched high out into the air.

10

SEEKING THE
WATER KEEPER

In order to practice singing the fibers I needed to find a very private place where I would not be interrupted or, god forbid, observed. The redwood forest that surrounded my home and the college seemed the obvious choice.

I started hiking out into the relatively undisturbed second growth to the north and west of the college campus. There were little canyons and gullies, and remains of buildings and bridges from the loggers of the eighteenth and nineteenth centuries.

I loved that place. Sometimes I felt I could have stayed out there and never returned. This is where the Hetakas' way of thinking made sense. The plants, trees, boulders, and creeks were becoming my friends and confidants.

It was winter again and the rains were in. The little creeks had become very full and fast. There was one creek where the land was steep and rough, creating impressive rapids and waterfalls that dragged huge pieces of wood to the sea.

Once or twice a week I climbed down into the gully and sat next to the cascading water and practiced the making and singing of the fibers, aiming them at the little waterfall.

It was very difficult to tell whether I was producing them correctly or not. But once in a while I would feel a sensation of a narrow current of energy, not unlike a mild electrical current, flowing up the center of my body and out my mouth. It was very pleasing and rejuvenating, but it took every bit of concentration and attention that I had.

Sometimes the mist of the falling water would swell and rise up, enveloping me. There was something exciting about it, even personal, inspiring. It felt a little mysterious and beguiling, and at the same time beneficent. I wondered briefly if it was a spirit of some kind that perhaps I was inadvertently communicating with.

Sometimes while I was out there my wind keeper friend would come. She would rustle through the trees and storm at me, pushing hard against my body. I could feel her intensity and was able to distinguish her presence very easily. On one occasion when she was surrounding me, I had a clear picture in my mind of Domano and Chea. I could not tell where they were or why I was picturing them, but I believed the picture came from the wind keeper. I wondered for a moment if I should try and find them, but my time was running short and I didn't want to leave the forest. I didn't give it a second thought and stretched out on the plastic sheet that I always brought.

The mist whipped around in the wind as I tried to sing the fibers. The Sun came out and shone through the trees. Everything sparkled. It was warm and comfortable, and as I lay there, I grew sleepy and dozed off.

I dreamed I was hiking down the watercourse toward the bay. The water was six feet deep in places, moving hard and fast. I clung to the cliffs and brush as I struggled down the edge of the creek. The rain poured in torrents. I was completely soaked, but not cold.

I reached another waterfall, somewhat bigger than the first one. A woman with very light blond hair was sitting toward the edge of it. She had on a dress that was almost white, but with a hint of blue-green. Its long skirt was hanging in the water, and she was barefoot.

She reached down, scooped up a handful of water, and held it out to me. It was clear and sparkled like jewels. I felt that I was slowing down. The woman greeted me, and I her.

And then she said, "I want to show you something. I'm the caretaker of the course and work of the water that comes here. Look."

Deep in the waterfall was an opening, a cave.

"Don't you want to go see?" she asked.

It wasn't dark inside the cave, and it was large enough to stand in. There were paintings on the walls. My curiosity was making me anxious. I could hear music that sounded like the tinkling and bubbling of water, and the smell of flowers was thick. I looked around and there were blossoms of all kinds covering the banks.

"Let me give you a hand," she said and led me through the cascades in the middle of the waterfall and into the cave.

Inside there was a spring that bubbled up from the ground and trickled across the floor of the cave. It was the source of the musical sounds that I was hearing. It almost pulsed as it sprang up.

"You like this little gully," she said. "It is my home. Since the beginning it has been my home. It's like you see it now because I and my friends of the land and air have made it to look like this. We're glad it pleases you enough to sing to us, so I offer you my water to drink in return."

I pulled off my shoes and walked through the spring to drink from its source. It was sweet and fresh, not like any water that I remembered.

I looked around the cavern. There were many alluringly lit passageways deep inside. Some were supported with stone-work up their sides and seemed very well worn, while others had cobwebs covering their entrances. Then, before I had a chance to look at them, the paintings shimmered as though under water and faded away.

I wondered about the stability of the whole cavern. Was it going to melt away also?

I turned to take another drink of the spring, and the woman said, "Drink all you want while you are here. The

196

waters are the seeds of the stars, and pure. You'll find it very renewing. But remember not to drink from the rivers outside. They have been defiled. Mankind has spit upon the blood of its Mother, its very own blood and life source.

"Would you be willing to help me and my friends to make the waters pure again?"

I was about to rise to the call and agree to almost anything she asked to help clean the waters of the planet, when suddenly I remembered what the Hetakas had said about promising spirits things you might not be able to accomplish.

"Tell me about the waters," I asked, instead. "I need to know as much about them as I can."

She was very gracious and hospitable and handed me a metal goblet to collect the spring water. We walked farther into the cave and sat down on boulders that lined the back wall.

"In the beginning of this planet, my friends and I came here to build our home. We collected the gasses and dust into a ball with the one who was to be our mother, until it was firm enough to walk on. We shaped the lands and pulled the waters apart from them to make the seas and the sky. And then many more came, and we all turned ourselves into myriads of different plants and animals, mountains, and rivers, and all kinds of wondrous things and places. Our waters flowed clean and pure, with honor and dignity, for eons after eons, until the people forgot where they came from.

"Now our blood is poisoned, and the land and sky are sick. Our bodies are dying. Even our beloved planet, our home, our mother. The people don't hear our voices any more.

"Will you be one who speaks for us?"

"I don't know that they'd listen to me either," I answered. "I wish I could help. But right off, I can't think of what I could do to make them listen to me. The only thing I can say for sure is that I will keep your message in my heart and when opportunities arise I'll be honored to speak for you, for whatever that might be worth. I can't promise anything. I guess I don't have much faith in my fellow humans."

She pointed outside to the sky. "There is something new coming near to our Sun, our home. We ask people to join us in cleaning the waters now, or we will fix our home by ourselves, as we have done before.

"I like your honesty. You are sincere. Please drink up."

The water was so refreshing and satisfying, like the best of foods and drinks all rolled into one. I was very thirsty for it. It filled a hunger in me that I hadn't known I had.

The walls started to move like water and flow down around me. The woman, too, began to shimmer and dissolve away.

"Wait!" I said. "I don't even know who you are. Will I find you again?"

"We'll meet again," she answered. "On that you can be assured." And then she and the cave and the spring flowed away, covering me in their path.

I choked for air and shocked myself awake. Looking around, I felt disoriented to find myself on my sheet where I had dozed off. The feeling of the dream was very heavy on me and didn't lighten for several hours.

Now I was going to be late getting home, and I still had to pick up something for dinner. I couldn't stop thinking about the dream, and it seemed to me that I even had the taste of the spring water in my mouth all the way home.

The next day I went to the campus as usual. I was walking from College Eight through the forest to College Five. The wind came up from nowhere, and rustling loudly, dove down to blow hard all around me. I was startled and felt the presence of the wind spirit. I thought she must be trying to tell me something, but I couldn't understand what.

I continued walking to the cafe at College Five, as was my plan, to pick up a cup of coffee to take to class. At a table inside sat the Hetakas. I was very surprised. They waved me over to join them. I wondered why they were there, if they were try-ing to find me.

"Hi," I said as I sat down. "I have a class in a few minutes. I can't visit long. What are you guys up to?"

"We came to get you," answered Domano.

"What for?" I asked.

"A little friend of ours tells us you have been talking to the river," he continued.

I didn't know what he meant.

Chea added, "This river spirit expects you to be questing to bond with her, because you practiced singing fibers to her. This is often done to begin a questing. Now every time you go to her home, she will greet you. She has offered her friendship to you. If you want her friendship, there are things you need to know about water keepers."

Then it dawned on me what they were talking about, and that I had bumbled into yet another adventure for which I felt completely unprepared. "I had a strange dream yesterday about the creek I go to, to practice. Does that mean anything?"

"Tell the dream. In every detail," Domano insisted.

I recounted it the best I could. I was surprised at how much I remembered and the intensity of the feelings that returned. They listened carefully, occasionally glancing at each other but never interrupting.

"Normally, you would not be approaching water spirits for several years yet," Chea explained. "They are highly com-plex and require an enormous amount of concentration and commitment to bond with. Your fortune is very great that she has taken to you and offered her friendship in spite of your inabilities and lack of understanding."

I was confused, and as usual, I didn't understand how they came to their conclusions. "But nothing has happened. I only had a dream."

Domano smiled gently, "You knew this keeper was there. You felt her. Think. Remember how you felt about the place."

I had forgotten about my passing thoughts and feelings that I was contacting some spirit in connection with practicing fiber making, and I wasn't able to make sense out of what they were saying.

Domano set his coffee down. "When we are beginning to learn these ways of being, our attention rarely is collected. Our thoughts wander, move erratically. They slip out of our remembering.

"You know how your wind spirit feels when she is near?" I nodded.

He leaned forward. "There is something like that, a feeling of something there. Something else. Some kind of intelligence. Most of all when you were falling asleep."

Now I began to feel uncomfortable. "Do you mean that that creek is a keeper also?" My feet tingled. I tried to remain objective, detached, struggling to avoid fear.

"Yes," they answered in unison. With the gestures of his face and hands, Domano was encouraging me to keep thinking and remembering.

"I take it the dream was important?" I asked. "How can a dream be important?"

Domano got up and offered to get everyone coffee. Chea put her hand on my arm and said, "In the shaman's world, everything is important. In dreams we can cross into the other realms, pass through many gates and observe and communicate with what is there.

"Now you have to learn to be responsible, to take notice of everything that goes on around you and in your dreams and figure out how they all fit into the total scheme of your experience. Everything is important. It is all a part of the whole. There are patterns to be seen. Knowledge and answers, just for the taking. Friendships and conversations waiting."

"Do you mean I was actually talking to that keeper? You can't mean that the events in the dream were real?"

"Yes," she answered. She was stone-faced.

I didn't want to be disrespectful, but I didn't believe it. I was feeling cornered and confused, and a bit foolish. I shook my head. "I don't see how."

"That is OK. You don't have to. Never take our word for anything! Consider it. Keep always your mind open. You will only find true knowing from your own experience. We are here to help you find the experience, not to make dogma. Take all those shoulds and must-be's out of your way. Let yourself see all the way to the horizon."

That felt easier and better. Without the restriction of having to believe in anything, I was left free to explore every aspect, every possibility, without needing to be right or verified. I could just look and experience for the sake of looking and experiencing, without the fear of failure or of being foolish. It was as if tethers, the bindings, were just falling away. They had instructed me in that before, but I had always forgotten it.

Then I remembered a sensation that I'd had when I was in the center circle of the Cowell College courtyard. I'd wanted to see and learn everything, but I hadn't cared what it was. I'd had no desire or need for the data to be any particular way or content. I was open and willing to learn and experience whatever was truly present. I'd had no expectations, no investments. It was wonderful, just accepting what was perceivable and not needing to make it into something else, knowing that when I accepted it for what it was, explanations and details would become observable.

I decided then that this attitude had a great advantage and that I would approach all my studies in this way.

"OK," I said. "The dream was a real event. A communication. I'll try that on. It feels about as alien as eating live grubs, though." Chea thought that was most amusing. We were laughing and making bad-taste faces when Domano came back with the coffee.

"They really taste very good," she said. "Fulfilling. I kind of miss them."

201

All this talk was making my gag reflex feel very touchy. "But Chea, don't you feel them wiggling and squishing in your mouth? Uh!"

"Oh, that is very satisfying." She laughed so much it was hard to understand her. "That's what makes them fun. They are so much better live than toasted! But don't take my word for it. You will need to try some sometime."

"Oh, sure!" I wished I hadn't used that analogy. She had succeeded, easily, in disgusting me. Now my poor little mind was completely preoccupied with hundreds of wiggling maggots.

Domano set the coffees down and leaned over the table. "The worms crawl in, the worms crawl out, the worms crawl up and down your spout . . . " He didn't finish, he just leaned back and laughed.

Where did he pick that up? He never ceased to surprise me. We laughed and joked for a few minutes, when I remembered that I was supposed to be in class. I was late. I agreed to meet them there as soon as it was over.

When I returned we continued to discuss the river keeper. They told me over and over how lucky I was to have a keeper approach me like that, and that she would always be available to me. But I would need to attempt a bonding with her, preferably soon.

According to them, in order to bond with keepers, makers, or guardians of waters, one must have extremely well-developed concentration abilities and a perfectly clear and honorable intent. They said that water spirits have the purest and most noble of characters, just like the integrity of the waters when they were new, the waters that brought and nursed the life on this planet.

Chea added, "They are like a woman who takes and cares for an infant, nurses it from her breast, and raises it to adulthood. This is their nature and how they feel toward the waters of our planet and all the things that live from the waters.

"The bonding may not be complete the first time. But this is OK. You will try again. And if you need to, again. Most shamans try more than twice in questing for water spirits. It is much easier to carry on a regular friendship. And this is good, too. It is your choice."

I was flattered, but I did not think I could live up to the job. I felt that I was still recovering from the quest for the wind keeper. This new affair made me anxious and apprehensive. My temples throbbed, and my stomach got nervous.

"Is it dangerous?" I asked very softly.

"Of course." Chea's face was stern and serious. "But you know who your enemy is now—your own thoughts and fears."

I nodded. "But don't I have a preparation time? Something to do first? Like take several years at least to learn to hunt and eat edible grubs?"

Chea's stone face cracked. She and Domano both laughed, and he said, "It is time for you to try, or this chance would not be here."

They smiled. Chea knocked her fist on the tabletop like a proud coach telling the champ to go out there and get 'em.

There was a silence. They just looked at me.

I wanted to slip away unnoticed as fast as I could. These studies were getting far too complicated.

"You will have to practice staying in your center by using the gifts of the directions," Chea finally said. "Every day, as often as possible. Wherever you are, except driving. And when you are in a place where you won't be disturbed, practice the leaf-on-the-river exercise. Work hard to fully feel every sense. You must develop your concentration abilities to their highest. And you must know why you seek this water keeper." She looked as though she were waiting for me to say something.

There was a silence again.

Finally she added, "You cannot go down to the creek in the meantime."

203

I had suspected as much. "But how long do I prepare?"

"Let's see how you are doing in two weeks," Chea answered. "And if you should practice singing fibers, sing them to your bed or your couch or something like that. Maybe that will keep you out of trouble." We laughed.

"I've got to go." I stood up. "Where and when?"

Domano touched my hand. "Wait just a little time. I have a quick story for you. Very quick." I sat back in my chair.

He smiled, leaning over the table, and spoke quietly. "Back in the beginning there was only water. First the water held very still. But then one day, it began stirring. Undulating. And from the deep came a great Dragon. It swam and danced. And as it shook its tail, lands formed. When it shook its head and hissed, the Sky and the Sun and Moon and Stars were shaped out of the waters that flew off its head.

"The Dragon circled the lands around and under. There were caves full of water. They were a good hiding place. And he thought he would like to coil inside them, when he was not roaming on lands and seas spitting out plants and animals and people.

"Sometimes he liked to shake the land and spit fire into the rock and make it burn high into the air. Sometimes this made him laugh, and one could hear him very far away, chuckling and talking to himself.

"From time to time he would splash some water up on the land. And it trickled into lakes and rivers. But it never seemed enough, because sometimes the Dragon would fall asleep in his caves and forget his creatures.

"So one day the Stars and Sun and Moon were watching. They saw the hardship of the creatures. Without water they forgot the Dragon. They got sick and weak. Struggled. And died.

"The Stars and Sun and Moon cried. Their tears fell and made rain. It is so that water is the most powerful and persistent of all things. This is because it was the first.

"It helped the creatures. And they are OK now, so long as this Dragon does not sleep too long and the Stars do not stop their crying."

I thought to myself, what an odd story. I was about to ask Domano what it meant when they stood up to go. I grabbed my bag and coat.

Chea gave me a sidelong glance and said, "Two weeks, this coffeehouse."

I smiled and nodded. "OK."

Domano added in a serious tone as he was starting to walk away, "You think on what it means to have water."

I wondered what he meant by that. We exchanged hugs and went our separate ways.

I worked very hard on the four gifts of centering: the song, the life energies, letting go of my thoughts, and experiencing the expansion of mind. I even tried to practice each one separately, but I was only able to do the song and the life-energy flow by themselves. I didn't understand why, but I could manage the letting go of thoughts only when I had at least the song or the energies flowing. And I couldn't get to the expansion of mind unless I had all of the other three working together.

The two weeks passed, and we met at the College Five Coffee House again. They had me do the complete centering exercise and decided that I should prepare a while longer before attempting the quest.

We walked all over campus in and out of classrooms, dorms, studies, cafes, and courtyards while I practiced the centering. It was one thing to do the exercise sitting quietly, undisturbed, with my eyes closed but quite another to be moving and among other people who were busy audibly carrying out their lives. Everything became a serious distraction. But Chea would gently and patiently guide me back to my easiest steps, my song and the energy flow.

She said that depending on one's state of mind and personality inclinations, it would be easier to find one of the four gifts than the others, and that this ease could change with the state of mind. So even though it was easiest for me at the moment to find my song, it wouldn't necessarily always be so. If it became harder, I should just go around the circle and try the others until I succeeded in producing a gift. Then, holding onto this gift, I should move around again until I had all four.

The hours rushed by and it was time to go. We agreed to meet in one week in the university library.

The following week they again decided I should prepare a bit longer. So we spent the afternoon walking through the campus as before, practicing the centering. I was improving, but only in very small increments. Domano explained to me that it takes a long time, years of persistent practice, to really accomplish things. He assured me that I was doing well and would be ready to try the quest for the river keeper soon.

During this last week I had several haunting dreams about traveling with a group in a desert. The wells on our course had turned up dry, and we had to ration the little water we had left. And as I moved on in the hot Sun I fantasized and hallucinated about the water of the spring that was hidden in the cave behind the waterfall back home.

When I told Domano and Chea about the dreams they said that the water keeper was talking to me, teaching me secrets about her realm. I had thought they were just a symptom of psychological overload from thinking about her so much of the time for the last several weeks.

Domano reminded me to contemplate hard the reason I wanted to pursue the water keeper and also the significance of water. He clarified for me that there were actually two beings to be dealt with here, the water keeper and the water she tends, just as with the wind there were both the wind keeper and the airs of the atmospheres that she maintains.

"Why is it so much more difficult to pursue the water than the wind?" I asked as we were about to part for the day.

Chea nodded and smiled. "Because the nature of air is so much more flexible. It goes everywhere. Gets into everything. With no trouble at all. We breathe it to live at every minute. A wind keeper can blow right through you. Your nature is a lot like the wind keeper, more so than the water.

"One does not need to hold the concentration for long periods with the wind, because she moves so fast. Water is slower, heavier, but persistent. You must be able to stay centered and in her field for a long time and not let the waves of thoughts or emotions or fears push you off. You must become as persistent as the water. Do you see?"

"Well . . . " I didn't really, but I didn't want to have to admit it.

"You will." She smiled and laughed softly. "Your thoughts do not yet understand, but your body does, and the greater part of your mind does. This is not a thing that can be formulated in the thoughts. It takes the whole self to understand. Just know that and let it be OK that you seem baffled. You have to learn to trust in your own ability to accomplish and understand."

"Yeah," I nodded. They had said that to me countless times, and yet, as with so many other things, I still continued to forget it. I felt very slow and very unexceptional.

We agreed to meet the following week, and I took off to catch the last of a lecture on ancient Chinese art. At least it was something familiar and immediately gratifying.

I had strange, compelling dreams almost every night of the week. In one of them I was in an endless ocean. Nothing else was swimming in it but me. It felt strange and wonderful. I could breathe in it with no difficulty and swam on and on through the depths. It was not dark anywhere. At one point I came out on huge waves and rolled and rode with them like a dolphin.

207

There was nothing there but water and light, yet everything was there. I was by myself but not alone. I felt whole and nourished, and so very satisfied. And every time I thought about that dream the feeling of it returned. I asked myself if this dream was the result of the water keeper trying to talk to me. If so, what was she saying? I couldn't find an answer. And I needed to know.

The week seemed to pass slowly. I could hardly wait to talk to the Hetakas to find out what the dreams signified.

We met as planned, and I eagerly bombarded them with everything.

"Wait! Wait!" Domano said in an excited tone. I wasn't sure, but I thought he was imitating and teasing me. I felt silly and laughed. He laughed with me and said, "We cannot make these answers for you. This you find for yourself. As you learn. You see, I bet you have an answer for one question all ready. Why do you seek this keeper?"

Without thinking I said, "To learn. To find out. To know for sure. To be her friend."

"And what does water mean to you now?" he added before I could think.

"The continuing of life." I didn't even know where that came from. I didn't think it. I felt it, and then it was in words. It was like a truth for me that I didn't even know was there, that perked up from a hidden place.

"Huh." He had an expression of acceptance. "You see how far you have come? We can take you to the river today."

I gasped involuntarily. "You mean now? Right now? Isn't this kind of sudden?"

"Sudden!" Chea laughed. "You have been preparing every day for weeks. Are you going to turn sissy on us again?"

"Yes ma'am." I hung my head in exaggerated shame.

"Come on! Let's get hiking," Domano said, clapping his hands. "We're wasting time." He grabbed both of us by the arm and led us toward the west side of campus.

"Oh God!" I was quickly developing a stomachache. My feet began to throb and tingle as we walked at a rapid pace through the campus and into the woods.

We stopped at the ridge just before the little river.

"This is as far as we go with you," Domano said. "You know all you need to make this quest. Stay calm. Trust. We will see you soon."

I knew I couldn't stop them. My heart was pumping fast. I felt as though I didn't know what to do, like a child that has been abandoned.

I watched them walk away and thought that at least this time it was daylight and I was very familiar with the terrain.

Everything was remarkably still. I could hear my heart beat and, not only did my feet tingle, my whole body tingled.

I took a few steps. My knees were shaking. I stopped and sat where I had stood. I just didn't feel capable. I sat there for a long time wondering if I should walk over to the creek and try the quest, and what would happen if I didn't. Or perhaps it would be better to come back tomorrow so that I would have time to prepare psychologically.

I didn't know what I would find over the ridge. I was frightened. My thoughts came cascading in on me. I couldn't tell any longer what was the right thing to do.

I got up and hiked to the top of the ridge and yelled down to the river that I would be back when I was ready. And then I walked back to my car as the rain began to fall.

I was disappointed in myself, but I knew I couldn't have done it. I wouldn't have had even the remotest chance in the frame of mind that I was in. I was going to need to build myself up to it. The next day that I could get the car, I would try it. I promised this to myself and to the river.

That night I slept very little and had fleeting dreams of the forest near the waterfall. I wasn't able to get the car for another three days, and my nervousness steadily increased. I knew my abilities were not as refined and proficient as an apprentice's would normally be when properly pursuing a water keeper, and that my chances were not high for a successful merge. But I did have a chance to deepen the remarkable relationship that had already begun.

In that sense I could not fail, but I remained stifled with apprehension. I didn't feel the consuming panic that I had had often before. It was a dull weight, an inertia. My world had changed so fast already, and I was frightened at what this would bring. I had no picture of what I was heading toward, what my world would look like when I finished studying with the Hetakas. And even though I had Chea and Domano as models, I still couldn't project how I would turn out. I liked the way the world looked to me just the way it was. I wasn't at all sure I wanted that to change again.

My biggest fear was for my children. How was my learning shamanism going to affect them, or my feelings and responses to them? They were my greatest joy. I would do anything for them. The last thing I wanted was to inadvertently cause harm to them. That would kill me.

I spent those three days completely consumed by those ideas, fears, and guilt, trying to sort out which ones were valid, just what my life was turning into, and how that affected my children, myself, and my husband.

I think I must have been lousy company. I slept little and ate less. I didn't listen well and moped at my chores and homework.

I decided to go because I had promised the river I would be back. But I think if I had not promised, I would not have tried the quest at that time. Things were moving much too fast for me. I felt as if I couldn't catch up to myself.

When I was able to get the car, I saw to it that I had the entire day to myself, from early morning till the school bus left the kids off. As I walked from the parking lot on campus to the river I shook as if I were on a giant vibrator. I hiked straight to the big waterfall. The Sun was out, but there were many clouds still in the sky. Everything sparkled with the light on the drops from the recent rain. It looked like a fairyland, with tiny rainbows flashing everywhere.

I looked all around. No one was there but me. I climbed down to the ledge of rock and dirt at the top of a huge redwood tree trunk that stood leaning at the side of the waterfall for almost its entire length. I called out to the river, "I'm here. Shall we begin?"

I methodically proceeded with finding my song and then each of the other gifts, one at a time. It was surprisingly easy this time.

I could hear and feel my friend the wind keeper. She had come to support me. My sense of aloneness left, and I began perceiving hundreds of life forms all around me. The feeling of all of our songs was euphoric, ecstatic, like being in love a thousand times over.

The water falling was like bells and drums. The sound and its feeling filled me. I couldn't tell the difference between what was inside me and what was out. Then I sensed another presence. It was the woman of the waterfall from my dream. I couldn't see her, but her presence got bigger and bigger. Her intensity made me shake all over again.

In some ways she was like the wind keeper, but in many others she was quite different. I related it to similarities within a species, yet distinctions between individuals.

She was not what I expected. She was considerably maternal and caring. There was a hugeness to her beyond what I easily perceived. She was in a sense the provider for all the life forms in her area. There was something incredibly beguiling about her.

As I stood there, the mist of the waterfall pulled together and created the form of the woman from my dream. I was startled. I began to breathe irregularly, and I lost my concentration.

She held her left hand out to me and smiled with acceptance and understanding. I knew that she desired my friendship in spite of my inadequacies, that she knew and received me for exactly who I was. She offered her assistance.

My mind became invaded with thoughts, and I soon lost my center. The image in the mist remained a while longer and returned briefly several times during the day as I attempted to concentrate and continue the quest.

I never regained my full centeredness that day, but I felt her there. She was comforting. And I knew that someday when I was ready, she would be there, happy to show me herself and her world. I was no longer afraid of her. I knew she had the concerns only of a mother or nurse for the welfare of her family.

When my time was up I said my gratitudes and goodbyes and headed back toward my car.

I was very relieved to have that behind me. The questions about my future had not been answered, but they didn't consume me any longer. I was satisfied for the moment, and at peace. I drove home planning my next trip into town to see the Hetakas.

11

THE SPIRAL

Although I had wanted to see the Hetakas and talk to them about my questing as I was leaving the water keeper, I came to feel that I wasn't in any big hurry. I was afraid that I had stupidly done any number of things wrong in the process, and I didn't want to hear admonishing. The school quarter that was ending had also been particularly rough. I still had one final left and then Christmas.

I needed a break—from *everything*. I had no appointment made with the Hetakas, so I decided to wait until after the holidays to contact them.

Once school was over I completely involved myself in Christmas with my kids and the family. It was so peaceful to not have to go anywhere or think about or do anything that I didn't feel like doing. It turned out to be a desperately needed reprieve.

My father had always told me that if something was worth doing at all, it was worth doing well, if not very well. So, like a diligent daughter, I was trying to do all things in my life exceptionally well. I didn't realize until later that I was burning my candle at both ends—and the middle.

But Christmas brought me some relief and a little time. I had no dreams that I remembered, did no practices, and thought very little about any spirits.

When classes resumed in January, I felt it was time to visit the Hetakas. I went to their apartment, and they almost seemed to be waiting for me. After our usual greetings and hugs we talked about the holidays and how the kids were doing.

Then I decided to talk about my quest for the water keeper. "You probably know, I failed the quest."

"Not so," Domano said and waved for me to sit down. "You have gained with her more than many shamans ever get with a water keeper. You have done very well, Kay. You have a great friend in her. Someday you might decide to try the merge again. But right now you have one of the greatest prizes in your hand and you do not even know it.

"With time and practice your abilities with your attention will improve, and the rewards, too."

"Can I go down to the river any more?"

"Whenever you like," he smiled. "Always say hello. Be grateful, respectful. And keep any bargains you make with her. That is all. She and the wind can teach you more than we can. And they can introduce you to other spirits as well.

"There is a gold mine you have there."

I fidgeted on my bench. "How will I know how to use it?"

Chea shook her head. "You do. Things will get clearer. Trust in yourself."

I nodded, but I hardly felt knowledgeable or experienced enough to trust myself.

Domano shook his finger at me, "Attention is the key. All the ability and power to do whatever you wish. It is tucked away safe, just there in the attention." And he pointed to my heart.

Chea handed me a little wooden tree with many branches that stood on a large circle which had been notched to the four directions. "This is like our perception. Each part is like a different way we can focus our attention, a different way to dance on the webs. The circle represents our usual range of attentions when we are awake or in meditations or daydreams.

The tiny footprints around the outer edge show the path of the people as they live their lives around the circle. The spiral that fills the circle is the path of the shaman which leads to the center.

"The center is the place of balanced awareness and use of the gifts of the directions. Our attention feels different here and sometimes gets enticed and drowsy by the branches of sleeping, which are just above. We know sleeping and usual waking very well, but we have to learn centered attentions in order to hold them and remember everything that happens there."

The Sun broke through the clouds and flooded down on me. I had to turn and look at it. It had been so cloudy that winter that I was beginning to feel desperate for any little bit of Sun I could get.

"Ah! That feels like heaven!" I leaned back up against the window. "Do you think it'll ever clear up? I'd love to go out, except it's so cold."

Domano just nodded from across the room and sipped his coffee.

"You just sit in the Sun and enjoy it from here," Chea said. "And we'll teach you about the tree."

I picked up my coffee and settled back. Chea sat on the floor next to my bench and pointed to the tree.

"Each of the branches above the ground grow farther and farther away from our usual, familiar waking, and it is increasingly difficult to stay conscious and remember with each one as you go up.

"The first branches are sleeping and waking dreaming, where you can begin to slip through time and space. Then comes the kind of attention that brings things into being. With each higher branch your attention grows sharper and the gifts of the directions increase. You reach farther and farther into the expanded mind and the above, and yet you remain connected to the circle and our Earth.

215

"Then on top—the place where you can choose to be no longer connected to our web, where you are free from the restrictions of time and space.

"The better you get with your attention and the higher you go, the greater your experience will be with all you attempt: questing, spirit journeys, understanding, gate travel, visitations, healings, teaching. This is what is in the mastery of the heart, the center, *ka ta see*."

A group of crows landed on the front lawn and began screaming. I turned to look. They were so loud and persistent that both Domano and Chea got up to look out the window.

"Boy, that one guy sure is excited!" Domano laughed.

The biggest one was hopping all over the yard from one crow to the next, screeching at each one. It reminded me of a snake oil salesman trying to rile up the crowd to buy his product. Folks were getting excited, but no one was buying. They were great fun to watch.

"Do you suppose he is trying to talk one of them into being his wife?" Domano joked.

"Who would have him?" said Chea. "He's too pushy. I'm surprised they just don't gang up on him and shoo him away."

We all laughed. The crow was very obnoxious and making a great fool of himself. Then all at once, just as Chea had suggested, the others all jumped at him and drove him off. We laughed and joked about them for a while. Then Chea returned the conversation to the tree, and Domano sat on the floor against his bench.

"You have reached the center of the circle. When you sleep, you move through the bottom branches and sometimes around the circle and even, once in a great while, up the tree a little. But you are almost completely unconscious through all this adventuring.

"In the act of dreaming you can take your attention through many degrees of time and space; you can travel, learn, grow. That is once you learn how to get to the branches and stay awake."

"Don't tell me," I joked. "That's what I learn next."

"Yes!" they said at the same time, enthusiastically.

Domano added, "You will always be perfecting the gifts, *ka ta see.* The arts of dreaming, they are just one way we use them."

"Oh, I'm so glad you clarified that for me." I didn't know whether to believe them or not. "You mean to tell me, that I constantly wootsie out, nearly died of fear a dozen times, failed at my last quest, and now you're going to teach me yet another difficult task?"

"You got it, tootsie," Domano saluted me.

"Oh, God!" I groaned, plopping my face into my hands. "I can't believe this is really happening to me."

Domano jumped up. "Let's go for a walk. Let us talk outside. I think the Sun is going to join us for a while."

We agreed in a hurry. I set the tree on the bench and grabbed my coat, and off we all went out the door. The traffic suddenly got very thick and as we were crossing the lawn toward the beach Domano grabbed my hand, hunched over, and began walking like a severely crippled person, even grunting and stumbling. He was miraculously convincing.

I was so embarrassed! Everyone was staring, and people slowed down to look. I turned to Chea for help, but she was stone-faced. I softly spoke to her to make him stop, but she ignored my plea and joined his little act in a supporting role. I wondered how far he'd take it.

As we toddled along, the humor of the situation became more apparent to me. I started to laugh, and Chea elbowed me in the side and gave me a very stern look. A couple had been walking toward us and saw me being reprimanded. As we passed them, the woman looked at me in disgust for having laughed at my crippled companion.

217

Now I was really having trouble not laughing. I pulled my hanky out of my coat pocket and covered my face, as if I were blowing my nose. It was a bit difficult with one hand, though.

We struggled our way down onto the beach. It seemed a lot of other people had had the same idea of catching the sunlight while it was out. Now that he had a closer audience, Domano decided to twitch and grunt even louder. Chea proceeded as if all were completely normal and began to talk about the tree and dreams again.

Domano was still holding my hand as though for support, and occasionally he fell over and struggled to get to his feet again.

"Don't just stare at him," Chea scolded loudly. "Help him up. Be thoughtful to an old man."

People would look at me with great disapproval. I could feel their judgment and condemnation, and even though I knew the truth and humor of the situation, the impact of their thoughts and feelings of me was quite uncomfortable.

"Keep your center and know your truth," Chea said softly. "Do not let the waves and currents of the minds of the people influence you and capture you. If you were untrained and weak, you would begin to believe those thoughts about you. You would accept them as your own. But now you can see and feel the difference. Remain always strong in your own song as the world appears to turn around you."

I should have guessed this was more than just teasing and joking. It was becoming apparent to me that the Hetakas did very little, if anything, that did not have a specific purpose.

Chea nonchalantly continued her discussion of dreaming. "When we collect our attention in the way of dreaming, usually we have only learned to be asleep. To use this kind of attention when we are awake takes training.

"First you must see that this attention has Death close at hand to guide you. Death will teach you to heighten all your senses and awareness. She will show all the places you can find joy and the many aspects of your song. She will make things be for you like they have never been before: music, art, nature, dance, ritual, relationships, everything. They will live with a vibrancy and power. Standing in your center, you can find her everywhere as your guide. She will change the world for you.

"Humans have a unique capacity for experiencing intense passion—an exploding zest for life."

With that comment Domano went down again and struggled more violently than ever to get up. The more I tried to help him, the harder he made it for me to help. Several people stopped to offer their assistance, and both Chea and Domano began speaking in their native tongue, pretending not to know English.

The strangers looked to me and asked me what they had said. Not knowing what else to do, I pretended to translate and told them that my grandfather would be OK, that we would be able to get him to his feet and all would be fine. I thanked them and said goodbye.

Then Domano started jabbering a mile a minute and waving the strangers over.

The gentleman asked if I was sure we didn't need any help, so I told him that now my old grandfather would like him to help him get to his feet. The stranger was delighted to be needed as a knight in shining armor. This opportunity seemed to do him a world of good.

Domano made it very difficult for him, and it ended up taking all three of us to get this little man to his feet. He flailed, flopped, grunted, and even farted. It took every ounce of willpower I ever even dreamed of having not to laugh.

Finally it seemed we had things under control again, and our Good Samaritan friend and his associates went on their way. And off we hobbled and wobbled down the beach toward the boardwalk, while Chea calmly continued about the dreams.

"Humans are unique in the way they can develop extreme individuality and unending curiosity. As a species we haven't always lived up to this. But with Death at hand, you will see.

"We will give you a new homework today."

"Do I still do all the others?" I asked.

"You will stop the leaf-on-the-water for now. And you will always do the gifts all together, as one homework, for the rest of your life. What I want you to do now is fun. And it should be very exciting for your painting and sculpture.

"First I want you to observe this beach in a normal way. Look around you at the sand, the water, the people. Remember how it is.

"Now, use the gifts and find your center. Let Death close to you so that she can show you how extraordinary and intense everything really is. Use all of your senses at once. Let the data flood in."

It was very difficult to hold my center while Domano was hanging on to me still playing cripple. We walked along slowly, and I had had only marginal success when we came to the mouth of the river. Domano acted as if he wanted to try to walk through it.

"You don't really want to try to go through it like this, do you?" I pleaded.

He grunted and tugged at my arm to follow him into the water.

I turned to Chea. "He doesn't really want us to try to take him through the river, does he? We'll never make it like this."

"Find your center and hold it. Just keep walking. Hold onto Domano. Go."

We must have been a sight, struggling across the water. Domano slipped and went under several times, almost pulling me with him. Amazingly enough, I actually stayed somewhat close to my center all the way across.

When we reached the other beach Chea patted my back. "Very good. Very good. Get well into your center and tell

Death to instruct you. Have her show you this beach. Use all of your senses. Notice all you can. Breathe in everything. Fill yourself with their songs. And remember."

We walked a little while as I observed. The feeling of Death close at hand was like a catalyst to feel and observe all I could while I still had the chance. Everything was brighter. The lights lighter, the darks darker. The smells came one on top of the other, and each seemed stronger than the last. Sounds seemed to move inside me. Things were where they belonged, in their respective places, and yet they all moved toward me. I literally felt everything I perceived through my entire body.

I didn't just see the tan color of the sand, it enveloped me and I sensed its color and nature with every cell of my body. I felt that I was vibrating with everything like a tuning fork. There was something about the whole-bodiness of this experience that reminded me of the way the roller coaster ride had made me feel.

"This is very good." Chea stopped walking. "Very good. Remember it.

"Now we will sit down here."

"Oh no," I interrupted. "If we sit down, we'll never get him back up again."

Chea laughed softly. "We'll manage. Go ahead. Let's sit for a while."

Domano just plopped where he stood. He was still holding my hand and pulled me off balance. I almost fell on him.

I sat down cross-legged next to him and Chea sat to my left.

"Now," she continued. "Close your eyes and recall both ways of seeing. Picture everything in your mind as vividly as you can. Feel everything with the same intensity. Hear, smell, taste. Feel the sand under your feet. Your body taking the steps. Domano pulling on your arm. Experience it all again."

I don't know how long we sat there while I remembered. I was amazed at the degree of detail and intensity with which

221

I recalled the experiences. I was very impressed with the difference between perceiving normally and perceiving from the center with one's song. It was like the difference between noticing a color and bathing in it, or seeing a picture of a hot fudge sundae and really eating one.

There was something remarkable about color. It had a nature all its own and radiated outward. Each color felt different and seemed to collect in different places within my body and the environment.

My mind began to distract me with random thoughts that lured me away and tried to convince me that these experiences were not real, but just a form of hypnosis or some other flimflammery.

Chea whispered in my ear, "Your only true adversaries are your own thoughts and fears. Let them pass by you."

In my mind I stepped aside, and all the thoughts just went on by. It was as though I watched them amble off over the horizon.

"That is part of the homework I want you to do. Observe, then remember. The other part is to remember your dreams, in detail and intensity."

I opened my eyes and returned to my normal state of awareness. "Should I keep a tablet beside my bed?"

"No," she answered. "No writing. Force yourself to remember. As soon as you start to wake up, make yourself remember as much as you can."

"But even dream therapists have their patients write the dreams in order to remember them," I complained.

"This is not dream therapy." She hit the sand with her fist and I jerked. "We are training your whole self to perceive and act in expanded ways. Writing will not help."

Domano moaned and struggled to get up. Of course, he had waited until he had the most people around him. I tried to pull him up and subdue him a little. It was amazing how heavy and awkward he could make his little body when he wanted to. Eventually he was up, and we headed to the pier.

He was truly masterful at his act. I had to admire him for that, even though I was becoming awfully frustrated with him. He jabbered and groaned and flailed. Once he drooled on the shoe of a concerned passerby.

At that point I jabbered back at him in nonsense sounds, using a scolding tone of voice and shaking my finger at him. I leaned close to him with my hanky to wipe his face and whispered, "It's getting so we can't take you anywhere."

He smiled and let out a huge yelp. I jerked back. When I caught my balance, I jabbered back at him again.

A man had been watching us from the edge of the pier. Domano dragged us over to where he was. He and Chea were speaking back and forth in their native tongue. I leaned over to Domano and jabbered to him, using exaggerated tone inflections, hoping he'd understand what I was thinking.

The man seemed very interested in us. He stepped over and introduced himself and asked what language we were speaking, how did I learn it, and would I mind telling him what I had just said to Domano.

I squeezed Domano's hand and said in a thick accent, "I told my grandfather that if he didn't behave himself I'd kick him off the pier."

I apologized for his behavior, saying that he wasn't responsible for his actions any longer, that he was senile. And then I said goodbye and yanked Domano around to head back to the apartment. I was amazed at myself. I couldn't believe I actually had said and done that. It was wonderful.

Domano stayed in character all the way back. When we finally got to my car, we laughed and laughed. I felt as if I needed to laugh for a month.

They reminded me to do my homework several times a day, and I'd see them there in one week.

I laughed all the way home and then periodically through the evening. My son asked me what I was laughing at. I told him that in town I saw this guy who made a big fart in public and I couldn't laugh without being rude, so now I had to laugh. That was probably not the best thing to have said. As kids will do, he wore out the joke till well past bedtime. But I couldn't really scold him effectively when I was laughing as hard as he was.

When we next met I drove the three of us over to Capitola to a little cafe with tables outside overlooking the bay. It was sunny and warm, and the water was calm. Little birds were hopping all over the terrace picking up scraps and crumbs.

"Now, tell me," I asked. "What does this perceiving and visualizing homework have to do with dreams?"

Domano seemed pleased with my question. "It is a preparation. A training. In order to control dreaming awake or asleep, you must have great concentration and visualizing. All parts of the work of the shaman depend on this.

"But enough on dreams today. Today we enjoy the Sun and I will entertain you with a story."

"Ah," I smiled. "This is a beautiful setting for a story. Just so long as you don't do anything embarrassing."

His expression was one of perfect innocence, and he raised his arms slightly and said, "Who, me?"

"Yes, you!" I laughed. I got a funny feeling in my stomach, and I hoped that I hadn't instigated another siege of bizarre behavior. His show of innocence was so well done that he almost made me question my own experience to the contrary.

The waitress came to get our order, and he said, "You just sit back and watch the sea. And enjoy. I'll show you."

I held my breath and braced myself.

"Three coffees and chips," he said to her with a big, sweet smile. He was putting on his best cute-little-old-flirty-man act. Everybody around seemed to think he was a really sweet old cad. I watched him closely and just waited for the ax to fall.

He delighted in keeping me off guard and flashed me a side glance with a look of "well done."

"This is a story that fits this beautiful day. Lean back. Put your feet up. The Sun and the sea are beautiful. This is a time not for work, but for taking in.

"The Maker Man was walking on the new place he just finished making. Throwing a ball up and catching it. He was very proud of himself. He thought he was real hot stuff.

"He patted the land and said, 'I will call you Earth. That is a great name.' And he walked on and on. There was lots of rocks. Lots and lots. He kicked a few around. Then he patted Earth and said, 'Yes, daughter. You are great. I have done a marvelous job.'

"He was about to leave when he heard this sobbing, sobbing. He looks around. But there is no one there. He yells, 'Who cries here?'

"And Earth says, 'It is me, father. Earth.'

"'Why do you cry?'

"'I will be all alone. You will go. And I will have no one to talk to, but Sun, who lives so far away I have to yell as loud as I can.'

"Maker Man thinks, what can I do? Oh yes! My poor daughter should have a husband. If I don't find her a husband she will never know the bearing of children. This is my duty to make her happy.

"So he tells her not to worry. He is a good hunter. He will hunt her a virile husband who will make her very happy.

"He travels to many worlds and looks and looks. No one, he thinks, is good enough for my daughter. A long time passes. Earth thinks maybe he has forgotten her, and she becomes very sad. Every day is another burden for her.

"Meanwhile, her crazy father turns down suitor after suitor. He says, 'He is too ugly. He is too stupid. He is too poor. He is too selfish. And he is too mean.'

"The years pass on and on and still he finds no one. There are hundreds and hundreds of suitors left behind. They think this is a bad deal. They decide to go hunt for Earth and persuade her to take one of them as her beloved.

"They divide into six groups, to cover the six paths of the land of stars. None of them are ever heard from again. They probably found someone else to take as wife.

"Meanwhile there was this young fellow named Sky, who heard stories about Maker Man's picky hunting for a husband for his beautiful daughter Earth. He thinks to himself that it would be far better if he found Earth himself, than to go to her father. So he was clever. He had heard the stories of the other suitors, how they never returned. He got an idea to find Earth quickly. He told Maker Man that he heard of a group of suitors that had found Earth on their own. They were there with her now, persuading her to marry one of them.

"Maker Man was furious. He set out at once to return to Earth, to protect his daughter. And Sky followed behind him, careful not to be seen.

"When Maker Man got to Earth he found his daughter alone.

"'Where are the suitors?!' he yelled.

"'What suitors, Father? Did you send suitors for me?' She was happy at this. She had thought he forgot her.

"'No one has been here?'

"'No one, Father. Are you bringing me a husband before I grow old?' She was becoming a bit displeased with him, again.

"'Yes, yes, Daughter. As soon as I have found one worthy enough.' And off he went again, now that he was convinced of her safety.

"Once he was gone, Sky came out of his hiding place. When he saw Earth his heart leaped. Oh, if he could only win her heart and convince her to marry him.

"He approached her slowly. She watched him come close, and she got very curious about him. She thought he was pleasing.

"He introduced himself and told her of his desire to become her husband. She liked him and they spend much time together. She tells him that he will have to ask her father for permission to marry. And when Sky tells her of the hundreds of suitors her father has already turned away, Earth thinks of a plan to trick her father.

"She sends a messenger to find and tell Maker Man that Earth had taken sick and was calling for her father. He returned at once. And Sky hid nearby.

"As her father cared for her she asked, 'Father, I have fear that I will never marry. Tell me, how do you hunt for a husband for me?'

"He gave her a long story of all the lands he travels and how hard he hunts.

"She says, 'How do you decide if they are worthy? Is there a test?'

"'Oh yes. Only the very worthiest of all can have my beloved daughter. I wish to take good care of you, and see that your whole life is full and rich.'

"'But Father, so far, most of my long life has been sad and lonely. Waiting for a mate. What is this test of yours, Father?'

"'I ask them to bring me the knife of the spider from the land of shadows. They all refuse and leave. You see, they were not worthy.'

"'But Father, how would you know if it was the right knife?'

"'Oh, I have been told that the blade is long, and sharp on both sides. The handle is bone. And the image of the shadow spider is carved on the palm. This is a secret known only to a few, so I will know when it is brought to me. Your husband will be very great. I will see to this.'

"Earth told her father that she now was recovered, and wouldn't he *please* go see to finding her a husband before she was dead of old age.

"Sky heard the whole secret. He told Earth not to worry. He would not be fool enough to risk going to the land of shadows. The place no one returns from. He said he could make a knife like the one her father described.

"Earth was excited. She had grown to love Sky very much and would die herself if he tried to go to the land of shadows. Now, she would soon be joined with her beloved.

"Sky worked hard to make the perfect knife. And he did well. He took it to Maker Man and asked for him to bless his union with Earth. Maker Man was mighty happy to finally find someone worthy for his daughter. To this day they have never been apart.

"Their union produced many, many offspring. And their remarkable fruitfulness was known far and wide through the land of the stars."

Domano tilted back in his chair and picked up his coffee. He smiled at me like the Cheshire cat. "How are your homeworks going? You do them every day?"

I smiled back. "Yes."

"Good," Chea added. "Be diligent. Consistent. Everything may depend on it. Even your life. Do the singing of the fibers, also. Only be careful where."

"Can I sing down at the river?" I asked.

"If you wish." Then she shook her finger at me. "But you know now how intense a communication it is. You don't realize how well you do at it. Life will respond back. And now you need to be responsible for all your actions. To pay attention to what happens around you. You can no longer do things haphazardly. Or blindly.

"It is time for us to go now. We are going to walk. But stay if you like."

They said goodbye and Domano winked at the waitress as they left. I stayed for only a few minutes longer and then rushed back up to the campus to finish some work that I needed to catch up on.

It would be several weeks before we were to meet again in the Cowell College courtyard. Meanwhile I had far too much to do and was having serious trouble trying to fit it all in. Then I decided to combine homework, and I began doing the Hetakas' while tending to my house and family. As my ability to do both things at once increased enough to make it a feasible way to accomplish my goals, I tried to incorporate the Hetakas' homework with some of my college work.

With the art classes it was a great boon, but with my science classes it was impossible. I needed to be linear and when I was successfully centered and using all the gifts, I wasn't able to incorporate the linear aspects of my mind.

When we met I asked about the linear qualities within the mind and if they were, indeed, something that could be used simultaneously with the gifts.

Domano sat on the wall and motioned for us to join him and said, "Oh, you have tried this. You know it is tricky. But it can be done. You need to pull yourself, with gifts in use, toward the south. To use the linear mind with big results means you think in sentences. But the sentences of your choice. Not mindless chatter. You control the direction and content of the thoughts. Not the old ideas and fears leading you by your nose.

"When you do this, the linear part of your mind becomes your tool, not your dictator. In the greater part of your mind, where perceiving is in whole pictures, you can learn to act out your experiments. Experience wondrous new things. Then it is the job of the linear to translate it as best as it can into the sentences.

"You do not have to fuss about this. If you want to work them at the same time, it will eventually come. Right now you are doing very well."

"Well?" My eyes popped open. "But I can barely hold the center for more than a moment at a time when I'm doing another action, like walking or painting or cleaning."

"Sometimes you expect too much of yourself," he reassured me. "Stop beating yourself up. You are very fortunate that you can get the center at all. These things take time. Even years. Shamans spend their whole lives perfecting them. And just when they are really getting a grasp and can really understand and affect things, it is time for death.

"I am telling you now that you have too much stress on your body. You must ease up on yourself."

"But how can I? How can I not do the things I'm committed to?"

"You can do them." He leaned closer. "All of them. It is in your mind that you are weighted down. You think that you do not do well. That you do not do enough. No matter what you gain it is not enough to meet your demands.

"Your body and your mind are capable of doing all the things you want. But not if you keep punishing yourself. Be proud of what you do. Find joy in it all. . . . instead of turning it into a struggle that is full of guilt and fear.

"I'll give you a new homework that will help. You lighten up on all your others and try just to find joy in whatever you are doing."

Chea took my hand and added, "When we think we do not like something or that we are not supposed to like it, we close our song off. We try to shut it out. Because we want to believe we are correct that we don't like this. If we were to feel our song at that time, we would not feel the sensation of dislike any more. And then what would happen to our belief that we have worked so hard to nurture?

"Our joy can always be found. It is always there. Our notice of it can be triggered by anything. It makes everything OK. And the body does not have to carry the stress. It can perform miracles when it is freed from the stress."

I started to cry. I felt as though I couldn't do anything right. It seemed that I was failing at everything. I was used to getting the equivalent of A's, and this quarter I was getting a C in biology. My house was a wreck. The laundry pile was big enough to eat Santa Cruz. My marriage was stressed. I wasn't spending enough time with my kids. I didn't cook properly any more. I rarely spoke or wrote to the rest of my family and friends. My abilities with the work of the Hetakas was almost nonexistent.

Domano got up. "Here. Let me find you a real good stick to beat yourself with."

I understood what he was trying to say, but I couldn't help the way I felt. It didn't seem to me that I was asking too much of myself. I believed that if I couldn't do it all and do it well, then there was something wrong with me, not with the amount of things that I piled onto myself or my stressful attitude toward performing them.

Chea put her arm around me. "You ease up on your homework. Only do what easily presents itself. And like Domano said, put your attention into feeling your joy wherever you are. This will help. I promise."

I cried and cried. All my feelings and fears of being a complete failure came to a head. What an awful sensation. And it hurt throughout my whole abdominal region.

Domano suggested that instead of trying to shove the experience away, I should let it exist, let it have its moment.

He said I should feel it, allow and acknowledge all of its aspects, not question or deny it. He said that there would come a time when the feelings would all make sense to me, but that didn't matter now. What was important was the acknowledgment and the experience.

We walked up into the woods, and they stayed with me for several hours until I felt better.

I agreed to ease up on the homework and concentrate on finding joy. We set the next meeting for almost a month later at the Stevenson College Coffee Shop.

I can't say that I was any better at the next meeting than I had been at the last one, except that I had managed to bury all the feelings about failure.

I got a coffee and soup and sat down at a table to wait for the Hetakas. It wasn't long before they showed up. The reggae music was cheerful and light. Chea came and sat down while Domano went to the counter.

I had been able to relate much better to Chea lately. She understood me, and I was able now to see genuine concern in her for my wellbeing. Her lack of superficial actions still unnerved me. I was now beginning, I believe, to see her actual personality. She was enormously compassionate, but she didn't gush. Her psychic abilities appeared to be extensive, but she showed absolutely no judgment. I was beginning to suspect that she was happy most of the time, even though her face so often seemed expressionless.

I didn't understand these combinations of behaviors and appearances. They didn't fit together for me. And even though I was becoming fond of her and dependent on her in many ways, she still scared me a little.

She asked me how things at home were, and I told her they were not great, but not too bad, either. We chatted a bit before Domano came to the table.

He sat down with his coffee and said, "We are going to talk about the tree today. About the branches of dreaming."

"Oh, good," I nodded. "I don't grasp that concept very well."

"The largest branches belong to dreaming," he said. "There are more of them than of the others above them. But that is because of its many parts." He looked over at Chea.

She spoke up. "By learning to sensitize all of your senses and focus your attention on them, you have been training yourself to experience and remember in dreaming. You will notice that things you concentrated on in the day will show up in your dreams at night. And eventually things you see in your dreams will show up in your waking.

"Another part of what we call dreaming is when the attention is aimed in almost the same way as when you are in a sleeping dream, only you are awake. At first it is difficult to not fall asleep, but you will learn to overcome this with practice."

"I don't understand what you mean. How can someone dream when they're awake? Do you mean a daydream? A fantasy?"

"No," Domano answered, tapping his fingers to the reggae music. "Daydreams are part of normal attention. Out on the circle. This is when you have centered yourself with the gifts and then turn your attention in such a way that it feels like dreaming. Only you are conscious. You can direct yourself within it."

"What do you do when you're there?" I was thoroughly amazed. Such a thing had never occurred to me before.

"You can go on spirit journeys." Domano smiled like a cat that just swallowed the fish. "Or hunt for knowledge. Talk to spirits. Play with time and space. Do healings. Gate travel."

"Are you guys putting me on?" I looked at Domano's eyes intently for some clue to the truth.

He stared right at me, shook his head, and said, "No. These things are for real."

"Spirit journeys?" I asked. "You mean astral projection?"

"I don't know astral projection," he shook his head.

Well, neither did I. "I think it's when your spirit leaves your body to go places, only you don't die."

He nodded and smiled. "Yes. That is a spirit journey." He laughed and raised his eyebrows. "See?"

Confusion was starting to raise my blood pressure. "Can you do all those things in sleeping dreams?"

"Yes," he said. "Only it takes many years of preparing and doing waking dreams before it happens. There is nothing you can do to make it happen, except prepare. Then, one day, it is just there."

I nodded. "Oh."

There was a silence. They must have been waiting for me to ask a question, but I was overwhelmed. I struggled to think up something. "Is all this necessary? Isn't there any easier way? Or something like a mini course?"

Chea hesitated, then said, "No. But there is always some idiot who thinks they can take a shortcut so they don't have to learn the lessons of all four directions and master the gifts.

"Instead of walking around the long spiral, they stand out there in the circle and jump up, trying to grab onto the branches to pull themselves up.

"But they are not balanced and there are many things about the circle, the spiral, and the tree that they do not understand. They usually think they do, but they don't. They think they can stay selfish and cruel, and avoid the heart.

"Sometimes they can even get powerful and cause harm to themselves and others. They are always out of whack. Things never go quite right for them. They get sicker and sicker and fall from the tree.

"You see, they never learned that had they stayed on their path, they would have become the circle, and the spiral, and the tree. From a seed to a giant, branch by branch.

"They remain desperately lonely and separate, full of fears. They will eventually attack everything in sight. They never give themselves the chance to become united with all of life and creation. And they never understand this. They never really even get to know their own song."

"Well," I said. "That puts a damper on any shortcut plans I might have had."

They laughed. They both seemed very delighted with themselves. Even Chea was grinning ear to ear.

"You guys are teasing me," I said, "aren't you? Astral projection and stuff like that. You do telekinesis, too?"

They looked at each other to see if the other knew what it was.

"You know," I waved my hands as if that would help them understand. "You think something to move, then it does. By itself."

They smiled and nodded. "Yes. Dreaming."

Domano laughed. I think my mouth was hanging open again. "This is an art of dreaming. All shamans can learn this if they choose."

I nodded, "Yeah." I was completely surprised by this new set of abilities they were proposing. I suppose I shouldn't have been, judging from the odd things we had already done and the things I'd observed them do. But somehow these psychic issues seemed better suited to the weird but intriguing books at the back corner of the bookstore, or the woodgy-woodgy labs at Duke University. For some reason, I had never expected to find them connected to native shamanism.

"Well . . . " I asked, "How do you do this kind of dreaming? I mean, how do you make your attention different?"

I got the feeling that I had just been hooked. Domano looked like a boy giggling with excitement as he pulled in his first fish. "You change the speed that some of your song radiates out at." He gave me that big Cheshire grin.

"Ah!" I smiled and nodded with him. "Of course." I didn't have the slightest idea of what he was talking about.

"That is OK. Just remember my words. It will be important soon enough."

We chatted about family and my possible move from the mountains into town. They suggested I do my homeworks as they fit into the rest of my life, but not to do them under stress. If I felt stress I was to do only the search for joy.

We said our adieus, and I left for class.

By the time of our next meeting it was almost quarter break. My husband and I had decided to move to town and were accepted at the student housing on campus. We were to move during the break, but I suddenly became seriously ill, and my husband was forced to conduct the entire move without my help.

I couldn't keep our scheduled meeting but trusted that the Hetakas were aware of my condition.

My recovery was slow, but I made it back to school shortly after classes began for the next quarter, and I was able to participate adequately.

The next time I saw the Hetakas, I was sitting in the Sun at the Good Earth Cafe. I was finished with my classes for the day and was en route home. But halfway through the campus I had become completely exhausted and had to rest where I was, which was the coffee shop.

They waved at me from the parking lot and I signaled them to come join me on the terrace. It was so good to see them. They were like a dose of good medicine.

They showed concern about my health but said they knew I would be fine. We chatted about inconsequential things, and then Domano said he would entertain me with a story.

"This is better than television," he said. "Don't you think? Yes?"

I agreed, leaned back on the rail, and curled my feet up under me. It felt wonderful to be with them again and listening to one of Domano's stories.

"A very long time ago there was a little tiny boy. He had

many brothers and sisters. His family was very poor. Even though he was very little, he worked for food for his family.

"One day in their small field at the edge of the hot desert, he was playing in the trees after work was finished. He found a shiny medallion. There was a marvelous dragon on the front. Its eyes shined blue. It spit a long stream of fire. And it had great wings. With jewels all over them.

"It was so marvelous that he feared his family would take it from him. It must be very valuable, and worth much. They would sell it for farm animals and food, for sure. So he hid it.

"That night after everyone was asleep, he snuck outside to look at it in the moonlight.

"And he said, 'If I had a dragon, I would ride him to the moon.'

"And just then, swooping down through the sky, comes this huge dragon with eyes like blue fire. The boy gasps. He does not know what to do. What if someone wakes and sees this very huge dragon in the field? They would probably try to kill it, he thought.

"'You should not stay,' he says to the dragon. 'You will cause the people to be afraid and they will try to hurt you.'

"'Where do you want to go?' the dragon yelled. And bits of flame came out of his mouth and scorched some plants on the field.

"The boy was afraid if the dragon spoke much more he would accidentally burn their whole field. So he had him follow him into the desert.

"'Are you the dragon on my medallion?' he says.

"'Yes. I am your ride. Wherever you desire, in the whole world. Hop on my back. I will take you there.'

"'Even to the moon?'

"'Of course. No place is too far.'

"'Can you bring me back?'

"'The medallion will call me. And I can return you. Hop on, and hold tight. I will show you the moon.'

"So the boy slips the medallion around his neck and hops onto the dragon. He holds onto his skin with all his might, because when the dragon flew, the wind was great and cold.

"They flew over the moon and looked down on great white cities with jewel towers, and many odd people as they walked about their business.

"'Do you wish to visit with them?' the dragon says.

"'Oh yes. Can we do that?'

"'Of course, little lord. I will set you down on the edge of the city.'

"And so he did. And the boy had a very good time. He walked up and down the streets. Looked at the strange clothes and buildings. And talked to the people. A boy even gave him tea and they played.

"After a while the boy got very sleepy and decided to go back home. He went to the edge of the city to call to the dragon, who came and took the boy home.

"He kept his treasure hidden again . . . until late on the next night. Then he called the dragon and told him to take him to faraway places to see strange things.

"They had a good time until one night the boy got careless. He fell off the dragon. When he hit the ground his medallion was lost from his neck. Now he was stuck, alone, in a strange desert land.

"He called and called the dragon, but he did not come. When the morning came he searched the whole day for the medallion. But it was not to be found. Hungry and sleepy, he walked to the village nearby. The people were strange, and he could not understand their language. But they felt sorry for him. They fed him and gave him work. And they let him sleep in the hay in the barn.

"Time passed and the boy was growing into a young man. Every week he had gone to the place where he fell and searched for the medallion. But he never found it. Finally he gave up. He learned the ways of the people of this village and was taken in by the old doctor man.

"The doctor man was good to him and taught him his craft. Finally the day came when the old doctor man could work no more and it was time for the boy to take his place in the world.

"When the old man was about to die he tells the boy he wants to be buried out in the desert country. At the foot of his favorite tree. The boy agrees to fulfill this wish. He fixes the body all up just the way the old one wanted, and takes it out into the country.

"The boy thinks, this is funny. This tree is very close to where I fell from the dragon. This is nice. Then he begins his long work of digging and preparing, to fulfill the wish.

"When he is all finished, he lays down on the ground at the foot of the tree, next to the grave. He rests and says good-bye to the dear old man for the last time. When he looks up into the great branches. There. Stuck way up high, is the medallion.

"He laughs, and climbs the tree to get it. And he yells, 'If I had a dragon I would fly to the moon.'

"The dragon returns. And off they went . . . to see many worlds.

"As the boy becomes a man he settles for good in the old doctor man's village, to heal the sick. But every now and then he was not to be found. And some of the village people would say he was off flying on a dragon."

I was tickled by the story and the attention, and I felt much better. Domano's stories always delighted me. That day I was easily carried away to the desert land of dragons.

Domano offered to get me coffee, but I turned him down. It didn't sound as though it would sit well on my stomach. As we talked, I remembered a question that was bothering me. I had never fully understood their concept of the web, and now with the new idea of the processes of dreaming, I could draw no correlations between these and anything else I knew.

Chea said, "The web is what radiates between things. The songs of hearts flow out into the world like tiny spiraling, waving threads. They meet and cross, weave the world we know. When we do dreaming, we can move these threads around. Attach and detach ourselves, rearrange things."

"Radiate? Like atomic waste?" I jabbed Domano with my elbow.

"Yes. Yes," he said. "Something like that. You can be the first one on your block to glow in the dark." We all laughed and made jokes about why some would glow more than others, and whether something like deodorant would help.

It was getting very late, so they helped me walk to the trolley that would take me home, and we made our next appointment. They stood under the trees and waved as the trolley drove off.

My life was taking one rocky turn after another. Before our next meeting, my husband asked me for a separation and moved out.

It took me completely by surprise. I was devastated. I realized that I had seen in our relationship only what I wanted to. Somehow, I had managed remarkably well to keep myself from seeing what was uncomfortable and painful. I knew we had problems, but I had believed they were only as serious as the average problems of most couples. Now it seemed that, under the guise of not wanting to cause hurt, we forgot how to talk to each other and widened the gap between us until it was too big to repair.

I forced myself to keep my work up and not fall behind in school.

I wanted to see Chea. I felt that she would understand and be able to help me. I went over to the Hetakas' apartment several days before our appointed time. They were there and invited me to sit in the sunlight of the window. Their concern was apparent, and they tried to comfort me.

Chea sat beside me, and just as I'd thought she would, she understood. I told them that I had had strange dreams for several nights since my husband left, and the oddest one had been just the night before. I was being hunted and chased by a huge, dark jaguar.

Chea nodded. "Your spirit friends are trying to tell you that your life is moving on, as indeed it should. It is taking its own course. Look for the opportunities your new life brings to you. In our village they would say 'the call of the jaguar is on you.'"

"What does that mean?" I blew my nose again and wiped the tears.

"The jaguar is here." She tapped her heart and smiled. "She is the one that runs the show, the smartest, the most powerful. She can talk to the Creator. She is magical and is the one who calls a person to be a shaman. She has called you.

"It is even said that some shamans turn themselves into jaguars from time to time to roam the forest."

I felt a strange anticipation in my body, like the kind I'd had just before the roller coaster ride. My feet tingled, and I felt electricity all over my back.

"Your young man has his own course to take. Let him go." Chea's voice was almost a plea. She made it feel easier and natural to separate our lives. I actually felt relief.

They brought me coffee and sandwiches. I stayed there most of the day, until it was time for me to be home to meet the kids from the school bus.

12

THE SHAMAN'S CAVE

Through the next couple of months I practiced both finding the joy in everything that I could and the perceiving-visualizing exercise. I believe that they helped me rapidly through the mourning period.

I began to see and feel incredible beauty and peace in everything around me, which manifested in waves between the moments of grief and loneliness.

I was living in one of the most beautiful places in the world. My apartment was small but exceptionally nice. The redwood forest was to one side with cow pastures that rolled to the bay on the other. There were racquetball courts across the street, and from my living room terrace I could see across the entire bay.

It was spring, and the fields and forest were filled with wildflowers and insects. I walked everywhere I needed to go. And it didn't take long for the moments of joy and exhilaration to outnumber the moments of sadness. It was becoming a truly happy time for me.

Domano and Chea recommended that I take some kind of exercise class that taught about physical balance and energy flow. But it needed to be fun. I was not to let it become something morbidly serious. So I signed up for aikido and belly dancing classes. They were a great deal of fun. Both of them even had ancient mystical origins, and it was fascinating to learn bits and pieces of these concepts and traditions. I was surprised at how similar they were to what I had learned from the Hetakas.

As the spring quarter neared its end, I saw less and less of my husband. And that felt fine. This was the first time in my life that I had ever been completely on my own. I was learning to live without him or any other adult, and I liked it.

In early June I met with the Hetakas on campus, and we walked through the fields in the Sun. I had been to a lecture a few days before about primitive art. The professor had mentioned a belief among some Amazon Indians about shamans who have developed an ability to travel great distances in moments without the aid of a vehicle, in other words, to teleport.

I could hardly wait to ask the Hetakas about this.

"Does this surprise you?" Domano asked.

"Well, not that there are legends like that," I answered, "but that the possibility might actually exist. I know that there are a lot of things that can't be explained, but something like this just seems too fantastic. It's impossible."

Domano smiled and gave a little chuckle. "It is gate travel. A gate in the web to another place."

"Are you serious?" I was sure he was teasing me. "Now, come on. You're teasing me, aren't you?" I looked back and forth at both of them, expecting one of them to indicate the truth to me. They both laughed.

"This is dreaming," Chea said, as though she were trying to make everything perfectly clear.

"You mean this is a dream? Right now?"

They laughed. "No. No. No," Domano said, catching his breath. "Traveling through gates, this is a part of dreaming."

I still didn't believe him. "You're telling me that people actually disappear from one place and reappear in another place, far away, all at once?"

"Yes," they both said together. They seemed very sincere.

"This is for real," Domano said. "Truly. It is one of the arts of dreaming. The most difficult one."

"Where does one go to?" I asked.

"Oh," Domano clapped his hands, "wherever you want. But you have to know the place you go to well. Know the songs and the feel of it. That is how you find it on the web and make a door there."

I must have had "that look" on my face again, the one with my mouth hanging wide open. They both chuckled.

Domano tried very hard to make me understand. "A gate is when you change your attention, very intense, in a certain way, so it forces the web around you to become a door. You think extremely clearly of the place you want. And then the door is formed in that web, and out you step. See?"

"You are serious." I looked at each of them again, back and forth. "Do you do this?"

"Yes," they both nodded.

I didn't know what to think or believe. I was afraid to ask if they were going to be teaching this to me. "What does it look like?"

Chea thought for a moment, hunting for words. "It looks like the energy of a place collecting together, drawing in."

"Does it ever happen in nature, by itself? Without humans making it?"

"Sometimes," Domano answered. "But not much. Sometimes a person can make it appear and not know it. This happens every once in a while to apprentices. They are shifting themselves and they aren't completely aware of what they are doing. They don't have very much control. If it happens, it is a good idea not to go into it by yourself, unless you know you have the place you seek perfectly clear in your mind."

"What happens if you don't?" I asked.

"You could end up someplace . . . else." He seemed unable to find the words he wanted.

"What do you mean, else?"

"Oh," he patted my arm, "gates can be made to anywhere. On our world. Other worlds." He looked at me straight in the eye for a moment. "There are many worlds besides this. We build our web and hold our attention in a way that keeps us from these places. But they are there. Just like the wind keeper is there."

We walked over to a little gully where the cows collected under the oak trees and sat on the big boulders. There were dozens of different tiny flowers everywhere in the grass and among the rocks. Birds sang back and forth across the field, and there were butterflies, dragonflies, and many strange little brightly colored insects that flew from plant to plant.

A dragonfly landed on Domano's hand. "Ha! See here. A visitor. He has come to listen to our talk. Maybe he has something to teach about gates, too. He sure is a friendly guy. He reminds me of my teacher. Look, Chea. Doesn't his face remind you of our teacher?"

Chea leaned over to look closely at the bug. "Yes, it sure does. Do you suppose that is him?" We all laughed, but I wasn't sure what I was laughing about. I wondered if they had some reason to suspect that their teacher could actually visit them in the form of a bug. But I decided I didn't want to know and said nothing.

Domano, still holding the bug, said, "I will never forget the time my teacher first pulled me through a gate. He had not told me very much about it before the gate appeared and he yanked me through. I was not understanding what was happening.

"I sure was scared. All of a sudden everything looked like it was moving. Then it wasn't the jungle place we were in. For the smallest moment, it was not anything. And then it moved itself into being a place high in the mountains.

"I yelled and grabbed my teacher. He had said we were going somewhere. But he did not tell me how. I shook all over. Everything felt electric. And he says to me, '*Tla ikt la wano wa ka ta see.*' It is good, is what he means, you're learning well the balance of the world.

245

"I didn't feel so good, though."

I was confused by his reference to the foreign language. "Is that language yours or your teacher's?"

"That is the language of the star people. A language our teachers spoke and taught some of it to us. You know some of the words already."

"Yes," I nodded. "I always thought that was your tribal language."

"No," he said. "This is different. It is better suited. More accurate."

Chea picked up an odd-shaped rock. "You don't need to worry about gate traveling just yet. It takes years of training to develop that art of dreaming.

"Today we are going to show you how to do the first dreaming art, spirit journeying. This kind of dreaming is done while you are awake." She handed me the rock. It looked like a little cat. I studied it and then handed it back to her.

"This is like you said," Domano picked up the conversation. "Going someplace and leaving your body behind. It is the shaman's way. It is the shaman's job to go to places that are very hard to get to and find knowledge to bring back to their people. You can find things in dreaming that can be found no other way. You can even learn more about dreaming.

"When you go on a spirit journey, you need to pay attention to every detail that you can perceive. Watching, listening, feeling, smelling, touching, paying attention to your own reactions. Everything is of critical importance.

"Experience every moment to its fullest and keenest, expecting to remember. Let your senses bathe in all that is there. The more intense and thorough the experience, the more thorough the learning and remembering.

"Sit down on the dirt here and lean back on the rock. Get comfortable. But not so much that you will fall asleep. Now breathe very full. Fill yourself completely with the life that is around you.

"Close your eyes, and find your center.

"Stay sitting on the ground. It will be your spirit that moves. And you must feel this with all your senses. As if every muscle is moving. Do this as intensely as possible.

"Now, stay centered, no matter what, and make your spirit rise and walk with me to the cows over there.

"That is good. Come. Feel every step. Feel the weight of your body on your feet. Come closer. Reach out and touch this cow. Feel the fur on your fingers. Smell it. Keep centered, and experience these things with the intent to remember.

"This is good. Very good. Now reach down and pick up a little rock. Feel your body bend. Smell the flowers. Feel the rock as you roll it in your fingers. Taste this rock."

This was a most unusual experience. I could feel everything as though my whole body were performing the actions. I stayed easily in my center, and every experience was exciting, as though new. It was almost as if I were doing these actions and feeling these experiences for the very first time. And yet there was something oddly familiar in it all, something that didn't have to do with the physical.

I could feel every muscle working as I bent over to get a rock. The smell of the cow was of dirty wet fur, and the flowers were sweet. I rolled the little rock in my fingers. It had smooth and sharp sides. I looked down at it, and it was a little piece of quartz.

I thought that it was a peculiar request to have me taste it, but I did anyway. It tasted like salty dirt.

Domano continued, "Walk with me up here. You will have to climb this gully. Come. Look at what is over the rise here."

Again I followed him. He looked as if he had a glow about his body. Everything was more intense in color and light. Even the dirt had a kind of glow to it.

I felt the muscles in my arms and legs pulling my body up the gully. It was wonderful, the feeling of exercising them. I looked at everything, and all the little objects were nestled together, like a community. They had an interaction going, some sort of symbiosis.

When I got to the ridge I looked all around at the view, and then at the plants and rocks. I smelled them and touched and listened.⁣ᵗ

Then Domano had me walk back with him, holding his hand, observing and feeling everything along the way.

"I want you to remember," he said. "All the things you perceived. Sit back down into your body."

I turned and saw myself sitting on the dirt. I could feel myself standing and sitting at the same time. Seeing myself like that was a little disorienting. My awareness of Death close by was sharpened. More than anything I did not want to die, but I was not afraid of it either. I could feel clearly how she sharpened my awareness and appreciation of all things. I stepped over and sat down.

"Settle yourself inside your body. Feel it again. Adjust inside."

It was like putting on an electrical body glove and reconnecting all the circuits. It took a moment to readjust. My body felt heavy and clumsy.

I was still in my center, and I opened my eyes.

Domano sat down next to me. "Recall everything. Every detail."

I went through every sensation and observation that I could remember. Sometimes I remembered out of sequence or skipped whole sections, but with their questions, I was finally able to remember most of the experience.

Then they had me physically retrace my steps. I couldn't believe how accurate my observations had been. There on the ground in front of me were the same rocks and patterns in the soil, the same little plants, even over the ridge of the gully. I was fascinated.

"How can this be?" I turned to Domano.

"This is our nature. Our heritage." He smiled his big toothy grin at me.

"Can this be done without being in your center?" I asked.

He shook his head, "Not really. There is no clarity in observing without the center. One's thoughts cloud and distort what is there. Remembering is difficult, if not impossible. The center is the key. The tree grows in the center. The gifts join together at the center. That is *ka ta see*. The job of the shaman is to bring *ka ta see* to the world. Bring balance."

I nodded. "I'm just blown away. I can hardly believe that I just did that. It's amazing. And I can't explain it any other way than astral projection, or I mean, spirit walking. It's really real. I really did it. I just can hardly believe it."

They laughed. Chea agreed with me. "Yes. It is pretty amazing. Especially at first. It will become more natural for you."

I felt so successful. Satisfied. "Can we do it again?"

"You bet." Domano raised his fist, striking the air. "Let's go right now."

"Go?" I interrupted. "Leave? Right now? But . . . "

"Go on a spirit journey," he laughed. "A real journey to a distant place. A shaman's journey to find knowledge."

"Really?" I was a little intimidated. I wanted to try this rare opportunity, but this seemed like a rather large jump.

"Yes," Chea said softly. "It is time. You're perfectly ready. Find your center. Trust in yourself. Breathe deep. Get up against your rock again and relax. Breathe. Feel your body."

Chea sat down with her back to a big rock. She was just a few feet to my left.

Domano sat facing me, just slightly off to my right. "Close your eyes, and feel your whole body. Just like before, I want you to rise up out of your body and stand up."

When I stood up in my spirit body Chea was standing to my left and Domano to my right.

"Take our hands," he continued. "We will walk a few steps and then we will step up and lift into the air. Keep your center. Observe everything. Observe to remember. We will be with you on this whole journey. Follow the directions we give. We will be guiding you."

We walked a few steps toward the cows and then lifted up into the air. They held onto my hands and stabilized me. We flew around over the fields several times, then they let go of my hands and let me fly free. It was surreal. I felt just like I did when flying in a sleeping dream. The degree of freedom that I experienced was beyond anything I had ever imagined. I could even feel the wind on my body, and the coolness of the air.

I followed Domano's instructions, and we headed south. We rose very high and began to travel at an incredible speed. He directed me to turn my attention away from feeling the wind and temperature while we were in the air and had me concentrate on the sensation of flying and the view of the land far below.

Within minutes we were above Baja California and then across the little bay and over to central Mexico, and south again. We traveled rapidly over Central America and the northern part of South America, until we reached the central southern region of Brazil.

We came in much closer and circled above an immense area that looked like rolling plains of grass. We followed this south until we came to a series of abrupt narrow canyons that cut into the plains. One of them seemed quite deep and long.

We followed it very close to its rim for a number of miles. Then it turned sharply to the left, and then again to the right. As we came around the corner of the cliff, there on the east face was a ledge and a large entrance to a cave.

We landed on the ledge. The Sun was low enough in the west to be shining a short distance into the cave. I could hear birds of prey screeching high above us and smell grasses and wild herbs in the air. I was barefoot and could feel the gravel under my feet. The air was hot but not very humid, and there were no clouds in the sky. I could see a short distance down the canyon in either direction. In one spot I could see to the little river at the bottom.

A wind came up. It felt special. I thought perhaps it was a keeper, like my friend back home. I suspected that she was being friendly and curious, extending her greetings and support.

I looked at Domano and Chea. They had a glowing quality, just as Domano had earlier on our little walk. I looked down at my hands and legs and they also were bright, with a slight luminescence.

Domano instructed me to enter the cave. He and Chea would be right behind me. He said that this cave was very special and had been used for centuries by shamans from all over to initiate their apprentices and to search for secret knowledge. Their teachers had brought them, and some day I would bring someone too.

The sunlight lit the first ten feet of the cave. The colors on the rock walls were vibrant rusts and ochres. There were paintings of stick figures, animals, and hands along one side. I wondered how long ago they were painted there, and who painted them.

And then I came to a different kind of figure. It was a man with antlerlike projections out of the top of his head and a bodysuit or halo type of covering over his entire body. His eyes were clearly and accurately drawn, looking straight out at the viewer, intensely. The other drawings were simple and very ordinary, but this last figure was superb. I asked Domano what he was, what he meant.

"It is a painting of one of the many spirits that come here. This place is special because of the energy that is bent into it and all the spirits that collect here."

I touched the painting and then moved on. The Sun was getting lower in the sky and shining farther down into the cave in long shafts. The gravel under my feet gave way to solid rock that was smooth in most places, as though water worn.

Deep inside the cavern it was completely dark, but I could occasionally see something shiny. I couldn't tell what it was. We kept on walking slowly as we moved out of the light. After a few yards it became so dark that I had to touch the side of the cave in order to find my way, and the temperature was getting much cooler.

Finally we reached a huge gallery. My eyes had adjusted to the dark, and I could just barely see indications that the walls and ceiling extended quite far. There were things in the cave that were like obstacles or obstructions. As I moved carefully through the gallery, they occasionally caught light and glimmered for a moment.

Domano told me to feel carefully through the entire room and then pick a spot to sit down in. He said that it was necessary for me to be in the gallery by myself, that this journey, this quest for knowledge, was mine alone. There was no telling what kind of knowledge would be shown to me. They would be waiting out on the ledge. I was free to explore the entire place, to feel and observe all that I could, and to take as much time as I needed.

At some point I would feel the need to sit in the spot that I had picked and observe very quietly. They each hugged me, and then they left me with the great room.

I walked and felt my way around the whole space. The obstacles, I decided, must be stalactites and stalagmites. There were places on the floor and walls that were very sharp and hard. I tried to avoid walking on those, but that was tricky.

This place felt strong and powerful. I was alone in the cave now, but I did not feel alone. The whole thing seemed to be alive, breathing, watching, moving.

I suddenly thought I should sit down. I had forgotten to pick a spot, so I scanned the whole room quickly and decided on a location next to a large stalactite, and sat down.

I put all my attention to observing and feeling the room. A tension grew. It felt as though many living beings were converging on the cavern. There were flickers of light. For a moment I thought I heard singing.

I sat still, breathing in the growing tension, feeling the songs of the many. And then it happened: the light of the setting Sun came perfectly down the cave and lit the entire gallery. It was a sight out of the dreams of fairy tales. The stalactites and stalagmites were huge, clear crystals.

The light shot everywhere in every color of the rainbow. I think my breath must have stopped. It was like being in a room surrounded by thousands of huge, glistening diamonds. The back of my neck and head tingled.

I heard steps behind me. I turned to see what was there and the crystal I had been leaning on was glowing as though lit from within. A small man stepped forward from around the crystal. The beams of light and color shone all over him. His head was like a jaguar's, but his face was human. He smiled and came and sat down close to me.

We looked at each other for a few moments, and then he said, "Welcome to our lodge. This is a place of power. Some things have the ability to either increase or decrease your energy. This place increases it. You have succeeded in getting here in the way of the shaman, and so we offer to share this with you."

I gave a single nod of acceptance and gratitude and remained silent, waiting for him to speak again.

"When a person comes here, they come for the sake of the children. All the children and all the generations to come of all species.

"With each generation through the past, one has come to learn how to be a voice and guardian for nature, to provide this link for their people.

"Today we ask many to come and learn. We wish to teach all the people to speak with us, for the sake of the children.

253

"People have lost their trust and loyalty in life. A relationship with themselves and with all things greater than anything they could imagine awaits them on the horizon.

"Tell your people that we are coming. We await meeting in peace and joy, in the name of those yet to come."

The sunlight hit the cavern in just the right way to create dozens of direct reflections and spectral refractions of the Sun straight into my eyes. All the crystals glowed. The light was so tremendous I couldn't see anything else. And then the crystals began to resonate, to make a chorus of exquisite and strange sounds. The whole cave resonated and echoed. I felt as if the lights and sounds penetrated me until I also vibrated with them.

And then the Sun set, and everything was still and dark. I looked around and the spirit man was gone. It felt that it was time for everyone to leave. I sat there for a few moments longer and then started back down the cave.

I felt very light on my feet, as though I could float away quite easily. I was aware of my center and my state of balance. I reached the opening, and Chea and Domano were there sitting on the edge, waiting for me.

Without a word we lifted into the air and flew back to the little gully in the cow field back home. When I opened my eyes the Sun was still up, a few hours from the horizon.

We had been in the field almost the whole day. It must have been getting close to dinner time, and my kids were probably home by now and wondering where I was. I looked at Domano to ask him about the journey.

He smiled and put his finger to his lips. "Do not talk on this just yet, even to yourself. Just remember as much as you can. Feel it.

"It is time to go. We will be up to see you soon."

We hugged goodbye and walked in our separate directions. My centeredness lingered for hours. And even through the dishes and children screaming I could still see the pervading eyes of the spirit man and hear the sounds of the crystal cave clearly in my mind.

13

QUEST FOR THE MASK

Several weeks had passed since I had seen the Hetakas and experienced my first spirit journey. My dreams were becoming very intense and usually didn't make much sense to me. One, however, grabbed my attention.

I was on a barge with many cabins. I explored the whole vessel. In each room there was a completely different elaborate decor, and sometimes there were people engaged in some activity. Some of the cabins were outlandish, and it was impossible to believe that they might be real.

I had a friend on board, and I took her with me to search through the rooms again, to see if they were all actually there. As we walked through the cabins, I expected some of the most outlandish ones to be either somehow different or completely gone.

To my bafflement, at least half of them were still there, as bizarre as ever. And what was even more puzzling was that some of the more sensible rooms, ones that I had taken for granted to be normal and real, were gone, disappeared entirely from the boat, walls and all.

When my friend and I went on deck to discuss it, I saw pieces of the missing cabins sinking down into the waves behind the barge. I pointed them out to her, but she could not see them.

The dream stuck with me for several days. It seemed to echo my thoughts and my sense that I could no longer say with complete surety which things were real and which were not. I needed a more extensive map of reality than the current version presented to me by academia.

It wasn't as though I were losing my grip on sanity, it was that my picture of what existence was had become far too small to include all of my experiences with the Hetakas. Sometimes I felt certain of which worldview was correct. But since the journey to the cave, I had no longer been able to explain things away and package them up in neat little categories in my mind. The harder I tried to hold the old puzzle pieces together, the less they fit.

In spite of the fact that while we were practicing spirit walking before the big journey, and I had walked back over the same area and discovered that my perceptions had been remarkably accurate, I still had a very hard time believing that the cave experience was real, and not some daydream or hypnosis.

The effect of that journey had been profound. I couldn't deny it, and I couldn't accept it. The concept of dreams being real was very difficult for me, not to mention the idea of astral projection being thought of as the same thing as dreaming. I thrashed through these concepts over and over again in my mind trying to understand, trying to arrive at some kind of a world structure in which everything fit.

My conclusion was that I didn't have all the information, and as badly as I wanted to understand I would have to just hold the data in question and wait for the remainder to come.

After spending those several weeks mentally harassing myself, I remembered that the Hetakas had told me not to think about this yet and not to judge rashly or jump to conclusions, that there was a time for thinking and a time for not thinking.

With that, I finally gave up in mental exhaustion. It was still morning and I went out to sit on the terrace of my apartment. There were two figures walking in the distant pasture. I thought they might be Domano and Chea, so I went downstairs and walked out through the field to find out.

The wind came up from nowhere. It was my friend from the mountains, whom I hadn't seen much since my move. It was nice to be with her again. She walked with me clear across the field to where I thought I had seen the two people go over the rise. And there, not far, were Domano and Chea. The wind blew very hard around the three of us, then disappeared.

Domano yelled, "Hello, hello. You are free this afternoon? Yes?"

"The kids are busy for the day. Yeah. I'm free. What did you have in mind?" I rubbed my hands together and thought, oh boy, more fun and games and confusion.

"It is time for you to quest for the mask." He smiled. Then Chea smiled.

A little hesitantly, I smiled too. "Is it fun? And safe? Don't forget safe."

They laughed and nodded their heads.

Chea looked me dead in the eye, "Oh yes. Yes. Of course." She sent a chill straight up my back. "Just about as fun and safe as the roller coaster, I'll bet."

We laughed and joked. They tried to set me at ease, but it was too late. Somewhere inside me I had already decided it was going to be at least frightening, if not dangerous.

Domano pointed into a secluded little gully. "You are going on another shaman's spirit journey to Brazil. This little place here will be very good. Let's sit here. You have to remain centered to do this. Fear will only pull you off. End your journey. No matter what happens, you must remain in control. In the center. Do not let surprise or fear or old thoughts pull you off. Sometimes they come. They happen. But you can let them be, and go on their own way. Do not attach to them. Do you understand?"

"Yes," I nodded my head. "You seem so serious."

"That is because you are in a mood to think so much," he said. "To learn, sometimes we just need to be reminded a lot."

"Some of us need to be reminded a whole *very* lot!" I laughed and bumped Domano with my elbow.

He laughed and nodded, "Yes." Then he pointed to a comfortable little spot by a boulder for me to sit down.

Chea sat in front of me. "This is a quest into the west. Domano will take you on the journey he took with his teachers into the mountains to search for the mask. You recall, we told you that in dreaming, one can bend time. This is what we will do. On the journey it will be like it was many years ago. And there will be many days passing.

"Remember, the more the detail and intensity, the more you learn.

"Are you ready?"

"Yes," I answered.

Chea moved toward my left. Domano sat facing me on my right and said, "Get very comfortable. It is a long journey. But don't go falling asleep, or I will have to kick you."

We all laughed. After scooting a number of pebbles out of the way, I was at last ready to begin.

Domano took several deep breaths, and I copied him. "Be centered. Stand up out of your body. Come. We fly to Brazil. To my village."

I stood up out of my body and lifted into the air with just Domano. I turned around for Chea, but Domano shook his head. "She needs to be there."

I understood and turned back around. We then flew rapidly over the landscape and came down into the forest of western Brazil.

We walked into the village and no one seemed to see us. A small group of men were about to leave on a trip. Domano said we would join them.

"We will follow these ghosts of the past," he said. "And I will tell you how it was for me.

"I was very young. I had only studied with my teachers less than two years. This quest was planned by the old tribal shaman, who was my first teacher for about a year. This quest is a tradition of our medicine people for countless generations.

"That man there is the old shaman. And this one here is one of the leaders of our people. He is a very strong warrior and well respected. Those other two are my teachers. And the young one lagging behind is me.

"Come. The trails are narrow here. I will stay behind you. But you will have to walk fast to keep up with them. Just push the plants aside.

"Ah, listen there. The birds calling. And way up there— monkeys."

The foliage was remarkably thick and vibrant. Everything had a smell, and everything was damp. Under a cover of mosses and leaves the ground was thick mud that oozed up around my feet and between my toes. High in the trees there were screams and croaks and chattering.

Every few feet the smells changed, from sweet to musky to mold, then sour and pungent, and always hot, moist, and intense. There were bugs everywhere. The thought occurred to me that there were enough bugs here to carry away the humans.

I looked up into the treetops. It was another whole world up there. The warrior pointed to something up high. Domano said that he was showing the party a beehive that perhaps could be raided another day. The men did not spend any time looking at it, but kept their strenuous pace. It was hard for me to keep up: they just kept going on and on. I needed to readjust my attitude toward how fast I could travel.

Finally we stopped. The men sat in a little circle and took out what looked like pieces of some kind of bread from bags they had on their backs. They ate in silence.

Domano removed the bag he was carrying and reached in and handed me some of the same breadlike food.

It was rougher in texture than white bread and tasted fairly plain, a little like rutabagas. Then he handed me something else to eat. It was dark and had been pressed together, possibly cooked. The men also took out something dark, broke it apart, and passed it around to share with each other. It was chewy and crunchy and tasted like scorched meat fat. I didn't ask what either thing was, and I was glad Domano didn't volunteer to tell me. Before I had finished, the men were up and moving again. I ate as I walked.

For what seemed like hour after hour, the forest looked the same, and flat. I wondered how they knew where they were or where they were going. The heat and humidity became stifling. The wind was weak and didn't reach down to the forest floor. In places where the blossoms covered everything, the air was so thick with the sweet of their scents, I felt that I was hardly able to breathe.

Just before dusk the group stopped again and set up a little camp. They each collected a large handful of a certain kind of leaf and spread them on what I took for a kind of palm leaf to make a bed. Domano and I did the same. As we lay down I was surprised at how comfortable it was.

Domano leaned over and whispered to me, "You will be very tempted to fall asleep. But you must resist." Then he lay back down and was perfectly silent.

I lay there and listened to the sounds of the forest change and watched the fire the men had built die down to coals. Somewhere in the night I was sure I heard the light, rumbling growl of a jaguar as it came close to camp to investigate. I wished I could have seen it.

The daylight came, but I could see no Sun through the thick of the treetops. We rose and scattered our leaves into the forest. More of the bread was passed around and we all ate as we walked.

Every shape, color, and texture was there in profusion. It was an amazing place, but still, each acre looked very much like the last. The only things that were changing were the creeks and the little rivers that we either turned at or crossed. I saw no sign of alligators or piranha fish. One of the men did get something on him that seemed like a leech. It was removed promptly, and everyone kept on with the pace.

The men were able to walk through even the thickest foliage with very little noise, and they rarely spoke among themselves. They seemed content and at ease, yet aware of every movement and sound around them.

Late in the day we came to a river with deep pools. Two of the men took their spears to the water's edge and quickly caught enough for their dinner, which they cooked on a small fire.

Again they collected a variety of fronds and leaves to make beds.

I was very glad to stop. My body was sore and tired. It felt wonderful to lie down and relax my muscles. The leaves we were on this time were very fragrant and soothing.

I almost drifted off to sleep when Domano reminded me to stay awake and stay observing. Everything was so real, so complete in the experience, that I almost forgot we were spirit walking and not physically in the jungle.

I was feeling strained from the constant pace that we had been keeping. Domano said that it was normal for a group of hunters or warriors to travel that way, and I had better adjust mentally to increase my stamina, because we had many days ahead of us. He said that he himself, when he was young and without much training, had had trouble maintaining that pace. Even in this early part of the journey I noticed how his young body was tiring and showing pain.

For two more days and nights we hiked on like this, until we came to the foothills of the Andes. Then the inclines began, with sharp ravines and rapids. The dirt underfoot was drier, and the vegetation seemed to open up and let the sunlight touch the ground from time to time. There was a thistly type of plant that grew there. Sometimes it almost seemed to lie in wait for us and jump out to attack as we passed.

Hiking had become difficult. We came to slopes that had loose rock under a coat of mud. And just when I thought I had a secure foothold, either I would slip on the mud or the rocks would give way and down the hill I'd slide. With the multitude of plants to cushion and slow the fall, I wasn't seriously injured.

Before dark we reached a large river. It was deep and fast, making it impassable. The party was forced to follow it upstream to the next possible ford. The sound of the rapids as I walked was both peaceful and exciting.

The anxiety of the group mounted, but I didn't know why. Then Domano told me, "We are entering the land of a notoriously dangerous tribe. Soon we will come to the hidden trail. We will be safer, but to travel through it is very difficult."

The men walked more slowly and quietly, listening to everything and stopping periodically to look intently into the forest. We came to a formidable thicket of bramble and thorns. Three of the party spread out to stand watch while the other two carefully pulled away branches in the thicket to expose a hidden tunnel that had been carved into the bottom of the brush.

With great skill they took branches and brushed away all their footprints and scattered leaves for many yards leading to the tunnel, making the area look as if peccaries had been there. Then, when they were sure the coast was clear, they all entered the hidden trail and carefully rearranged the branches that hid the entrance. Domano and I did the same.

The tunnel varied in height and width from two to four feet, with a mud floor. It was dark inside and the air thick and stale. We had to proceed on all fours. Even though the Sun was setting, we crawled on as quickly and silently as possible. Domano said we had to get as far away from their enemies' frequently used trail as possible to avoid being heard, or if they had dogs, being smelled.

The tunnel cut along parallel to the river for many miles through enemy territory. It was the shortest and most direct path to the sacred sights in the mountains. The only other way, up the foothills and across the river, would take thirty to forty more days. They would have to go many miles around the violent and impassable tributaries of that area that emptied into the big river. The cliffs were often loose shale and rock and sometimes even leaned out over the rapids. Domano said that his ancestors had dug out this tunnel many generations before, when this violent tribe first moved into the area.

Suddenly the old shaman made a chirping sound, and everyone stopped. Far off outside the brambles we could hear steps. He passed down a handful of leaves. Each of the men took a few and silently rubbed them completely over their bare bodies. Domano handed me a few from his bag, and I removed my clothes and rubbed the leaves on myself. They were pungent, almost antiseptic in their smell.

We sat there in silence in the growing dark for perhaps an hour. Then, when the shaman signaled, the group continued to crawl on. I quickly put my clothes back on, shoved the leaves into my pocket, and scrambled along behind as best I could.

When we finally stopped, the old shaman allowed the eating of only one small root and several soft sweet leaves that all the men seemed to have a supply of in their bags. Domano handed me some to try. The root was soft and milky inside and tasted like sour grass. I brushed the dirt off and forced myself to eat it, trading bite for bite with the sweet honeylike leaves.

I tried to watch the group, but it had gotten too dark. I could only just make out the young Domano. He didn't seem very pleased with the dinner, either. When he turned around, positioning himself to lie down, I could tell he was sore and tired. He took out what was left of his pungent leaves and rubbed them on his knees and again all over his body.

The old shaman was crawling back to each member of the party. The young Domano handed him the crumpled leaves and lay down on his back with a finalness as if he would never rise again. The old man placed the pieces of leaves under Domano's body from his head to his toes and whispered to him. Young Domano seemed very worried about something, but the shaman was not concerned and pressed sternly on the young one's chest and gave him an order.

In a few moments, after the shaman returned to his spot, I could see what was upsetting the young Domano. There were bugs and crawling things of every description working their way into the tunnel. I gasped and froze on the spot. The older Domano told me not to throw myself off balance. "Do not succumb to fear," he whispered. "Remember *ka ta see*. These leaves are very powerful. The old man told me to calm myself. That I was giving my body away to the forest and its creatures. And they would surely take all of me if I did not do what he ordered. He says these leaves, when used by the shaman, have great magic. They will keep away all dangerous creatures and spirits of the night forest.

"Now you rub them on yourself and your clothes again. I will place them under your body. You will see.

"When I lay down that night, my escape from pain was indescribable. I was so sore and tired. I do not think I cared if something carried me off or not. I had no more strength to complain or fight. But these leaves have a strange magic. They felt like the softest hammock swinging in the breeze."

I followed Domano's instructions, and he placed the leaves under my whole body as I lay there on my back in the mud. He told me not to move, that the magic was temperamental and did not like to be stirred.

As the night passed, the darkness became so complete I could see nothing. I was not bothered by anything touching or crawling on me, and the ground seemed soft and warm.

When daylight came I was startled by the multitude of cobwebs and living things that crept in the bramble within inches of our bodies. I looked up the path at the others to see if they had been bothered by any of them. Apparently the magic of the leaves had worked, and everyone had slept well and safely.

Breakfast consisted of the same roots and leaves again. The tunnel went on and on at a slight incline. Nothing seemed to change. We crawled until dark and then set up camp as before, rubbing ourselves with and sleeping on the pungent leaves.

The next day in the tunnel, I could see the stress on everyone from having been confined on all fours for such an extended period. Young Domano seemed to be faring the worst. Each movement showed pain, and I could see blood on his knees from time to time.

Finally the terrain changed and gave us some variety. The slope of the land now jutted steeply up and down, with tiny springs running alongside or across the path. The mud was deep. In places, the head of the party had to cut back the new growth that threatened to block our way. The inclines were difficult to get up. We had to get a handhold on the thorny brush and pull ourselves up. But the declines were the reward. Most of the men slid down on their backsides, but the warrior went face first on his belly. They laughed and teased as if it were a game, but all with a marked degree of quiet.

Jettisoning down the slick paths like toothpaste from a tube was fun. I could feel the jolt of excitement throughout my body and the little quake in the stomach that feels as if you had left it back up at the top. It reminded me to stay in my center, to utilize the gifts. And as I did that my view of the tunnel transformed from dull, gloomy, and dangerous to luminous and full of countless breathtaking forms of life.

In midafternoon the old shaman stopped the group to instruct them at a bubbling sulphur well that was directly in the middle of the path. It was about two feet in diameter. Steam rose from it in profuse columns. The old man spoke very softly, pointing to his chest, the sky, and the spring. Domano said that he was telling the men about the spring and how a special kind of fire spirit lived in the hearts of humans and also in that spring.

While it was still just barely light we found a level spot where we could sleep the night. Leaves were rubbed and placed as before, and the night passed without incident.

Late the next afternoon, when it seemed that we might be crawling on forever, the tunnel opened up onto the shore of the big river. It was a shallow, smooth section, spreading out four or five times wider than it was downstream. After the warrior and old shaman checked the entire area, we all came out to wade across.

You could see on the men's faces that it was both relieving and painful to stand. The Sun lit the water with a blinding glare. It was difficult to see, but we couldn't waste any time. The party needed to get across the water as fast as possible and into the cover of the forest.

The river marked the beginning of the mountains. On the other side the forest shot up at a good sixty-degree angle. Domano said that at the top of this big forested hill was a rocky trail that bent around the mountain. Once we got to it, the hiking would be considerably easier for a while. It was our misfortune that this steep hill was especially thick with mud and difficult to ascend. He said it would be very bad for them if they did not make it to the top by dark.

Once across the river, the group started up as fast as it could, grabbing anything with roots that looked big enough to hold a person. I looked up the hill through the trees. The end seemed a million miles away.

The warrior took a running start, throwing his body around tree trunks and large bushes. He was far ahead of everyone when the bush he was climbing around gave way, and he slid almost the whole way down before he could grab a tree big enough to stop him. He signaled that he was OK, and they all continued to climb.

Everyone was slipping. The only things that could stop the feet from sliding were well-rooted plants. By the time we got halfway up, clouds had gathered and rain was imminent. The men all seemed worried. From the appearance of the ground, it seemed as if water would run over it in sheets during a heavy downpour. Reaching the top under those circumstances looked dubious.

They decided to continue. They used everything they could to assist them, pulling each other up with heavy vines and even with their own bodies; they would hang to a tree trunk and let another hoist himself by grabbing onto their feet.

It was dark when we reached the ledge at the top of the trees. I felt exhausted and battered from one end to the other. The trail, for what I could see of it, was rocky and level, with a wall of solid stone shooting up on the other side. We followed this cliff to a small enclosure and set up camp. They ate the end of the roots and leaves and went to sleep.

The night noises echoed out of the forest against the cliff. I heard deep growls, clicks, screeches, footsteps, but I could see nothing.

In the dawn we followed the ledge up and around the mountain. Plants grew where they could out of cracks in the rock. Occasionally there were patches of drier forest several acres wide where the land became level enough to hold soil. Tiny springs broke through the rock and cascaded down the cliff face. At one place a spring had eroded away what little ledge we had to walk on, leaving us a four-foot jump. And sometimes the ledge was so thin we had to scoot sideways, hugging the face of the cliff.

It was nice to feel the wind again. Sometimes it carried the smells and moisture of the forest below, and at others it was brisk and drier, with the smell of grasses and sweet highland brush. I looked down over the top of the forest canopy. It stretched green, fading into mist to the horizon. Far off there were several birds circling above the trees.

I could see signs that this trail was used frequently by many animals; the most prominent looked to be from the deer family. But at this point, the only four-legged creatures we saw were several varieties of small squirrels and mice that skittered all over the cliff and appeared to be curious about us.

That night, camp was set in one of the little outcroppings of forest. The men caught some game and built a fire, talking and singing. And then, as before, they rubbed themselves with leaves and peacefully fell asleep. It seemed odd, but there were very few noises through the night.

The next day the precipice that had been our trail ended, and we climbed several hundred feet up a gently sloping section of the cliff. I felt like a mountain climber digging my fingers into cracks in the rock and finding flat spots that would support weight to pull myself up. It was very hot. Fortunately, we were on the east side of the mountain, and most of this climb took place after the Sun was off the cliff.

When we got to the top the land spread out for perhaps a mile. It was rocky and windy, with only grasses and small shrubs. Bordering this area on the far side was forest. It rose in the distance into huge whitecapped mountains that stretched on to the north and south. The sky was a pale blue, and many different birds flew back and forth screeching and singing. Odd-colored lizards sat on rocks in the Sun and ran off as we passed by.

We set camp in the center of the clearing. The warrior caught a small peccary, and they ate around a little fire. As the coals faded they lay staring at the night sky, talking quietly among themselves. The stars were numerous and shimmered more than I had ever seen. When they fell asleep, I heard nothing but the honey-smelling wind.

They were up at dawn again and into the mountain jungle. It was different up there. The foliage was less dense and the dirt of the forest floor seemed dry. There were sounds everywhere and strong odors. Even though the terrain was steep, hiking was relatively easy. The men found a bed of large grubs and ate them down with relish. The older Domano offered me my first opportunity to try them, but I declined. I found it rather disturbing to watch them shove live wiggling things that looked like maggots into their mouths. I turned and looked at the monkeys in the treetops instead.

This part of the jungle was quite varied, with openings and then dense patches. Huge rock formations jutted up through the greenery, sometimes with caves. There were petroglyphs and occasionally a rock that had been completely carved into an enigmatic image. The style was crude, boxy, and abstract enough that I couldn't tell what they represented. The men paid the carvings little attention. Domano didn't volunteer any explanation of them, and I didn't ask.

I had hoped it would be cooler up there, but it wasn't. It actually seemed hotter. As the Sun was about to set, we camped at the first flat location we came to. There was an unusually large number of monkeys high in the trees. After we were there a short while, the youngsters grew less cautious and came within ten or twelve feet of us. Then the darkness forced them back to their treetops to rest for the night.

For two more days we pressed on. We passed three cascading creeks and many more carved stones. One of them had a necklace of different-colored beads strung around its neck. The old shaman stopped in front of it and examined the beads. He looked carefully at the statues nearby and then ordered the group to set up camp at an open area a few feet away.

Everyone gathered leaves and plants in silence. They made no fire and ate from what they had collected.

"We are just outside of the sacred grounds," Domano said, pointing to the statue. "We will spend the night here. They prepare for the ceremonies of this next day. This is why everyone is silent and no fire will be built."

Before the men went to sleep they all took a piece of tobacco out of their packs, and chewing it, walked off into the jungle by themselves.

The next day we scattered our leaf beds and hiked up just a few hundred feet onto a flat treeless plateau that was dotted with lichen-covered ruins. Many of the buildings were still intact. They had been built with huge stones that were carved to fit together perfectly with no mortar. Some of the largest boulders were sculpted with reliefs that were similar in design to the stones we had passed on our way.

It looked as though more than time and erosion had been beating away at this place. I wondered if it had once been vandalized by zealous missionaries or conquistadors.

The first structure we came to was a platform raised in steps. Monkeys scattered as we climbed up the old broken stones to its flat top. I could see the whole city from there. It was surrounded by the rain forest. I wondered why there were no trees and only very small plants and mosses growing inside, why the forest hadn't reclaimed that spot.

I looked down at the huge stone blocks I was standing on. They were captivating. The more I looked at them, the more extraordinary they became. It was almost as though I could see into the stone; that is, its opaqueness was becoming transparent to me. Every grain became radiant and multicolored. It even seemed to me at that moment that the stones I was standing on were weightless.

Domano clicked at me to get my attention. The men had all taken off their bags and were heading for the center of the city. As I stepped down into the path I could see the remnants of a paved street. I could feel what was left of the thoughts and actions of the centuries of people who had passed there before me. This was a sacred ground. People came from very far away seeking what this place had to give. And now there was no one there but us and the monkeys.

We walked down the narrow old street until we came to a small building, with its roof and rooms in usable condition. Inside there were baskets on the floor with paints and feathers in them. The men said nothing and began to paint designs on themselves and tie different-colored feathers in their hair and on their arms. Domano pointed with his chin for me to do the same.

When they were finished the old shaman led them outside to an area of rubble. He told them to pick up as many rocks as they could carry and take them to the courtyard at the center of the city. There he directed them to build a spiral of specific proportions. They made several trips back and forth before it was complete. Then each man found a small pair of rocks that fit well in his hands to hit together as a percussion instrument. Domano signaled for me to find a pair also.

We all sat around the outer edge of the spiral and the old shaman talked. Domano translated his explanation of the spiral and the ceremonial dance we were about to do.

"This stone spiral," he began, "is a temple. The old one says that it is as much a sacred temple as the big stone buildings here. And so is the ground when it is set for ceremony with any other things, like dirt, leaves, water, fire. These are temporary. Meant only for this moment. While the stone buildings here are meant to carry through many generations of your grandchildren.

"Here we will do the spiral dance. We will weave fibers between the spirit world and our world. We will bring what is there into our lives. To make it part of our perception. When we are finished we will return all the rocks back into the rubble they once were.

"One by one," Domano added, "they will all dance down the spiral path and back, banging their rocks together, while the rest sing and beat out the rhythm. You will follow my young self, and I will follow you."

The warrior went first, calling and striking out with his fist from time to time. Domano said he was opening the way, warning all in the path that we were coming. He said that he was the strong one and must clear the path of all tricksters and potential dangers.

He moved slowly and forcefully from the opening of the outer rim into the center, where he danced in place and sang a long prayer to each direction. The Sun was getting high in the sky and hot. The monkeys were becoming very curious about us and collected in closer and closer to watch. They jabbered among themselves like gossiping teenage girls, pushing and shoving for the best vantage point. And then the warrior addressed the spirits surrounding us in this little city, and every animal became quiet and still.

He pulled his arms up to his chest six times and with pomp and dignity stepped backward round and out the spiral.

The young Domano was next, and accordingly each man took his turn. Domano nudged me to follow suit, but I wasn't sure what to do. He nudged me again. I still just sat there. Finally he leaned over and whispered for me to dance down the spiral and tie the worlds together for myself, so that I may have the resources of both of them freely at hand.

"But how?" I stood up.

"So you did not see any of the fibers the men had?" he asked.

"No."

"They are pulling fibers through the different webs. When you start down the spiral you must pull this world with you. Then when you are in the center, push these fibers through the center point and grab the fibers from the other side. From the world of spirits. Pull them into our world and hook them to each direction. Then hold them tight, and pull all the way back out with you. They will be for you.

272

"I will dance next. Then we sit and watch. The spirits will dance last.

"Keep in your center and reach out with your song so that you will perceive all of it. Go now."

I concentrated for a minute and stepped into the opening of the spiral. I could feel my whole body pulling something behind me into the spiral temple. The farther I went the harder I had to pull. I could see the spiral formation that the energy in the air was taking. It got smaller and smaller as it went down into the middle. There was something there in the center point like a window about the size of my hand.

I began the anchoring of the fibers by taking a handful of them from my body. I could see them clearly now. They were tiny threads of vibrating light. As I shoved my hand into the window I could feel a sensation like static electricity cushioning around my arm and hand.

I placed the fibers on the other side and grabbed a new handful to pull back through. I held them up to each of the directions, and they latched on as though through an invisible hook. Then I remembered the warrior tapping his chest six times before returning. I did the same and the fibers connected to my body. They brought a sensation of something that I could only sense, something that was remarkable from the other side.

I stepped backward, trying to maintain my step and beat, but I was clumsy and unfamiliar with dancing. I wanted to be graceful and rhythmic like the men. Their naturalness with the whole procedure made it look so beautiful and easy. I was out of step and out of beat and tripped on my own feet.

The farther out the spiral I got the harder it was to pull the fibers, until I got to the outside, and then they suddenly had no pull at all. I could still see them. They hadn't changed or detached. They had just stopped tugging.

I turned around to Domano. He signaled to me to sit down. He took his turn, and this time I saw him working the fibers. After he sat down the air around the courtyard began to stir with the presence of many beings. They were like wisps of color and shimmering air. They moved down the spiral and back. Sometimes I could see fibers, but mostly just the air shimmering, and I could feel them manipulating the webs. Some didn't return, and I believe I saw new ones coming through the center into the spiral. They were beneficent and pleasant. When it was all over, the men got up and dismantled the spiral. We followed them back to the building where the baskets were to return the feathers and freshen up our paint. Everyone seemed deep in contemplation. Not a word was spoken.

When the Sun was just above the horizon nearing dusk, we all followed the old shaman out to a structure that looked like a step pyramid with its upper half missing, and we climbed to the top of it. There the men sat their young apprentice in the center. I sat with my back to his. The old Domano was facing me, squatting near the edge. The old shaman was opposite him, facing the young Domano. As the old shaman spoke, Domano again translated to me.

"The old one says it is time for the questing of the mask," he said. "This is a shaman's walk to find what ways of being we carry, that we put on and off like skin. These are our images of ourselves. Some we even loathe. They are our shelters, shields, crutches — our world. They are our personalities, the way we react to all things. The old one says that Death is fresh and new and alive. It is the old masks of habit that are the 'living dead.' Decaying, heaped in disarray.

"Until we learn to use the gifts of the directions, our masks remain our habit. They rule us and our perception."

"You mean like our thoughts?" I interrupted.

"Our masks are made of our thoughts." He smiled at me. "On this journey you will travel deep inside yourself to the place where masks are found. Watch closely. They will show you all about themselves and how to be their master. How to pick and choose what mask to wear at your bidding. Not theirs. How to keep them alive.

"Close your eyes. From your center take your attention inside yourself. To the central channel, go down the channel to the upper part of your belly. Face front. There you see three caves: left, center, right.

"Go to the righthand cave. Remove all clothings and objects off of your body.

"Go ahead now, inside."

The caves were tall, about seven to eight feet in height. It was dark inside and dank. I could hear my breath and my footsteps on the dirt and stone. There were paintings on the walls, and as I walked in farther I could smell the dampness of the cave. There were bones imbedded in the dirt and rock. I reached my hand out to steady myself and almost touched the spiders that were running off into the darkness.

I walked on and on. The cave became smaller and the mud was thick on the bottom. It shifted under my feet, and in the dark I could just barely make out a snake wiggling away from under my foot. I wanted to panic and scream, but my center made the feeling just slip away.

As I went on, there was barely any light left and the cave was getting small. I was forced to bend way over to continue. Something sticking out of the cave wall scratched me. I looked closely at it. It was a large broken thigh bone. I could hear faint, unidentifiable noises from down in the cave.

Whatever I touched was moist, and the cave was beginning to smell of something spoiled. The ground took a slant downward. It was lumpy and wet, and I was glad I couldn't see what was there. Walking was precarious. I was growing more uneasy with every step. I could sense something nearby.

Suddenly a shadow darted by me down the wall. I jumped involuntarily. As I struggled down the cavern, the noises droned like the beating of my heart. Now I had to bend over so far that I decided to crawl. Whatever it was under my hands and knees, I didn't want to know. It felt disgusting and smelt worse.

The decline became more severe, and I crawled deeper and deeper. There was a faint beam of light that came into the cave from a shaft above, making the paintings on the walls visible. I thought I saw them moving ever so slightly, and then I heard a whisper nearby. I turned to look behind me. There was nothing. I heard it again to my right. It came from the painting on the wall.

My anxiety was building. I was slipping off my center. Something fell on my back. I screamed and reached around to brush it off. It ran down my back and over my leg. I realized I was letting fear get the better of me.

I stopped, took a deep breath, and forced myself back into my center, bringing each gift into focus, one by one.

I came to a place where there were crevices going off in several directions. There must have been a tiny light shaft in one that allowed me to see what looked like human attempts to enlarge it.

I became fascinated by the prospect of all these caverns and their contents and stopped focusing all my attention on the cave I was in. So when the floor took another sudden, steep dip, I slid uncontrollably through the muck. I tried to brace myself with my hands and feet, but everything was wet. I could get no traction.

Suddenly the shaft opened up. There was light. I was skidding into a huge cavern that dropped off steeply to my right. I was terrified. I couldn't stop myself from sliding. I grabbed at the rock to get a finger hold, but my momentum carried me off my ledge into the huge bottomless cavern.

My stomach rolled. It felt as if I were falling forever, plummeting down and down. There was light in places that lit up paintings on the cliff. They moved and sounds came from them. I recognized these images: they were my masks.

As I fell I saw myself with no illusions. The virtuous, the ugly, the out-of-control, with all their shoulds and absolutes and different images of the world and me. I jetted through every emotion and every extreme. I saw the dozens of faces I took, or rather that took me, to interact with the world. I recognized and acknowledged all of them.

Now I suspected that I no longer had a need to respond to the world without a choice of what mask to use.

I felt free. I fell faster and faster. Everything grew very bright. And suddenly it all stopped, as though I had hit a bottom to the cavern. I heard the old shaman's voice and Domano's. The monkeys were chattering in the distance.

I opened my eyes with a start. I was sitting on the stone platform, the young Domano to my back, the old one facing me. The old Domano that I was coming to know so well smiled, and so did I. The Sun was down and it was almost dark.

"Rise," he said.

I could feel the young Domano getting up behind me. I stood up.

Domano looked happy for me. "The two of you will dance now. This is the dance of the mask. You must pick different masks, one at a time, and put them on. Masks you use. And masks that you have never known.

"Give it breath and make it come alive. Feel its personality. The way of its movements. Keep conscious that you are the mask maker. It is said everything is like a performance. It is the touch of the dancer that brings it to life."

The men had begun singing. The young Domano was dancing dramatically around the platform and down the steps. I danced through each of my masks and then tried on the unfamiliar. I laughed and yelled. I was having so much fun. I looked over at the old Domano, and he was laughing and singing. As the night wore on, I gained more and more of my center. Things began to luminesce. I sensed the life around me: hundreds of living things everywhere, and all were dancing and singing. I was euphoric.

Shortly before dawn it was time for the ceremonies to end. We left the pyramid platform and returned to the place where the men had left their bags. They were undisturbed. I was surprised that the monkeys hadn't raided them. We rubbed ourselves with dirt from the ground to remove the ceremonial paint. Then some of the men took fresh paint from their bags and decorated themselves in their usual manner.

Domano put his hands on my shoulders. "This is where we leave them. It is time for us to return to Santa Cruz." He reached for my hand.

I looked around. I didn't want to go. I loved the jungle and the ruins. I felt as though I had been there for weeks. But I remembered then that it was a spirit journey, that time had been altered to pass by at a different pace. I thought perhaps one day I would return.

I held Domano's hand, and we walked up the broken stone steps. The men put their bags on and disappeared into the dark of the forest night. We walked a few brisk steps and lifted up into the air. The ruins glowed behind us.

It took us only minutes to reach the meadow by my apartment. I could see our bodies below, just as before. It was a strange feeling. I wondered why we were made this way, in pieces that can come apart.

I heard Domano's voice telling me to settle myself inside my body, to allow myself to readjust and feel all the senses. Again my body felt awkward and heavy, clumsy to maneuver. I opened my eyes and got up to move around.

Domano hastily told me not to walk yet. But it was too late. I was up and starting to amble, when my legs gave out underneath me. It was as though they didn't belong to me any more.

"Go slow," he said as I landed on my bottom. He and Chea laughed. "You need to give your body time to adjust. Let things get flowing first."

I laughed. I must have looked pretty funny. Then I realized why my legs had given out. They were completely asleep. The feeling had been so dead in them that I hadn't even been aware they were asleep. Now they were beginning to tingle painfully, from the bottoms of my feet to the top of my fanny. I yelled some obscenity and asked them to make it stop. It became excruciating. I sat there moaning and laughing at the same time.

"Rub and pat your legs like this," Chea said, laughing and pounding on my feet.

That made them feel even worse. I hoped that her actions would speed up my recovery, but it didn't.

Domano leaned over with a gleam in his eye, "You can get up and walk now."

"Oh no, no, no," I answered. "You must be kidding." They grabbed me by my arms and yanked me up. The feeling was indescribable. Holding on to me by my armpits, they made me walk. I felt ridiculous. We laughed hysterically while I floundered in my pain. I had almost no control over my lower muscles.

Within just a few minutes I was back to normal. The Sun was setting, and I needed to get back home to meet the kids and prepare dinner. I was joyful but tired.

"You have done very well, little one," Chea said, smiling, as we were preparing to go our separate ways. They looked at me proudly, and that made me feel that I had really accomplished something.

"Do not think on this yet this time." Domano shook his finger at me. "Remember and feel. But do not let your mind churn away on this. Bye-bye, now. We will see you soon. Do your homeworks."

We hiked off in opposite directions. I could see my kids playing in the grass by the apartments. Images of the jungle and the masks on the cliff filled my mind. I could hear the men singing in my head. I suddenly realized I was exhausted, as though I hadn't slept for days, and I wondered as I reached the apartment how I was going to stay awake long enough to feed the kids and get them to bed.

14

THE GIFT OF THE ADVERSARY

For the next several days I slept an inordinate amount, at least twelve hours a day. I didn't dream. I felt suspended between worlds. I remembered Chea telling me that I had to be able to learn their traditions in the middle of the city, in the middle of my ordinary life, or I would not be able to do them at all. It seemed to me that I was struggling far more than I should be, and that maybe I wasn't cut out to learn their shaman's traditions after all.

They had told me many times that I needed to come to terms with both ways of living, to balance and integrate them together within myself. But no matter how I decided to utilize them, it needed to be in a way that acknowledged and utilized the best from my own heritage as well. I was not to throw either one away.

I could see how it would be far easier to succeed at being a shamanic apprentice if one had grown up with those concepts, or even if one were to leave for good the normal daily life and become a recluse somewhere, away from the world, to study those things. Then they would become one's whole life, and there would be no cultural or ideological conflict. But the Hetakas said that all of our cultures were changing rapidly into a world culture, one that encompassed and bonded together all the others. As with the other religious systems, the knowledge and use of shamanism had to become universally accessible, and that meant understandable and usable in the everyday lives of modern humanity. The times of isolation had passed.

And here this knowledge had been available to me, but my life-style as an American housewife and mother seemed to be almost in opposition to it. I had no idea how to reconcile this. How can I possibly appreciate and interact with the miraculous spectacle of life forms on our planet, or find the joy of my song, when I am in the middle of a traffic jam on an overly hot day with two screaming, hungry kids in the back seat beating on each other, with bills overdue, with my scholarship check late, with a parent-teacher meeting in less than an hour, and with a term paper three days late? In moments like those I didn't think about utilizing the gifts and centering myself, I wanted to swear and honk my horn, and threaten my kids with restrictions and no computer time. I didn't think of the equity and peace between all things. I wanted to bite, kick, and spit nails. That's the American way, isn't it? Swear now and ask questions later? Even if you do it in silence? I knew it well.

When I quested for the mask I saw that habit woven into my reactions. I expected my life to be frustrating, and so automatically, with no forethought or choice, I reacted with massive frustration and blind hostility. I hadn't even been aware that I had been hostile. Swearing at and belittling anything that was in my way, even though the words were left unspoken, seemed as natural and ordinary as eating dinner. But now I could see that this frustration and pent-up anger had injured my health and there was no real need for it to exist. It had no redeeming reason to be conjured up. It was just habit.

The quest had taken the wind of that habit right out of my sails. There I was several days after the quest, with a perfect opportunity to be infuriated when the kids were having a fight with my only supply of dried beans, and I just couldn't muster up any anger. I tried, but the habit wasn't there. I found myself faced with an array of possible responses, and I couldn't choose. I didn't know what to do. I just turned around and left the kitchen. The kids were so shocked that they stopped the fight and started cleaning up the beans. They snuck a peek at me in the living room with worried looks on their faces. I was sure they thought I was cracking up.

That night they both got mad at me for not punishing the other one. I was afraid to. Justice wasn't what it used to be for me. I needed time to put the world in perspective, to figure out how to respond to life with choice instead of habit. I felt like an animal that had been born and lived all of its life in a cage and suddenly had the door left open.

The following day, I found that sometimes I would react as though the door were closed. I would go about living for a few hours as I always had, until I was right in the middle of my automation. Then, with a sensation like a bubble popping, all the power would be gone from the reaction. Suddenly, I would no longer be compelled to respond in my old ways. It made me feel as if I had just woken up from sleepwalking.

I avoided seeing people unnecessarily, especially my husband. I didn't know how I would respond to them. I felt very inconsistent and a little out of control. I wasn't sure what was happening to me. I realized that most of my responses to the world were automatic. They spent all my energy in ways and on things that were of no value to me. I was unconsciously polluting the environment of my children, my husband, and my friends.

I wondered why I drifted back and forth from conscious to unconscious living. I wanted to see the Hetakas and have them cure me of these ills. I went down to their apartment to find them, but they weren't there. I assumed that I wouldn't be able to see them that day, and I walked across the street to go sit on the rocks and look at the sea.

I was despondent, and I sat there staring at the waves as they splashed near me. Something caught my attention. I turned my head to the left and looked down the shoreline. Not far away were Domano and Chea, sitting on the rocks looking at me. They didn't smile or wave. I wondered why, what was on their minds. I walked over to greet them.

"Oh, I'm so glad I found you!" I said as I walked up and gave them each a hug. "I think I'm losing my grip."

"Nonsense!" Chea was expressionless.

"What's happening to me?" I looked at Domano. "Why are you so serious?"

"A shaman's journey is very powerful." His eyes were clear and direct. "It will change your life. It would take you years to understand your masks in your culture's way. Maybe you never would. With a spirit journey you learn and change in months. Weeks even. It forces you to pull attention together and use all your potential. Most people walk all their life in a haze. A sleep."

"But I'm not thinking like I used to," I complained.

"Thank goodness," he laughed.

I was relieved to see him laugh. It wasn't often that he was that serious. Now I felt that things were normal. "So I'm not crazy, huh?"

"No." He smiled and shook his head.

"Why can't I think right?" I asked. "I'm afraid I won't be able to take care of my kids. They were fighting and I couldn't find any *wrong* in what they were doing. I didn't get angry. I couldn't think normally. I couldn't figure out what would be the right way to punish them. So I didn't do anything. Boy, were they shocked! They thought I was nuts."

They laughed. Chea motioned for me to sit down next to her. "The same thing happened to me," she said, "when I was a young apprentice. It seemed like all of a sudden the world changed for me. My family looked different. My people. I was different. Nothing was black and white any longer. I could see the two sides of life in all places. They danced together in infinitely different patterns. One day the world had many grays and many colors. It was breathtaking, but at first I did not know how to live with this. In time it showed me. It showed me the countless choices we have at every moment. We do not have to limit ourselves to one narrow existence. Like a kind of blindness. All the worlds are open to us to experience. Explore.

"The doors are open for you now. You are waking from the hazy sleep. That's all."

Domano stood up and started to climb around the rocks. The tide was coming in, and the waves were splashing higher and spraying right up onto us. He popped his eyes open and hooted like an owl. "Hoo! That is cold!" His expression was so cute.

I laughed and said, "Yeah. This ain't the tropics." He laughed.

He was climbing with his back to the water. Chea and I could see a huge wave coming in. We looked at each other and said nothing. It came crashing up and completely covered Domano. He gave out an astounding scream, waved his arms in the air, and looked as if he had lost his balance and was being swept out to sea.

His eyes were almost bulging all the way out of his face. Chea started to laugh. I was appalled. I got up with the idea to somehow help him back onto the rocks.

Chea stopped me. "Look," she said.

I turned to her and then turned back to Domano. He was wavering back and forth, throwing his arms in all directions. He would have looked comical if he hadn't seemed to be in such danger.

Then I noticed that his balance point was actually perfect, moving directly under the center of his weight at all times. I involuntarily stopped thinking, and my song became apparent. I could feel the energies begin to flow automatically. And as my mind reached out, I could see the fibers and energies that flowed from Domano's body to the entire area. It was like a dance.

285

Another huge wave splashed over him and onto us, and with that he lifted his body backward away from the rocks and into the sea, landing butt first. His scream when he hit the cold water could have been heard above the waves for a mile. He flailed his arms and legs wildly and crossed his eyes, and under he went.

Chea was laughing. I was worried about him, but I couldn't help laughing, too. A moment later he rose back up out of the water in the same position, yelling in waving crescendos. He was hilarious. I laughed hard enough to make my eyes tear. Then down he went and back up again in another position.

Chea could hardly catch her breath. "He is so funny. He makes me laugh so hard I'm going to wet my pants!"

I couldn't believe she had said that! Now I was just about hysterical. It was so surprising and out of character for her. Every time I thought I had her figured out, she'd blow my image of her all to bits.

Domano climbed back up on the rocks. He had no trouble at all. His agility and physical prowess always astounded me. I almost reached out to help him up, but I was afraid he'd pull me into the water with him.

The two of them could be so much fun. Sometimes I wondered what I did without them in my life. Since I'd met them things were never dull. I think I was actually learning to expect the unexpected, something that they had been telling me to do all along.

Chea was on her back, holding her stomach. She was laughing so hard she made no sound except for a few desperate gulps for air. Seeing her like that, I could have laughed for days. It felt so good.

She looked up at Domano as we laughed, and their eyes spoke to each other of a lifetime of love and friendship. That was the first glimpse I had gotten of their personal relationship. They had never shown overt affection in front of me before.

And, although I was still laughing out of control I was touched by the obvious love they have had for each other all these years.

Domano plopped down on the rocks just about the time we stopped laughing, bulged his eyes, and made another horrific yelp. It was so unexpected, I screamed and almost lost my balance. And then I saw something that I had never seen before. It was as though time shifted into slow motion, and I observed his actions penetrating outward at his command from his center. I watched him purposefully execute the actions of a mask. It was like somehow following a piece of his consciousness as it moved inside him.

I stared at him until my thoughts began to analyze this new experience, and then it was gone.

"Let's go to the house." Domano clapped his hands, then said, as though there were no reason for it, "I am freezing!"

As we walked back Chea said, "You are becoming too lax and dependent on us. You are expecting us to fix what is out of kilter in your life. You cannot do that. Self-reliance is the most important aspect of a shaman. You must learn to be confident in your own abilities to understand and take action.

"You have learned a great deal. But it takes time to be able to utilize it all. To make it part of you. Our teachers were wise. They gave us enemies and challenges to force us into learning. We could not take anything for granted or at face value. Now this is the same gift we must give to you."

I didn't understand what she meant. I expected her to explain what this gift and the challenge would be, but as we reached their apartment she just told me to learn to live in the state of expecting the unexpected, to be ready to act without reacting, and to utilize the vast resources that were available to me. And then they hugged me goodbye and said they would be seeing me soon.

I drove off, wondering what she had meant. The word "enemy" came back into my mind. I started to get nervous. Did this mean I was going to have an adversary in my life?

What would an enemy generated by them be like? I thrashed it back and forth in my mind until I got a headache. I could feel danger collecting all around me. I felt weak and trapped.

I decided I needed to think by myself for a while where no one could find me. I parked my car at my apartment and walked off into the woods in a direction I had never gone before.

I didn't like feeling afraid and without control over my life. It seemed that I never knew what was going to happen. Lately I'd make plans, goals, and schedules only to have them turned topsy-turvy by outside influences.

At that moment I became afraid that some kind of danger was stalking me. I had hoped that hiding in the forest for a while would help me alleviate what appeared to be irrational fears, but it didn't work.

I started walking up a deer trail when I heard a low grunting noise off to my left. I stopped to listen and look through the trees. The sound seemed to come from just a few feet away, but I could see only bushes and trees. I tried to stay calm, but my fear was gaining. I could not recognize the sound or see a source for it. I could feel the fear growing in my throat and stomach. I felt as if I were going to choke or throw up. I wanted to say "Who's there?" but like in a bad dream, I couldn't get any sound to come out. I had trouble moving, as though all my circuits were jammed.

There was another groan, and another. I gagged, but nothing came up. My whole body shook. I could feel Death very close, and I wondered if this were going to be an undignified end to my apprenticeship and my life. I was terrified. I was trying to convince my body to run, when the sound came from my right. It seemed louder and more threatening.

I managed to move back down the trail toward my apartment. My stomach wrenched in waves. I was unable to think or feel anything but the fear. It seemed that not even in meeting Death and Destiny had my terror been this great. I wanted to be able to do something, but I felt completely powerless.

Then the noises came from all directions. I could feel the hot breath with every groan. I panicked and tried to run back toward the campus. The sounds stayed right by me. I couldn't get away from them. I went completely out of control, crying and gagging.

I couldn't see straight through all my sobbing, and I tripped and fell. The sounds pounded in around me and I curled up shaking in a little ball on the ground, just barely able to mumble, pleading for it to go away.

After a horrendous time, it stopped suddenly, and there was dead silence. I was afraid to move. I held my stomach and tilted my head up just slightly to look around. I didn't know where I was. I thought I had run back down the same path I had come up and should have been somewhere near the Empire Grade Road by Kresge College. But the land and trees where different. They were bigger, and the forest was much denser and darker. There was even a steep hill to my right. I didn't remember any of it. I stayed there curled up and shaking for a long time. I didn't dare move anything but my head, and that only a little. My stomach hurt so much that I didn't think I'd be able to straighten out if I wanted to. Every part of me ached.

As I lay there my fear subsided enough to let me think. I wondered if the sounds had been made by some kind of spirit being or if it had been Domano and Chea. I believed they had something to do with it, one way or the other. I felt my trust in them disappearing. I didn't know what to do.

Finally I decided to get up and try to walk back home. I was terrified that whatever had been after me was still there and would attack me again at any moment.

I looked all around and could not recognize my location. I knew that the apartments were downstream from where I was, so if I headed along the watercourse I shouldn't be too far off.

Everything was too quiet. I didn't even see a bird or squirrel. My body was still shaking as I walked, and I wondered how a mousy little housewife could end up in a situation like this.

The wind blew up around me like an explosion. I jumped and screamed involuntarily. I desperately hoped it was my friend. If ever I needed one it was then, even if I didn't understand her. When I tried to feel her presence to identify her, I realized how drastically far off center and scattered I was. I had let myself be carried off nearly to the point of my death. It worried me greatly. How could I trust myself to handle a crisis, if this was the best I could do?

I stopped walking and tried to center myself. My song eluded me, but with effort I was able to feel the energies flowing through me from the Earth. In my state of trauma I was not able to stop my thoughts, and I never even tried to feel the expansion of the mind.

As I began to concentrate on the feelings of the energies, I noticed my fear backing off enough to ease the pain in my stomach. The wind came up again, this time pounding on my back, practically pushing me over. I tensed up and lost my concentration. If it was my old friend, why was she treating me so strangely? Why didn't I feel her?

I had an immediate urge to get out of that spot as fast as I could, and I started running down the watercourse with the wind at my back.

As I ran I wondered if the weird sounds would return and what I would do if they did. It was getting late and cold. I hadn't come to the road yet, or to the creek or anything familiar. I wondered if I would ever see my kids again, and I started to cry. I wasn't ready to leave them or the rest of my life.

Why was I in such bad shape? What had I done wrong? Or had my mistake been to study with the Hetakas in the first place? It wasn't long before I was out of breath and struggling to go on. I slowed to a trot, then to a walk.

The watercourse became full of boulders and logs, and I had to climb out of it and proceed along its upper edge. I still couldn't figure out where I was. The thought occurred to me that maybe I'd end up at the beach and have to take the bus back home.

I was still in a state of great anxiety and fear. Every sound frightened me. I felt victimized by everything. I just wanted to get home and fix my kids some dinner and maybe clean the house a bit, or talk on the phone. At that moment I felt way over my head in the bizarre and I desperately wanted just the ordinary.

As I was jogging along, I heard footsteps rustling the leaves. At first I thought it was me or an echo, but then it changed its rhythm and got louder. My heart started to beat hard and fast. My fear grew again and swallowed me as if I were a quick and easy morsel.

The noises grew louder and the groaning was among them. I panicked and stomped ahead, disregarding the life that was in my path. At some point I began screaming as loudly as I could. The noise and the fear seemed to go on escalating forever, until I unexpectedly charged into a break in the trees. I grabbed a branch to stop myself and held my breath. I couldn't believe it. I was at Highway 17 somewhere near Scotts Valley. My fear dissipated. I looked into the forest behind me. It was quiet and empty.

I was jerked back into another frame of awareness. Even though I felt completely ridiculous for running and screaming wildly through the forest, I had no explanation as to how I had ended up some six miles, as the crow flies, from where I had been.

The wind came up gently around me. This time I knew it was my friend. She seemed to settle my stomach, but I still couldn't stop shaking. It felt as though she were trying to speak to me. Images of duels and challenges filled my mind. I knew I had met my adversary and lost the battle, but perhaps not yet the war.

15

SEPARATED
ONLY BY TIME

It was winter again. I was spending a lot of my spare time sitting on my terrace looking out over the meadows and the bay. I hadn't seen the Hetakas for over a month, since the morning of the attack in the forest.

I had failed the challenge, but I had learned immeasurably from it, and that gave me a sense of success, of gaining. I was living on an edge with a foot in each world. I had given up for the moment trying to define the universe and was making a point of observing and feeling it. I watched it change from one microsecond to the next.

Domano had once told me that to live as well as possible one had to be able to change with the universe. As he put it, "In order to find and maintain our center of balance, *ka ta see,* one must be nimble and alert. Clear of focus. Clear of intent. Feeling equity and union with all there is. And with great passion, always to be ready and willing for a next step in the dance."

I thought I was beginning to understand what that way of being meant from a practical-application standpoint. I certainly hadn't achieved it. Conceivably it could take a lifetime to master. Sitting there on my terrace I couldn't think of anything better to do with my life, for myself, my kids, and those around me. What was so special about my beliefs or behavior that couldn't be improved by a little change? Not much.

I wondered if the quest for the mask was still in progress,

if the shaman's journey had been only the beginning of the search. I noticed the changes within myself even on an hourly basis. The world looked more hospitable and stimulating all the time. I wasn't as sure any more of my self-righteousness and my judgments of others.

I wondered what life would be like if the two worlds were integrated. I remembered Chea telling me that, though primitive peoples may not be able to read or have flush toilets, they often have a deep understanding for things like the passion of life. They see it in their world and respect it. If they kill a thing, they honor its passion for its life and its love for the world by accepting its joys, griefs, and strengths and offering theirs someday in return. They see stored in the flesh of a being all of its journeys on the path of its life, and all of its qualities. They believe they can gain them and share in its passion.

She had said that modern humans have no real place to learn or acquire passion for life, to learn to feel their own songs. They know that they are missing something, but they can't figure out what. This is why they are so enthralled with wild things, places, and peoples. They feel compelled to capture them and somehow absorb or consume their wildness. And when they don't succeed they get angry and destroy the very wildness, the passion, they lust for.

I wondered then if one of my challenges that the Hetakas had spoken of was to find a way to merge these two worlds, keeping the best parts of each.

The Sun was out. It was cold, but I thought it would be nice to walk along the beach at the boardwalk. There wouldn't be many people there, and I could enjoy the surf and think about my world and the spirit journeys. So I hopped on the next bus.

The wind off the water was freezing, but it felt good. The sand was wet and hard from the receding tide. There were very few people there, just some kids playing near the pier.

As I walked along next to the boardwalk looking at the water marks on the sand, I heard voices laughing and the splashing of water. In the background was music from the 1940s. I wondered what was going on in the video arcade and looked up to see a young couple walking along the boardwalk holding hands, dressed in 1940s clothes right down to the hair and a wartime naval uniform. I could hear them talking, and the young man said, "Swell."

They headed off for the big arcade room. I looked around and could see two different facades for each booth, and other men dressed in World War II uniforms. I heard more splashing and walked over to look inside the arcade.

I was seeing time layers again. Superimposed on the video machines was a swimming pool full of kids. The young couple walked straight through a boy and a video game.

I didn't know why this was happening, but I was delighted. I decided to try and make the best of it and to observe and feel all that I could without making judgments.

I turned and looked all around me. The pier was different, and an old car was parked out on it. There were funny old lamp fixtures and a pregnant woman with a polka-dotted parasol and a Ginger Rogers hairdo.

I asked myself what this could possibly have to do with what I had been contemplating for the last month. The only thing that came to mind was cycles and sequences of actions. I wasn't sure I saw any real significance in the scene, so I decided not to worry about it and just continue to observe.

As I walked along slowly, trying to take in everything, an amazing thing happened: another time layer appeared. This one was a shoreline before white men had arrived.

The cliff edges were farther out into the water, and there were ridges and small mesalike formations that the Indian people were utilizing as living and working places. There were maybe fifty or sixty natives very passively going about their daily lives. Some were fishing or collecting food and firewood, and children were playing.

I tried to look at everything and watch how the three layers overlapped. I found it quite remarkable that all the people appeared to continue without a thought of the others. We all shared this same place, separated by time.

I don't know how long I watched. Time seemed inconsequential. Then a fourth layer began to emerge, and bits of a fifth. The people of the fourth layer were dressed peculiarly. I didn't recognize the styles. There were other small changes. Some of the rides of the amusement park were different and very streamlined in appearance. I believed that this layer was from the future.

There was a woman in her sixties walking down the steps with a little boy. She looked disturbingly familiar. I walked up closer to get a good look at her.

The little boy said to her, "Gramma Kay? What are you going to do?"

Then I knew. It was me in the future with a grandchild. I looked fairly well, but my hair was so gray. I turned to the boy. He looked a lot like my son when he was seven or eight. I was delighted at the prospect of having a grandchild, someone I could dote on and have adventures with. I fell in love with him instantly.

As I followed them and watched the child, I begrudgingly remembered what Domano had said many times about the future: that it was in flux, changing with every movement the world makes. What we may see of it in vision or divination is only a product of all of our thoughts and actions collected together through time and projected accordingly into the actions then most likely to occur at the future point. These sets of future actions change as we change and take our next action. The bottom line being that I may or may not have a grandson, but it would seem likely that I would.

I wanted to get to know him. He sat down in the sand and I sat next to him. It felt like a deep truth that someday I would pass on all the traditions that I had learned to my grandchildren and maybe even great grandchildren. I wondered how that future me was handling it.

I was enjoying him so much as he sat there digging in the sand. Then in my peripheral vision, the fifth layer began to emerge. I turned toward the boardwalk to see it from the best vantage point. I think my breath stopped.

The boardwalk with all its rides, the streets leading up to it, and the bridge were all in decay and half buried by the sands and water. The land formations were different. I could see no people or animals, not even a single bird. Plants grew wild over everything. There was a quiet beyond the surf.

I froze on the spot and yelled involuntarily, "But what of my grandson? My grandson?!"

I felt a tap on my shoulder. And another.

"Kay. Kay," a voice said.

I turned and the time layers began to dissipate. It was Domano and Chea.

"Hey," Domano smiled and hit me on the shoulder. "How 'bout we trek this beach together for a while longer?"

I smiled and nodded. We started walking, Chea to my left and Domano to my right. I looked back, and all the time layers were gone except the image of the boy playing in the sand.

The End